# PORTUGUESE LAW
## an Overview

UNIVERSIDADE NOVA DE LISBOA
FACULTY OF LAW

# PORTUGUESE LAW
## an Overview

*Editors*
CARLOS FERREIRA DE ALMEIDA
ASSUNÇÃO CRISTAS
NUNO PIÇARRA

Linguistic Revision by PHILLLIPPA CANNON

PORTUGUESE LAW – an Overview

COORDENADORES
CARLOS FERREIRA DE ALMEIDA
ASSUNÇÃO CRISTAS
NUNO PIÇARRA

EDITOR
EDIÇÕES ALMEDINA, SA
Avenida Fernão Magalhães, n.º 584, 5.º Andar
3000-174 Coimbra
Tel: 239 851 904
Fax: 239 851 901
www.almedina.net
editora@almedina.net

PRÉ-IMPRESSÃO • IMPRESSÃO • ACABAMENTO
G.C. GRÁFICA DE COIMBRA, LDA.
Palheira – Assafarge
3001-453 Coimbra
producao@graficadecoimbra.pt

Junho, 2007

DEPÓSITO LEGAL
259752/07

Os dados e as opiniões inseridos na presente publicação
são da exclusiva responsabilidade do(s) seu(s) autor(es).

Toda a reprodução desta obra, por fotocópia ou outro qualquer processo,
sem prévia autorização escrita do Editor,
é ilícita e passível de procedimento judicial contra o infractor.

# EDITORS´ PREFACE

The initial idea of editing this book arose from our recognition of the need to provide accessible and systematically presented information about Portuguese law. To date no publication, either in Portuguese or in any other language, has offered a panoramic and comprehensive overview of the Portuguese legal system.

The principal target audience of this book is naturally a non-Portuguese readership looking for succinct and accurate information on the Portuguese legal system. Nevertheless even Portuguese lawyers might find it useful, as it offers accurate, up-to-date and clearly presented information on the major areas of Portuguese law.

The book is divided into three parts: general framework, private law and public law. Each part is in turn divided into chapters dedicated to a particular area of the law. These chapters reflect the common division of legal disciplines.

All authors are somehow related to the Faculty of Law of Universidade Nova de Lisboa, whether in their capacity as resident professors, invited professors or PhD students. This is therefore a collective work, imbued with a shared vision of the mission and goals of the Faculty of Law of Universidade Nova de Lisboa. One of its principal aims is to "internationalize" Portuguese law and the Portuguese University, promoting knowledge in order to achieve a rewarding and broader debate.

In this special year of 2007, when the Faculty of Law of Universidade Nova de Lisboa celebrates its 10th anniversary, this book is a symbol of the innovation that characterizes our faculty. It represents, moreover, a work of reference, evidencing the intention to enrich Portuguese legal literature.

Two final remarks should be added. Firstly, we thank Phillippa Cannon for her important work linguistically revising texts. Second, we would like to thank Almedina, our publisher, for the unstinting interest and support shown from the very first moment of the book's conception.

CARLOS FERREIRA DE ALMEIDA
ASSUNÇÃO CRISTAS
NUNO PIÇARRA

# TABLE OF CONTENTS

## I
### General Framework

1. Legal History
   *Cristina Nogueira da Silva* ..................................................................... 15
2. Portuguese Legal System
   *Vitor Pereira Neves, Carlos Ferreira de Almeida* ................................. 29
3. Legal Studies
   *João Caupers, Tiago Duarte* .................................................................. 43
4. EU Law and Portuguese Law
   *Miguel Poiares Maduro, Francisco Pereira Coutinho* ......................... 51

## II
### Public Law

5. Constitutional Law
   *Jorge Bacelar Gouveia* ........................................................................... 75
6. Fundamental Rights
   *Jorge Bacelar Gouveia* ........................................................................... 89
7. Administrative Law
   *Diogo Freitas do Amaral, João Caupers* ............................................... 99
8. Competition Law
   *José Luís da Cruz Vilaça, Dorothée Choussy Serzedelo* ...................... 113
9. Tax Law
   *Francisco de Sousa da Câmara* ............................................................. 131
10. Criminal Law
    *Teresa Pizarro Beleza, Frederico de Lacerda da Costa Pinto* .............. 147
11. Criminal Procedure
    *Teresa Pizarro Beleza, Frederico de Lacerda da Costa Pinto* .............. 167

## III
## Private Law

12. Contract Law
  *Margarida Lima Rego, Carlos Ferreira de Almeida* ............................. 183
13. Law of Torts
  *Ana Prata* ...................................................................................... 197
14. Property Law
  *Rui Pinto Duarte* ............................................................................ 207
15. Intellectual Property Law
  *Cláudia Trabuco* ............................................................................ 215
16. Family Law
  *Luís Lingnau da Silveira* ........................................................... 229
17. Law of Successions
  *José João Abrantes* .................................................................... 239
18. Commercial Law
  *Rui Pinto Duarte, Assunção Cristas* ....................................... 251
19. Company Law
  *Rui Pinto Duarte* ...................................................................... 259
20. Labor Law
  *José João Abrantes* .................................................................... 279
21. Private International Law
  *Eugénia Galvão Teles, Maria Helena Brito* ........................... 287
22. Civil Procedure
  *José Lebre de Freitas, Mariana França Gouveia* ................... 305

# AUTHORS

ABRANTES, José João, LLM (UL), PhD (Bremen), Professor of Private Law at the Faculty of Law, *Universidade Nova de Lisboa*

BACELAR GOUVEIA, Jorge, LLM (UL), PhD (UNL), Professor of Public Law at the Faculty of Law, *Universidade Nova de Lisboa*

BELEZA, Tereza Pizarro, LLM (Cambridge), PhD (UL), Professor of Public Law at the Faculty of Law, *Universidade Nova de Lisboa*

BRITO, Maria Helena, LLM (UL), PhD (UL), Professor of Private Law at the Faculty of Law, *Universidade Nova de Lisboa*; Judge of the Constitutional Court

CAUPERS, João, LLM (UL), PhD (UL), Professor of Public Law and Dean of the Faculty of Law, *Universidade Nova de Lisboa*

Costa Pinto, Frederico de Lacerda da, LLM (UL), Visiting Professor at the Faculty of Law, *Universidade Nova de Lisboa*; Legal Adviser at the Portuguese Securities and Exchange Authority (CMVM).

CRISTAS, Assunção, PhD (UNL), Professor of Private Law at the Faculty of Law, *Universidade Nova de Lisboa*

CRUZ VILAÇA, José Luís, Visiting Professor at the Faculty of Law, *Universidade Nova de Lisboa*; Attorney at law, Partner with *PLMJ – A.M. Pereira, Sáragga Leal, Oliveira Martins, Júdice e Associados*; Former Advocate General at the European Court of Justice and President of the European Court of First Instance

DUARTE, Tiago, PhD (UNL), Professor of Public Law at the Faculty of Law, *Universidade Nova de Lisboa*; Attorney at law, Senior Associate at *PLMJ – A.M. Pereira, Sáragga Leal, Oliveira Martins, Júdice e Associados*

FERREIRA DE ALMEIDA, Carlos, LLM (UL), PhD (UL), Professor of Private Law, former Dean of the Faculty of Law, *Universidade Nova de Lisboa*

FRANÇA GOUVEIA, Mariana, PhD (UNL), Professor of Private Law at the Faculty of Law, *Universidade Nova de Lisboa*

FREITAS DO AMARAL, Diogo, LLM (UL), PhD (UL), Professor of Public Law and former Dean of The Faculty of Law, *Universidade Nova de Lisboa*; Former Minister for Foreign Affairs, former President of the United Nations General Assembly

GALVÃO TELES, Eugénia, LLM (UL), PhD student at the Faculty of Law, *Universidade Nova de Lisboa*

LEBRE DE FREITAS, José, LLM (UL), PhD (UL), Professor of Private Law at the Faculty of Law, *Universidade Nova de Lisboa*, Attorney at law

LIMA REGO, Margarida, MJur, MPhil (Oxford), PhD student at the Faculty of Law, *Universidade Nova de Lisboa*; Attorney at law, Associate with *Morais Leitão, Galvão Teles, Soares da Silva e Associados*

NEVES, Vitor Pereira das, PhD (UNL), Professor of Private Law at the Faculty of Law, *Universidade Nova de Lisboa*; Attorney at law, Junior Partener with *PLMJ – A.M. Pereira, Sáragga Leal, Oliveira Martins, Júdice e Associados*

NOGUEIRA DA SILVA, Cristina, Masters degree in History (UNL), PhD in Legal History (UNL), Professor at the Faculty of Law, *Universidade Nova de Lisboa*

PEREIRA COUTINHO, Francisco, PhD student at the Faculty of Law, *Universidade Nova de Lisboa*

PIÇARRA, Nuno, LLM (UL), PhD (UNL), Professor of Public Law at the Faculty of Law, *Universidade Nova de Lisboa*

PINTO DUARTE, Rui, LLM (UL), PhD (UNL), Professor of Private Law at the Faculty of Law, *Universidade Nova de Lisboa*; Attorney at law

POIARES MADURO, Miguel, PhD (EUI Florence), Professor of Public Law at the Faculty of Law, *Universidade Nova de Lisboa*; Advocate General at the European Court of Justice

PRATA, Ana, LLM (UL), PhD (UP), Professor of Private Law at the Faculty of Law, *Universidade Nova de Lisboa*

SERZEDELO, Dorothée Choussy, *Avocat à la Cour*, Associate at *PLMJ – A.M. Pereira, Sáragga Leal, Oliveira Martins, Júdice e Associados*

SOUSA DA CÂMARA, Francisco, LLM (UCP), Visiting Professor at the Faculty of Law, *Universidade Nova de Lisboa*; Attorney at Law, Partner with *Morais Leitão, Galvão Teles, Soares da Silva e Associados*

TRABUCO, Cláudia, PhD (UNL), Professor of Private Law at the Faculty of Law, *Universidade Nova de Lisboa*; legal adviser at the Portuguese Competition Authority

SILVEIRA, Luís Lingnau da, LLM (UL), Visiting Professor at the Faculty of Law, *Universidade Nova de Lisboa*; President of the Data Protection National Commission

# TABLE OF ABBREVIATIONS

| | |
|---|---|
| ACE | *Agrupamento Complementar de Empresas* |
| CA | Competition Authority |
| CC | Civil Code |
| CPC | Civil Procedure Code |
| CPR | Constitution of the Portuguese Republic |
| CSC | *Código das Sociedades Comerciais* |
| DTT | double tax treaties |
| EC | European Community |
| ECJ | European Court of Justice |
| EIRL | *Estabelecimento Individual de Responsabilidade Limitada* |
| EPE | *Entidade Pública Empresarial* |
| EU | European Union |
| FDUNL | Faculty of Law, Universidade Nova de Lisboa |
| GAAR | general anti-avoidance rule |
| GTL | General Tax Law |
| IMI | immovable property tax |
| IMT | transfer tax on immovables |
| IRC | corporate income tax |
| IRS | individual income tax |
| LC | Labour Code |
| OJ | Official Journal |
| PC | Penal Code |
| PPC | Penal Procedure Code |
| SA | *Sociedade Anónima* |
| SAAR | specific anti-avoidance rule |
| SpQ | *Sociedade por Quotas* |
| TEC | Treaty of the European Community |
| UCP | *Universidade Católica Portuguesa* |
| UL | *Universidade de Lisboa* |
| UM | *Universidade do Minho* |
| UNL | *Universidade Nova de Lisboa* |
| UP | *Universidade do Porto* |

# I
# GENERAL FRAMEWORK

# CHAPTER 1
# Legal History

CRISTINA NOGUEIRA DA SILVA

SUMMARY: *1. Roman law heritage 2. Medieval legal pluralism and "modern" emergence of royal statutes and charters 3. Law, reason and reform in the 18th century 4. The liberal law: enforcing the State power, liberating civil society 5. The* Estado Novo, *authoritarianism and organic society 6. "Democracy, Decolonization, Development" and the European Union*

## 1. Roman law heritage

The first *corpus* of written law whose enforcement is fairly well documented for the Iberian Peninsula is Roman law.

Roman civil law was, in theory, applied throughout the Roman province of *Hispania*, which by and large corresponded to the Iberian Peninsula, and within which the continental territory of Portugal is situated. However, in *Hispania*, as in other provinces of the Empire, Roman civil law had to take account of and was strongly influenced by the customs of the indigenous people, as well as various pre-Roman legal traditions, giving rise to a "vulgarised" Roman law.

This Roman law survived in the law of the Visigoths, the Germanic people who replaced the Roman authorities in the Iberian Peninsula, in 466 A.D. The Visigoth kings, who were already Romanized and Christianized, replaced their ancient Germanic customary law with written law, most of it derived not only from original

Germanic legal principles but also from the Christianized civil law of the Low Empire. Visigoth law was also influenced by the Roman provincial custom, as well as by the law of the Church.

This Visigoth law was codified in three law codes of different characters: *Code of Eric* (476 A. D.), which contained the above described Germanic law; *Lex Romana Visigothorum* (506), which in turn contained extracts of Roman law; and the *Codex of Reccesvindus* (later named *Liber Iudicum*, 654), incorporating a large number of Roman legal rules as well as the legislation of the Visigoth kings.

All these codes intended to record old customs and not to create new law. However, none of them had much relevance in the daily realities of life in the peninsular territory. Everyday life continued to be ruled by unwritten legal principles and communitarian norms of behaviour accepted by peninsular Gothic-Roman communities.

## 2. Medieval Legal pluralism and "modern" emergence of the royal statutes and charters

By the time of the independence of Portuguese Kingdom (1143), inhabitants of the Portuguese kingdom lived in autonomous communities, ruled by their own norms. Later, many of these communities were officially recognized by Royal and Seigniorial Chartas (*forais*). Through these *forais,* the King or the local landlords recognized the local customs and traditional authorities. As many of these *forais* aimed to promote settlements, fiscal and administrative privileges were granted, giving origin to the *Concelhos*, or boroughs with jurisdictional autonomy, whose officials were involved in the administration of justice. Local law was also collected and recorded in the *Posturas*, resulting from neighbour's agreements, as well as in the *Estatutos* and *Foros longos*, which represent written collections of local legal traditions.

In scholarly circles, the authority of *Liber Iudicum* still held sway, being quoted and applied in courts until 13th century. Until such time Royal statutes, most of them reproducing palatine court decisions, were of limited importance.

Another legal order was composed of the law of the church, canon law, and its jurisdiction over the entirely Christian people. The ecclesiastical courts judged ecclesiastical people as well as all matters related to spiritual concerns, which included questions related with marriage, inheritance and family relations. Furthermore, anyone could submit voluntarily to the jurisdiction of ecclesiastical courts, even though kings throughout medieval and modern times tried to confine and contain the Church's jurisdiction.

From the 13th century onwards, Visigoth codes lost their influence, namely due to the predominance of the Roman law of the Byzantine Emperor Justinian (*Corpus Juris Civilis*). At this time Roman law became the European common law, through the influence of the interpretative work carried on by the Italian Glossators (11th century) and Commentators (from the 12th century). These Italian jurists, using the scholastic method, integrated Roman law, canon law and local law, such as the law of the kingdoms, within a homogeneous body.

Roman doctrine and legislation were acknowledged and enforced in Portugal from the early days of the monarchy, first through Castillian sources (Afonso X's *Fuero Real* and *Siete Partidas*, both dating from the late 13th century) and, later, by way of the direct influence of Glossators and Commentators. The *Glossa Ordinaria* of Accursius (1220-1234), the work of Commentators (especially Bartolus' opinions, 1313-1354) and, later, the *communis opinio doctorum*, became texts of authority for Portuguese lawyers, as well as subsidiary law in Portugal. The very concept of a "common opinion" expressed rather well the dialectical and barely probabilistic character – in an Aristotelian sense – of European juridical knowledge in those times.

Roman Justinian law shaped royal legislation, which also became a factor in the Romanization of Portuguese law. In fact, Portuguese royal statutes and charters were drafted by jurists who had studied in Italian universities. Therefore all royal legislation was interpreted within the context of the common (or Roman) law texts. Nevertheless, the opposite phenomenon could also take place. In political core zones, common law was often corrected by royal legislation. In fact, from the 15th century onwards, royal legislation acquired a growing importance. The first codifications of Portuguese law were published: *Ordenações Afonsinas* (1446), *Ordenações Manuelinas* (1514-1521) and *Ordenações Filipinas* (1603), presenting the first example of European Early Modern codifications. The later remained in force until 1867 (Portugal) and 1917 (Brazil, the most important Portuguese colony during 17th and 18th centuries).

In medieval and modern times, the coexistence of several jurisdictions and various legal systems created a situation of legal pluralism, which mirrored the plurality of political entities. All over Europe, several different legal orders were in force, each one with its own legitimacy and range, but all of them sharing the same social space (the church order, the monarchical order, the municipal order, and the seigniorial order amongst others). At the same time, limited legal autonomy continued to be extended to non-Christian religious communities, namely the Muslim and Jewish ones, who lived in self-regulating communities, mainly situated in the main cities.

In view of this pluralism, the kings tried to organize the legal orders existing within the kingdom, in order to establish the supremacy of Royal law. Thus, *Ordenações Afonsinas* stated that the kingdom's law (statute law, jurisprudence and customs) should prevail as the main source of law. Canon law ruled on spiritual matters and certain temporal matters according to a criterion defined by Bartolus. Roman law was valid as subsidiary law in temporal matters, according to the common law principle of the ultimate supremacy of local norms, within their range, over general norms.

In the final resort the King was vested with the authority to supplement the law.

In the subsequent *Ordenações Manuelinas*, common law doctrine gave way to the common opinion, bestowing upon the courts the last word in the determination of the relevant law. Guided by common opinion, judges were liberated from blind obedience to the Italian jurists and began to devise new solutions, better able to fit new normative needs.

The solemn decisions (*Assentos*) of palatine courts (Casa da Suplicação and Relação do Porto), as well as of the overseas high courts (Goa, Baia e Rio de Janeiro), were registered and had a binding effect.

Outside the palatine courts local customs still prevailed amidst the "rustic judges", who did not know, or even read, the learned law. These customs were recognized by the official legal system as a valid source of law, providing they met some basic pre-requisites.

## 3. Law, reason and reform in the 18th century

During the closing years of 18th century, the rationalism and voluntarism of European modern natural law changed the underlying assumptions of pre-modern law. Natural law, rooted in reason, became the basis of every legal norm. The enlightened will of the monarch, bestowed with the mission of rendering positive the law of nature, became the preeminent source of positive law. Legal knowledge turned into a science, able to establish legal truth.

Within this framework, a statute of 1769 (*Lei da Boa Razão*) reformed the hierarchy of sources of Portuguese law, reasserting the primacy of royal statute law, as well as the merely subsidiary value of Roman law, filtered by the criterion of rationality. Common law doctrine ceased to be applicable. Canon law was abolished as a source of law in civil cases. The value of jurisprudence was restricted and, finally, custom was practically excluded from the set of valid legal sources. Significantly, political, economic, commercial and maritime matters came under the influence of the law of the "Christian, enlightened and civilized Nations", an article which allowed the enactment of reformist legislation as well as a kind of "doctrinal experimentalism", inspired by the French Civil Code of 1804, and favoring the enlightened political reforms of the late 18th century and first years of the next century.

During this period an effort to reform the *Ordenações* (*Project of a New Code*, 1778-89) was initiated, although the new European political context rapidly and rather soundly aborted it.

## 4. The liberal law: enforcing the State power, liberating civil society

Following the Portuguese Liberal Revolution (1820), constitutional movements ensued. Portuguese Constitutions from the period of liberal monarchy (1820-1910) were marked by their individualism, consecrating civil rights, national sovereignty, a representative system and the division of powers as a way of limiting powers, monarchical government, and the stipulation of a census to the exercise of electoral rights. However, important differences marked the various Portuguese constitutional experiences that followed. Although simplifying here a complex situation, we can perhaps characterize these constitutions according to their proximity to two ideal constitutional models.

One asserted the primacy of national sovereignty, the broadening of electoral rights, the supremacy of parliament and mono-cameralism (unitarian representation of popular will). To this model belongs the first liberal Constitution (1822-23 and 1836-38).

The second model was characterized by conservatism, the "monarchical principle", restricted electoral rights, sharing of power between the king and national representation and bicameralism. To this model belongs the Constitutional Charta (1826-1828, 1834-1836, 1842-1910), issued by the King after three years of civil war (1823-
-1826). The Charta was inspired by the French Constitutional Charta of 1814, and tried to conciliate the principle of national sovereignty with the monarchical principle. A novel inclusion was the institution of a "moderator power" (Benjamin Constant), bestowed upon the king, comprising namely the legislative veto, as well as the power of dismissing the Parliament and nominating members to a High Chamber (*Câmara dos Pares*). This Constitutional Charta embodied the permanent liberal-conservative compromise until 1910, although its text was slightly revised several times; in a democratic sense (1852, 1885) broadening of electoral rights, reform of the high chamber), or in a conservative context (1896).

In spite of its importance within the liberal political programme, codification occurred quite late in Portugal. Therefore, the *Ancien Regime*'s legislation remained in force during several decades of the 19th century, along with foreign law, namely the French Civil Code of 1804, and other early European codifications, such as the Prussian

*Allgemeines Landrecht* and Austrian *Allgemeines bürgeliches Gesetzbuch*. These latter codifications were directly applied in innovative domains such as commercial law, or even in the core matters of civil law, when traditional situations and solutions clashed with the new spirit of individualism and contractualism. In 1832, a set of decrees adapted civil and fiscal administration, as well as the organization of justice, to the guiding principles of a liberal State.

Administrative reform was the first step to embody a new model of the State. Successive codifications (1836, 1842, 1878, 1886) changed administrative models, according to more or less centralized patterns. The aim pursued by liberal administrative reform was, to a great extent, reduction in the autonomy hold by the old peripheral centres of political power, subjecting them – namely the *Concelhos*, lands endowed with jurisdictional autonomy and ruled, with great autonomy, by elected city councils – to the State project. At the same time, justice was reorganized in 1832 (*Reforma Judiciária*), and underwent several other reforms thereafter (1836-37, *Nova Reforma Judiciária*, 1841, *Novíssima Reforma Judiciária*). Along with the enforcement of these judicial reforms judges were converted into career officials, most of them named by the government, having lost the autonomy they had in the *Ancien Régime*'s political and judicial system.

In 1877 the first codification of civil procedure appeared, with the Code of Commercial Procedure (1895) representing the next step. The rupture with *Ancien Régime* court's praxis was over, giving rise to the most visible consequence of all these reforms; the end of the "jurisdictional government" which had been led by the judges during the *Ancien Régime*.

Criminal law was the object of three codes (1837, 1852 and 1886), although the first had no practical implementation. These codes were inspired by a utilitarian and preventive approach, in spite the existing doctrinal reflection on the moral nature of the criminal action, on heightening guilt and on the "intrinsic justice of the punition". On the other side, doctrinal concern as to the corrective function of penal law gave rise to a reform of the prison system, associated with the idea of rehabilitating prisoners, and also with the abolition of cruel penalties within the Constitutions and the Civil Code. The death penalty would be abolished at a later date, initially for political crimes (1852, *Acto Adicional*), and thereafter for all crimes (Decree of 1 July 1867). Nevertheless it was still preserved in military criminal law until 1911 (Decree of 16 March 1911).

If public law – not only constitutional, but also administrative and criminal – underwent dramatic changes, which were demanded by the implementation of a new model of political organization, the same cannot be said of private law, where innovation was combined with tradition, due to the force of its Roman law heritage (from medieval to rationalist versions). The first branch to be codified was commercial law (1833, 1888). The Civil Code, the most relevant codification of private common law, appeared in 1867. The Civil Code was marked by an underlying liberal and individualistic philosophy, yet tempered by notions of solidarity, as well as "social unity and integration". Some of the innovations brought about by the Code included the demolition of communitarian rights as well as all the religious and moral restrictions that had previously imposed heavy limitations in property rights and contractual law. In the family law domain innovation encompassed the legal devaluation of the "domestic order", giving rise to a timid disempowerment of the *pater familias*, and the institution of the civil marriage for non-catholic Portuguese citizens. In spite of all the social, economic and cultural changes of the late 19th and 20th centuries, the Civil Code of 1867, combining foreign influence with national jurisprudence and doctrine, remained in force until 1966.

In the final years of the 19th century, new legislation on labour matters echoed the new, albeit limited, development of Portuguese capitalism. This new legislation was mainly directed towards the protection of child and female labour: setting a minimum age for workers of twelve years, reducing the maximum working hours, instituting maternity leave (four resting weeks for the parturient), and forbidding night work for children (Decrees of 10 February 1890 and 14 April 1891; Regulation of 16 March 1893; Decrees of 6 June 1894 and 20 October 1898). Other adult workers were subject to a regime of contractual liberty, unlimited working hours and no weekend or holiday allowances.

In 1910, the Portuguese monarchy was overthrown by a Republican revolution, and a new Constitution was approved (1911). This Constitution, in accordance with the democratic model, organized a lay and democratic republican regime. It preserved, however, some elements of the previous constitutional tradition: national sovereignty, separation of powers, a bicameral system, as well as a liberal vision of society, marked by near absence of social rights and by indifference regarding political parties, which would only be formally acknowledged in 1919, in a constitutional revision. A pure parliamentary regime was installed anew, whereby the powers of a President, elected by the Parliament, were very restricted in the face of strong parliamentary supremacy. Furthermore, the electoral regime was democratized with the institution of Universal Suffrage, although women continued to be systematically excluded, as were illiterate people. Even this enlargement of the electorate was later strongly restricted through electoral reforms.

It was only during the Republican regime (1910) that the administrative principle of decentralization was firmly established. Nevertheless, it would be short lived, because during Salazar's authoritarian regime (1926-1974, see below) a centralized concept of administration was reinstituted, which only came to an end with the democratic revolution of 1974 (see below). The same would occur with a famous law on the separation of the Church and the State (20 April 1910), which strongly contrasted with the mild laicism of the monarchical constitution, expressing the firm anti-clericalism of the leading circles of the Portuguese Republican regime. For the first time, the Catholic religion lost its status as the official religion of the Portuguese State, as endorsed by all the liberal Constitutions. At the same time, important changes to family law instituted the obligatory civil marriage, even for the Catholics, and the admission of divorce, as well as a clear statement in favour of the principle of liberty and equality between man and women in the conjugal society (Decrees of December 25, 1910 and November 3, 1910, the latter of which is known as the Divorce Law).

Nevertheless, the subordinated place of women, even in patrimonial aspects, was preserved, demonstrating that the republican family law had more to do with the political will to reduce the Church influence than with any kind of feminism, which was nonexistent. The imposition of the registry office for all Portuguese citizens (Decree of 18 February 1911) was another sign of that political will.

Finally, the institution of the right to strike (6 December 1910) and legislation on lease matters (*Leis do Inquilinato*), which helped poor industrial workers who lived in extremely overcrowded conditions to rent houses, were the most significant social measures of the Republican regime, the latter also aiming to counterbalance the social discomfort provoked by the Great War, in which Portugal aligned with the democratic powers.

## 5. The *Estado Novo*, authoritarianism and organic society

In 1926 a military movement instituted a dictatorship, which would call Salazar to the government. An authoritarian project of Constitution, prepared by Salazar, was later approved by plebiscite in 1933. Reacting against the parliamentary system of the former regime, this Constitution imposed what was at least in formal terms a strongly presidential model. Reacting also against the former individualistic philosophy of the liberal and Republican preceding period, it installed a Corporatist Regime, giving representative powers to so-called intermediate bodies, such as the family, professional corporations, the Church, and municipalities, through a corporative chamber.

Nonetheless, instead of a bottom-up organization, corporatism was an official top-down organized structure, whose leaders and representatives were appointed by the State. Whilst recognizing fundamental rights and liberties (even some of the political ones, like elections, freedom of thought and of demonstration), the Constitution severely restricted their efficacy, submitting them to the regulation of the ordinary (even governmental) law. Guided by moral criteria or the "interests of society", the legislator could restrict the exercise of fundamental rights in order to assure what the Regime considered to be their "social function". Meanwhile, the Government dominated political power, assuming not only the governmental tasks but also fundamental legislative functions.

Therefore, the *Estado Novo*, framed by this Constitution and developed by the political praxis of Oliveira Salazar, acquired a dictatorial shape, characterized by its anti-individualism, anti-parliamentarism and nationalism. Only one political party was recognized, the *União Nacional* (National Union, later, at the end of the 1960s, *Acção Nacional Popular*). Political policy was established in 1933, as was censorship and the regulation of the freedom of speech (April 1933). In 1936, a new Administrative Code put an end to the decentralized model of the Republican regime, establishing an absolutely centralized administrative regime, whereby all the municipal authorities were appointed by the government, normally from amongst the *União Nacional*'s affiliates. Although similar to other authoritarian European states of the period, Salazar's regime was a peculiar form of fascism, less populist and milder than Nazism, Fascism or Francoism. Salazar's deep Catholicism prevented him from adopting certain styles and measures (namely proto-Paganism and racism), which the Church formally condemned in the cases of Germany and Italy.

In what concerns the judicial system, two judicial statutes were approved (1944 and 1962), which allowed the government to control the entire system of nomination and promotion of magistrates, subjecting the whole judicial system to its influence. By declaring non-observance of the law to be impossible, even under the argument of it being unjust or immoral, these statutes also lessened the substantial independence of the judicial power. Contradicting, in this way, both the constitutional statement that the Portuguese State "was limited by morality and by the law" and the former possibility to recur to the "principles of natural law" when interpreting the positive law, admitted by the Civil Code of 1867, the new article clearly intended to prevent any kind of jurisprudential or doctrinal innovation.

Criminal law was also subject to considerable alteration, especially in the domain of political crimes. In 1929, a new Code of Criminal Procedure intensified the inquisitorial nature of the procedure and softened the defence guarantees, mainly in that which pertained to political crimes. A stronger intervention of the police forces during criminal investigations was another consequence of the new Code. In June 1933, political repression was regulated by a decree, whereby not only a special jurisdiction but also a special prison system was established for political prisoners, along with an extended list of political crimes. The establishment of a special criminal system for political opponents would conclude with the general reformation of the prison system in 1936 (*Reforma criminal*). During

World War II a new programme, designed to combat political criminality, was enacted, involving the foundation of a special court to judge these crimes and also granting a greater autonomy to the police to intervene during the gathering of evidence and to decide upon the application of security measures. The classification of new infractions and the introduction of heavier penalties to punish political crimes were other novelties introduced by this new programme (Decree 1943; Decree 1945). These policies were intensified once again in 1947, through the reform of the Penal Code of 1886. Other reforms, supported by old categories of social risk recovered from the positivist Italian theories of the 19th century, allowed for imprisonment without time limitations, and even without trial or judicial conviction of the practice of a crime (Decree-Law No. 35 007, 13 October 1945).

While public law was reshaped to fit an authoritarian version of the State, private law experienced some waves of conservatism, the first of which came with the signature of a *Concordata* between Holy See and the Portuguese Republic (1940). This brought an end to obligatory civil marriage and the legal distinction between civil and Catholic marriages. A strong restriction upon divorce for Catholics was one of the consequences of the *Concordata*, with great effects on Portuguese family law. Later, this branch of law would suffer another alteration, with the publication of the new Civil Code, in 1966. Inspired by what the contemporary justice minister considered to be "an organic conception of the civil society", this recreated the legal status of the "head of the family" in a Thomist vision of family hierarchy.

As a "social State", the *Estado Novo* tempered the individualism of private law by introducing some social legislation (framed by the corporatist organization), limiting the extreme individualism in civil law, namely by: establishing an official rate of interest, introducing a policy of low-cost housing (backed up by law), stressing the public limits of property (namely in the case of expropriation for public interest), and introducing an old-fashioned household regime to prevent the dispersion of family (*casal de família*, Decree 7.033, 16 October 1920). In the context of labour law, new labour legislation (the National Work Statute, *Estatuto do Trabalho Nacional*, 1933) supported the State's interventionism in labour and economic matters, allowing the gradual establishment of a corporative system. Guided by the idea of an existing solidarity between capital, work and property, the regime declared strikes and lock-outs to be illegal activities and promoted political participation in economic activity through corporative organisms supervised by the government. The National Work Statute of 1933 was then complemented by "anti--individualist" legislation, in some aspects similar to those of the contemporary Welfare States (limitation of absolute free will in individual work contracts, regulation of working hours, weekly rest and holidays, and measures related with accidents and ill wealth at work).

During the 19th and early 20th centuries, almost all the Portuguese Codes were enforced in the overseas provinces in Africa, India, Macao and Timor, albeit tailored to local circumstances. However, this kind of "assimilationism" was not radical. For example, the statute that extended the Civil Code to the colonies recognized the private law of the non-European inhabitants. During the Republican period the "assimilationist" nature of the Portuguese colonial policy was revised and a new regime of systematic administrative and legal differentiation for the colonies was established. This regime was semi-adopted by the *Estado Novo*, which maintained the legal differentiation – namely when approving an Indigenous Special Status (1929) – but instituted a centralized administration regime in colonial government. In the 1945 revision of the Constitution of 1933, a *Colonial Act* was integrated, creating the constitutional framework of Portuguese colonization.

## 6. "Democracy, Decolonization, Development" and the European Union

On April 25 1974, after a failed reformist period aimed at liberalizing the political and economical system whilst rejecting the decolonization, despite the background of international anti colonialism, a revolution, led by an army group of subaltern officers (MFA, Movement of Armed Forces), overthrew the government. Democracy, Decolonization and economic and social Development were the three main objectives of the MFA "constitutional" programme. In the next year a constituent assembly was elected, which voted upon the central principles of the new political regime (freedom of thought, speech and association, free constitution of political parties and unions, universal suffrage in free elections). The nationalization of banks and other basic economical sectors (transport, energy, assurance companies, communications and others), as well as a general programme of agrarian reform that included the collectivization of land property, were some of the means chosen in order to realize a socialist society. Nonetheless, this "socialist way", which was adopted in the new Constitution (1976), would be gradually substituted by another social and economic development model, which was similar to that followed by member countries of the European Community, to which Portugal would adhere in 1986.

**Bibliography**

ALBUQUERQUE, Martin, and Ruy Albuquerque, *História do Direito Português*, Lisbon, 1986. BARRETO, António, and M. Filomena Mónica (coords), *Dicionário de História de Portugal*, Lisbon, 1999. GOMES CANOTILHO, J. J., *Direito Constitucional e Teoria da Constituição*, 7th ed., Coimbra, 2003. HESPANHA, António Manuel, "A Revolução e os mecanismos de poder" in António Reis (dir.), *Portugal Contemporâneo*, Lisbon, 1990. Idem, *Panorama Histórico da Cultura Jurídica Europeia*, Lisbon, 1997. MARQUES, Mário Reis, "Estruturas Jurídicas" in História de Portugal (dir. José Mattoso), Lisbon, s.d., vol. V: "O Liberalismo". GOMES DA SILVA, Nuno Espinosa, *História do Direito Português*, Lisbon, 1992.

CHAPTER 2

# Portuguese Legal System as Civil Law

Vítor Pereira Neves
Carlos Ferreira de Almeida

SUMMARY: *1. Introduction and relevant historical background 2. Legal sources 3. The courts of law 4. Legal professions 5. Portuguese law as civil law*

## 1. Introduction and relevant historical background

**1.1** This chapter contains a preliminary description of the Portuguese legal system. The objectives of this description are solely those of presenting, from an introductory perspective, the most important structural elements of this legal system, setting out the system's fundamental characteristics and considering its place within the context of the extended families of Western law.

In pursuance of these objectives, the elements generally considered as fundamental to the characterization of any legal system are analysed, notably: (i) the system of legal sources, (ii) judicial organization, and (iii) the legal professions. To conclude, all these elements are brought together, thus allowing for the above-mentioned macro-comparative classification of the Portuguese legal system.

**1.2.** The limits imposed on the length of this text preclude a comprehensive account of the historical evolution of the Portuguese legal system (see chapter on *Legal History*). Notwithstanding reference shall be made, albeit from an introductory perspective, to those elements that are considered essential and, within this context, bear a decisive influence on the characterization of the Portuguese legal system as it presently stands.

Within this context, and in view of the deep and lasting impression that they left, particular emphasis shall be placed on (i) the shaping influence of the material solutions inherited from German customs and Roman law in their successive manifestations (and receptions), in relation to the early unification of the Portuguese State; (ii) the rationalization of the system of sources finally brought about by the absolutist monarchy, as materialized in the centralizing of State organization and in the 1769 *Lei da Boa Razão* (Law of Good Reason); (iii) the renewal of solutions and the systematic deepening of this rationalization of sources, in accordance with liberal logic, after the 1820 Revolution; (iv) the democratization that followed the April 1974 revolution, at the various levels where this trend is shown in the so-called modern democratic State; and lastly, (v) the accession of Portugal to the European Communities in the middle 1980s and its consequent evolution, which resulted in the Portuguese system submitting to the required convergence with European law, in terms of both the modernization of its material regime and, essentially, the progressive decentralization (or subordination) of its legal sources.

## 2. Legal sources

**2.1** In discussing legal sources within the scope of the Portuguese legal system, a distinction between immediate sources and indirect sources must be made. The first group of sources corresponds to methods of creating and disclosing legal rules. The second group lacks innovative capability, as it only involves methods for the disclosure of legal rules. According to the dominant consensus amongst Portuguese jurists, statutory law and (for certain authors) custom constitute the first group, whereas doctrine and case law form part of the second group.

**2.2.** Statutory law (*lei*) is unequivocally the most important source of law in the Portuguese legal system, as it is the legal source with true hegemony. Indeed, as the evolution of the Portuguese legal system reveals, statutory law is invariably sought to solve any concrete problem, based on the assumption that the adequate resolution of all problems will be found in it. At this level, we can therefore speak of seeking plenitude or comprehensiveness in legal regulations, based on a set of accepted methodological principles both for the drafting of laws (based on the great abstraction of legally enshrined rules) and for their subsequent interpretation and integration, which are essentially based on this implicit assumption that the interpreter will find all the express or implicit solutions he seeks in the law.

As for the applicable system of law, the Portuguese legal system continues to maintain its fundamental organization. Codes exist for practically all the main branches of the law. They systematize the regime, based upon criteria that are essentially doctrinal. In addition to these codes there are a growing number of specific laws regulating issues that, having arisen after the codes in which they could have been integrated were written, or having fallen outside the scope of the essentials of the regulations for a given sector, were not integrated in these codes.

Before the accession of Portugal to the European Communities and save for international treaties to which Portugal was already a party, the hegemony of the law as a legal source was constructed exclusively upon the basis of Portuguese internal law, based on the tripartite hierarchy headed by the 1976 Constitution of the Portuguese Republic, to which law formally approved by the Assembly of the Republic or the Government was subordinated. Lastly, subordinated to the law in the formal sense but still falling within the broad concept of the law as a legal source were those laws which, in the material sense, coincided with ruling decrees approved by public administration bodies within the scope of the powers conferred on them for this purpose. Today, given the principle of the primacy of EU law over the internal law of the European Union Member States, this hierarchy of legal sources must be considered as having undergone modification, considering that all legal provisions of internal law must conform to EU law.

**2.3** With regard to the importance of custom as an immediate source of law in the Portuguese legal system, there appears to be a clear contradiction between, on the one hand, the generally recognized principle of no opposition to custom as a source of law, at least in those cases not involving any *contra legem* custom, and, on the other hand, the extreme difficulty we encounter in identifying cases in which it is accepted that an actually implemented solution had custom as its source. There is therefore a stark contrast between the generosity with which most authors view custom and the practical relevance it actually assumes.

**2.4** At another level, case law (*jurisprudência*) and doctrine play a secondary role, even where principles are concerned, as sources of law in the Portuguese legal system. Indeed, as mentioned above, they are said to lack innovative capability and are used exclusively as a means of disclosing (or identifying and clarifying) pre-existing legal standards or solutions, generally from a legal source.

This case law and doctrinal framework, explicitly assumed correct by judges themselves and lawyers, influences the style of court decisions and of doctrinal texts or works. As regards the latter, it can theoretically be assumed, a few exceptions aside, that these texts or works can generally be classified according to the perspective on which they are based or, in other words, to the way in which they build their object. Some tend to take the form of in-depth studies of special legal problems, for which a given solution is sought, whilst others explicitly take the form of more or less extensive studies of legal concepts or sectors contained in the applicable legislation. In any event, notwithstanding this disparity, most doctrinal works and texts share an assumption – namely that solutions to all problems should be sought in law. Accordingly, these solutions invariably take the form of clarifications as to the meaning of the law, by which they are rendered lawful.

The structure and content of court decisions are characterized by, in succession, the object of the case in question, the assumptions of fact relevant to render judgement upon it, the issues on which the correct decision depends, and lastly, with particular relevance to the matter now being addressed, the solution to the case, with constant and express reference to the legal rules on which this decision is based. Although court decisions contain countless references to previous decisions (and doctrinal works) where the same legal issues were addressed, this reference almost always seeks to identify previous references presenting the same interpretation of the same legal rules and not references establishing *ex novo* solutions for the same problems. Here, once again, even these references are marked by the assumption that ultimately the goal is to identify solutions enshrined in the law.

Despite this official discourse, there is no doubt that doctrine and case law play a significant role, decisively surpassing that of mere auxiliaries in the discovery of the applicable law. Indeed, aside from the influence that each one brings to bear in the drafting of laws, reference should be made to the not insignificant number of cases where doctrine and case law have promoted the true *praeter legem* development of the legal system by upholding and divulging solutions that are generally accepted and not in any way supported by the law. Ultimately, this fact is implicitly acknowledged when, in considering the applicable law, reference is made to the need to fill gaps in the law, particularly in cases where no rule is applicable by analogy, thus making it necessary to resort to the so-called *analogia juris* or the rule which the legislator would have created within the spirit of the system, had the omitted issue or lacuna been provided for. In either case, strictly speaking, the issue is invariably that of resorting to legal solutions based on rules established by doctrine or case law.

## 3. Courts of law

**3.1** With regard to Portuguese judicial organization, a fundamental distinction should be drawn between ordinary jurisdiction and administrative jurisdiction. Administrative jurisdiction is composed of the administrative and tax courts, and is restricted to disputes arising from legal relationships classified as being of an administrative or tax nature (see Chapter on *Administrative Law*, n. 10). Ordinary jurisdiction comprises the judicial courts, the jurisdiction of which covers all civil and criminal matters over which other courts do not have specific authority.

**3.2** The judicial courts collectively forming the ordinary jurisdiction are divided into three levels or instances: (i) the first instance courts (which are in turn broadly divided into general jurisdiction courts and specialized jurisdiction courts); (ii) the Courts of Appeal; and (iii) the Supreme Court of Justice. The boundaries of the jurisdiction of each of these courts are drawn up by taking the following four fundamental criteria into consideration: subject-matter, hierarchy, value of the proceedings and territory.

First Instance Courts (*tribunais de comarca*), the geographical jurisdiction of each court corresponding to the area that is comparatively the smallest, are those (about 300) that in the first instance hear practically all disputes submitted to civil and criminal jurisdiction. Among first instance courts, the general jurisdiction courts are those that settle disputes not specifically entrusted to other courts, whereas specialized jurisdiction courts only settle certain types of disputes, the limits of which are established according to the subject matter in the case of specialized jurisdiction courts and to the subject matter and procedural type in the case of specific jurisdiction courts. The most important specialized courts are the Labour Courts, Family Courts and Commerce Courts. The intervention of the jury is not admitted in civil cases and is limited and unusual in criminal cases. Courts of Appeal (*tribunais da relação*) are second instance courts, having jurisdiction in geographical areas covering a number of judicial circuits and regions that correspond to all or part of the so-called judicial districts. The five Courts of Appeal that exist at the present time each cover a part of the national territory. The Courts of Appeal are divided into three chambers, each of which deals with a different subject matter (*civil*, *criminal* or *social*). Concerning civil matters, they have jurisdiction essentially over decisions on appeals against judgments issued by the first instance courts, in proceedings of a value beyond these courts' jurisdiction (which is now of approximately EUR 4,000.00), or in matters relating to the status of individuals. Where the Courts of Appeal uphold judgments on appeal new judgments are issued, replacing those previously issued by the first instance courts, without it being necessary for the proceedings to be sent back to the lower courts.

The Supreme Court of Justice, the seat of which is in Lisbon, has jurisdiction over the entire national territory. Like the Courts of Appeal, it is split into three divisions (civil, criminal and social). Generally, the Supreme Court of Justice only rules on matters of law and is not allowed to take cognizance of matters of fact. Concerning civil matters, it has jurisdiction over decisions on appeal from judgments of second instance courts in proceedings of a value exceeding these courts' jurisdiction (which is now of approximately EUR 15,000.00). As in the case of the Courts of Appeal, as a rule the Supreme Court of Justice does more than revoke or confirm appealed decisions, as it can at once issue replacement decisions, without it being necessary for the proceedings to be sent back to the Court of Appeal.

The Supreme Court has no power to choose the cases that it will decide, but it has the possibility to harmonize jurisprudence in matters where there is no consensus within the superior courts.

**3.3** Aside from these two jurisdictions and laying outside their frameworks, the Constitutional Court, the Court of Auditors, the Jurisdiction Disputes Court (which settles disputes between civil and administrative jurisdictions), the Peace Courts and the Arbitration Tribunals (private courts not specifically considered herein) complete the scheme of the Portuguese courts.

The Constitutional Court has the specific power to administer justice in cases invoking or disputing rules or principles of a constitutional nature. The Constitutional Court is specifically responsible for deciding, either preventively or *a posteriori*, on the possible incompatibility of legislation with the Constitution, either on the initiative of political agents to whom the Constitution of Portugal confers legitimacy (abstract control) or at the behest of the parties in dispute before other courts (concrete control).

The Court of Auditors (*Tribunal de Contas*) is the supreme body entrusted with supervision of the lawfulness of public expenditure and the scrutiny of public entities' accounts. The law requires that information relating to public expenditure and public entities' accounts must be submitted to this court.

The Peace Courts (*Julgados de Paz*) were introduced in 2001 as dispute settlement tools, capable of contributing to social peace. These courts perform duties far beyond the scope of merely applying the law. The different operating "logic" of these courts requires the promotion of *mediation* prior to the settlement of a dispute submitted to any peace court. In these courts it is possible for disputes to be settled based on *equitas*, in those cases where issues involve lesser values and the parties to the dispute accept that the decision should be issued in accordance with such a criterion. Peace courts are only entitled to judge disputes of a lesser value, their jurisdiction being materially restricted to judging issues relating to assets (deriving from the law of obligations and rights *in rem*) and to compensation in connection with certain criminal offences. The jurisdiction of peace courts is only of a declaratory nature and, therefore, in order to enforce decisions issued by the peace courts, the parties have to resort to the first instance courts of the civil jurisdiction.

## 4. Legal professions

**4.1** Legal professions, broadly speaking, are understood to be those open to Portuguese law graduates and those around which the operation of the Portuguese legal system revolves. They may be divided into two categories: institutionalized and non-institutionalized legal professions. To draw this distinction, two criteria must be considered: (i) whether further education to complement law degrees is required; and (ii) whether these professions are subject to specific legal regulations.

"Non-institutionalized legal professions" coincide in generic terms with the provision of legal advice by law graduates to employers, under the terms of employment contracts. This activity is performed by an increasing number of law graduates, but does not require any specific training and is regulated by the provisions generally governing the legal labour relationship, subject only to a limited set of legal rules applicable to legal professions, which define the acts that are legally reserved to these professions and assert that the duty of obedience to which the workers in question are subject cannot impair their technical autonomy.

Institutionalized legal professions encompass judges, magistrates from the Public Prosecutor's Office, attorneys, solicitors (including executive solicitors), notaries, registrars and judges of the peace courts.

**4.2** Judges, who are responsible for administering justice and promoting the enforcement of their decisions, are organized into two separate bodies – the judges of the ordinary courts and the judges of the administrative and tax courts. The distinction between these bodies is based on the different jurisdictions where these judges perform their duties. The most outstanding feature of the judges' statute concerns their independence (and a number of guarantees are set out, aimed at ensuring this independence), given that they are required to decide only according to the law and may not be held subject to any orders or instructions.

Access to the profession of judge presupposes a law degree completed at least two years beforehand, and the successful completion of aptitude tests and training courses. The *Centro de Estudos Judiciários* (educational institution under the auspices of the Ministry of Justice, with legal personality and administrative and financial autonomy) is the entity responsible for providing this training. The access of judges to the higher courts is usually decided by way of a contest, in which merit (assessed by way of periodic evaluations) and seniority are taken into account.

The appointment of judges and most of the decisions relating to the profession (e.g. appointments, promotions and disciplinary actions) is the responsibility of the Supreme Judicial Council (*Conselho Superior de Magistratura*), a higher management and disciplinary body for judges, which is presided by the Chairman of the Supreme Court of Justice and composed of further sixteen members, appointed by the President of the Republic (two), elected by the Assembly of the Republic (seven) and elected by the judges (another seven).

The judges of the Administrative Courts tend to abide by the rules applicable to judges of the ordinary courts, despite the fact that they form an autonomous body. Exceptions may apply in relation to a limited number of rules set out in a specific statute and the pronouncements of a specific Supreme Council for administrative judges.

**4.3** Parallel to but separate from the judicial magistracy is the Public Prosecutor's Office Magistracy (*Ministério Público*), which is composed of hierarchically subordinated magistrates who are generally responsible for (i) representing the State in proceedings to which the State is a party, (ii) defending certain interests (mainly of unfit persons and collective or diffuse interests) defined by law, (iii) participating in the implementation of criminal policy, and (iv) applying penalties in legal proceedings, oriented by lawfulness criteria. Without prejudice to the consequences arising from the hierarchical structure of the Public Prosecutor's Office, its statute is close to that applicable to judges, particularly in respect of the independence guarantees from which the magistrates benefit.

As a rule, access to the profession of magistrate is subject to the same requirements applicable to judges. The Superior Council, which is superior body of the Public Prosecutor's Office, is responsible for appointing the Public Prosecutor Office's agents, for organizing and assessing the performance of the magistrates, as well as for exercising disciplinary powers. Access to senior positions in the Public Prosecutor's Office is gained via promotion, which takes into consideration both the merit and seniority of magistrates.

**4.4** Attorneys (*advogados*) are lawyers whose profession consists of performing acts before the courts under a power of attorney and providing legal advice. From a legal standpoint, and notwithstanding their aforementioned characterization as liberal professionals, lawyers are associated with the administration of justice and are responsible for representing parties in litigation, enjoying technical discretionary powers and being bound solely by criteria of lawfulness and the deontological rules applicable to this profession. The Bar Association (*Ordem dos Advogados*), in its capacity as the professional association that represents all lawyers, is responsible for verifying the observance of these rules and for exercising disciplinary powers.

In order to practise their profession, attorneys are required to register with the Bar Association after passing a public examination at the end of an eighteen-month training course. Lawyers may practice their profession either individually or in firms, the sole object of which is the joint performance of their profession.

**4.5** Solicitors are liberal professionals who perform legal acts on the behalf of third parties, essentially by representing their clients before the public authorities. Under the mandate conferred on them, solicitors perform acts considered to be of lesser relevance, or involving legal issues in relation to which there is no legal requirement for a lawyer to be appointed. With regard to the requirements to be fulfilled prior to practising this profession, not all solicitors have a degree in law. Graduates with a bachelor's degree in solicitors' studies can also gain access to this profession. In any event, in order to practise, solicitors are required to register with the Chamber of Solicitors, which provides a specific training course for candidates prior to official registration.

Solicitors with over three years' experience are also offered the possibility of performing the duties of executive solicitor, provided they successfully complete specific training courses for executive solicitors. Executive solicitors, who are appointed for each case by the respective creditor or the court registry, are required to complete a number of formalities in executive proceedings, such as the service of notices and requests for publication, under the relevant judge's supervision.

Solicitors can, like attorneys, set up firms to practise their profession jointly. In its capacity as the professional association representing solicitors, the Chamber of Solicitors is required to monitor their activity, to confer the title of solicitor or execution solicitor, or remove it, and moreover, to exercise disciplinary powers.

**4.6** Notaries are now liberal professionals (who therefore act independently and impartially and are freely chosen by the interested parties). They confer authenticity and public faith upon certain documents, which, according to legislative policy criteria, are considered to be of great relevance. Notaries furthermore ensure the due filing and lawfulness of documents, and provide clarifications to the contracting parties on the meaning and consequences of the acts they are performing.

The requirements for access to this profession are: (i) the successful completion of an 18-month professional training course, which includes a number of written and oral examinations, organized by the Notaries' Council, integrated in the Ministry of Justice; (ii) registration with the Notaries' Association; and (c) obtainment of a licence from the Ministry of Justice to open a notary's office.

The Notaries' Council is responsible for most matters relating to the appointment, organization and performance assessment of notaries. The Notaries' Association is the professional association that represents the interests of notaries and is responsible for ensuring that their activities are compatible with the applicable deontological rules.

**4.7** Registrars (*conservadores*) are civil servants responsible for registering certain legal situations, with a view to their public disclosure. In addition to performing the acts required for the proper functioning of official documentation systems, the duties of registrars essentially consist of verifying compliance with the legal provisions applicable to a wide range of legal situations relating to the status of individuals, the vicissitudes of commercial companies and certain assets (such as real estate, motor vehicles, and ships).

Access to this profession is subject to an admission procedure, which comprises four eliminatory stages: (i) aptitude tests; (ii) further education or training courses (of approximately 6 months); (iii) an adaptation period; and (iv) final examinations. The Directorate General for Registry and Notary Civil Service (integrated in the Ministry of Justice), with which hierarchical appeals can be lodged against decisions made by Registrars, is responsible for most matters relating to the appointment, organization and performance assessment of Registrars.

**4.8** Judges of the peace are those professionals whose responsibility it is to seek conciliation between parties in dispute, on matters falling within the jurisdiction of the Peace Courts. This profession is reserved for law graduates over the age of 30, who are recruited by contest, curricular assessment and public examinations. The Council for Monitoring the Establishment and Opening of Peace Courts, which is accountable to the Assembly of the Republic, is responsible for most issues relating to the appointment, organization and performance assessment of judges of the peace.

## 5. Portuguese law as civil law

**5.1** From the foregoing analysis of the fundamental features of the Portuguese legal system we may clearly conclude that this system falls within the scope of the so-called Roman-German (or civil) legal family. The main traits of this legal family result from the practically uniform historical and cultural evolution of the Western European legal systems, based on German customs and Roman law and on the dissemination of the main ideals of the French Revolution throughout Europe.

Nowadays, the kinship between these legal systems has been strengthened by the fact that the great majority have reached a relatively similar stage of evolution, thereby contributing to the standardization of the meta-legal factors that most influence their characterization. Particular emphasis must be given to democratic organization representing the State, supported by written Constitutions and by the prevalence of the so-called market economy, both of which are reinforced by the integration of these systems in the European Union and the harmonizing consequences derived therewith.

**5.2** Whilst the integration of the Portuguese legal system within the civil law systems is clearly apparent from our analysis, it should however be noted that it is essentially in terms of the system of sources that its integration is most obvious, given the prevalence of the statutory law as a legal source to the detriment of other sources, albeit to different extents. Moreover, and as already mentioned in connection with the Portuguese legal system, consequences are derived from this prevalence of the law that are also common to civil law systems. These systems tend to set out general and theoretical legal rules in codes organized in observance of essential doctrinal criteria, aimed at providing comprehensive regulation and thus contributing to the discovery of the applicable law. These rules are invariably built around the interpretation of solutions enshrined in the law and, in the absence of these, around the innovative support of doctrine and case law. Knowledge of these sources is therefore essential in order to acquire an adequate understanding of these systems, notwithstanding the fact that this knowledge is generally undervalued in official legal discourse.

## Bibliography

DAVID, R. and C. JAUFFRET-SPINOSI, *Les grands systèmes de droit contemporains*, 11th ed., Paris, 2002. FERREIRA DE ALMEIDA, Carlos; *Introdução ao direito comparado*, 2nd ed., Coimbra, 1998. FREITAS DO AMARAL, Diogo; *Manual de Introdução ao Direito*, vol. I, Coimbra, 2004. OLIVEIRA ASCENSÃO, José; *O Direito. Introdução e teoria geral*, 13th ed., Coimbra, 2005. ZWEIGERT, K., and H. Kötz; *Einführung in die Rechtsvergleichung auf dem Gebiet des Privatrechts*, 3rd ed., Tübingen, 1996 (*An introduction to comparative law*, trad. by T.Weir, 2nd ed., Oxford, 1992).

CHAPTER 3

# Legal Studies

João Caupers
Tiago Duarte

Summary: *1. Historical survey 2. Academic framework 3. Innovation in* Universidade Nova de Lisboa's *Law Faculty*

## 1. Historical survey

Legal studies in Portugal date back more than seven hundred years. Pope Nicholas IV's Decree of 9 August 1290, which founded the first Portuguese University, was already mentioned in the teaching of Canon Law and Roman Law.

Very few documents concerning legal studies in those distant times have survived. In 1309 the University had three professors; two teaching Canon Law and one teaching Roman Law. By the beginning of the sixteenth century, when the first University Statute was approved, that number had doubled.

During the reign of King John III (*Dom João III*), the Portuguese University achieved institutional stability. In 1537 it was settled in the city of Coimbra (previously it had, like the royal Court itself, a peripatetic existence). A period of consolidation, expansion and modernization was inaugurated. European influence increased dramatically, with the employment of several well-known professors, both foreigners and formerly expatriate Portuguese. The University

Statute was reviewed several times during the sixteenth and seventeenth centuries, up to 1772 when the so-called New Statute was approved.

Within the Portuguese University two law schools existed: the Canon School, where the *Corpus Iuris Canonici* was studied; and the Law School, dedicated to the *Corpus Juris Civilis*. In the latter case teaching was divided into eight subjects, reflecting the eight parts into which experts divided the *Corpus Juris Civilis.*

The New Statute retained those eight subjects whilst adding some more: Natural Law (including the *Jus Gentium*) and, for the first time, Portuguese Law. The most important change brought by the Statute, however, concerned not the subjects taught but rather the teaching methods employed. Instead of using the traditional analytic method, dissecting and commenting upon the rules to their most insignificant detail, the Statute compelled the University's professors to conceive a plan for each subject, in such a way that a body of essential knowledge could be taught during the academic year. The Statute also urged the professors to publish handbooks for each subject.

The New Statute was revoked in 1836, shortly after the end of the civil war between the conservative monarchists and liberals. The two schools were merged into a new Law School. A first law degree continued to require five years of study. Law teaching was, in a way, nationalized, since Portuguese Law was divided into several modern subjects: Trade Law, Criminal Law, Administrative Law, Economics, and Legal Pathology. During the eighteenth century other subjects were added: International Law, Civil Procedure Law and Colonial Law.

The beginning of the twentieth century witnessed a reorganization of legal studies, heralded by Decree 4, of 24 December 1901. The most noteworthy aspect of this reform was, as an impressive sign of the times, the major importance given to sociological subjects.

The Portuguese monarchy fell on 5 October 1910, to be replaced by a Republic. In 1911, the School of Law proposed a new reform of the legal studies, which received the approval of the Republican government. It was indeed a modern reform, capable of putting Portugal in the vanguard of European legal studies. There is evidence that this reform had the general support of the European law *intelligentsia.*

*Legal Studies* 45

In that same year of 1911, the government was engaged in fundamental reform of the Portuguese educational framework. This astute reform recognized the need for two new universities, as a *sine qua non* for the development of the country: one in Lisbon, and the other in Oporto. In 1913 the University of Lisbon established a new law school.

Legal studies were twice reformed in both law schools (Coimbra and Lisbon) during the period known as the First Republic (1910--1926): in 1918 and in 1922. The lack of political stability minimized the effectiveness of these reforms.

In 1928, under the authoritarian regime known as *Estado Novo* (New State), further reform was approved. The major change was the reduction of the period needed to obtain the first law degree, to four years (*bachelarato*). After a fifth year a student could obtain their second law degree (*licenciatura*), necessary for entry into the most relevant legal professions, namely those of attorneys and judges.

In 1972, close to the end of the New State, legal studies underwent a new reform. The Decree-Law No. 364/72, from 28 September 1972, introduced two major changes; legal studies in both law schools were organized on a semester basis (instead of an annual basis), and the first degree (which retained the name *bachelarato*) was delivered after six successful semesters. The following four semesters conferred the second degree (still named *licenciatura*).

After the 1974 Revolution the law stopped imposing standard parameters on legal studies. The *bacharelato* ceased to exist and the *licenciatura* became the first law degree once again. Each university – whose autonomy was fully recognized in 1988 – could choose its own programme and implement specific rules in line with its conception of legal studies. The number of law schools increased to twenty. Unfortunately teaching and researching levels did not develop and improve in line with this growth.


## 2. Academic framework

**2.1.** Portuguese legal studies are nowadays organized according to a three degree model: the *licenciatura,* the m*estrado* (Master's) and the *doutoramento* (PhD).

The *licenciatura* is the lower law degree. In order to obtain such degree, one must apply to a law school – after having successfully completed twelve years of education – and complete the specific examinations demanded for each university. Compulsory subjects are Portuguese and History, and the examinations, rather than being held by each university, are organized at the national level and are considered to be part of the secondary studies.

There are five law schools belonging to the public sector in Portugal; two in Lisbon, one in Coimbra, one in Oporto and one in Braga. Two schools belong to the Portuguese Catholic University (Lisbon and Oporto) and there are thirteen privately owned law schools. Taken together they teach some 20,000 law students.

At the present time – that is before the reorganization of legal studies in accordance with the *Bologna Statement*, which is now underway – a student must complete ten academic semesters (or 300 credits, for those schools already complying with the *European Credits Transfer System, (ECTS)*). Programmes are approved by the respective bodies of each university. If the universities are State or Catholic Church-owned, there is no legal or administrative constraint concerning the subjects to be taught. Privately owned universities must submit their programmes to the Ministry for Science, Technology and Higher Education for approval.

Nevertheless, following the Portuguese legal tradition (and also due to some lack of imagination...) law schools' programmes have not tended to vary significantly, although one can identify some increasing divergences during the last few years. As a matter of fact, law schools have recently started to offer their students a wider range of subjects, so that they can acquire adequate skills and knowledge to face the professional challenges that grow every day.

Nowadays, the moot issue is *Bologna* and its effects on the structure of legal studies. Since the Government passed a decree on the subject, all Portuguese law· schools have had to divide legal studies into three cycles. Law schools belonging to the Portuguese State adopted more or less the same framework. The first degree, the *licenciatura*, requires 240 credits. The second degree, the *mestrado*, requires a further 90 to 120 credits. The requirements for a doctorate are still being discussed; candidates may be required to attend classes on a variety of subjects and the approval of an original dissertation is mandatory.

**2.2.** The Law School of the *Universidade Nova de Lisboa* (FDUNL) was created ten years ago. A first degree studies programme was set up, which has, since its beginning, a duration of ten semesters. The programme operated on a credit system basis (different from the ECTS, however, which did not exist at that time). Conversion to the ECTS was accordingly easier than in any other Portuguese law school.

The programme includes both mandatory subjects and elective subjects. The former include the main law subjects, deemed to be essential for the common training of all lawyers: Constitutional Law, Civil Law, Administrative Law, Criminal Law, International Law, Contract Law, EU Law, Civil Procedure Law, Criminal Procedure Law, and also subjects in the field of economics, such as Microeconomics and Macroeconomics. Within this group of mandatory subjects special reference should be made to some innovative subjects that bring together academic knowledge and professional practice, namely Ethics for Lawyers and Cross-Disciplinary Legal Practice.

The programme offers a wide range of elective subjects, to be chosen by students according to their individual preferences and, if requested, with guidance from their tutors. These subjects fall within the scope of legal science, enabling students either to deepen their understanding of subjects they have studied before (such as subjects within the field of EU Law), or gain access to new fields such as Information Technology Law, International Criminal Law, Consumer Law, Competition Law, Environmental Law, Securities Law, Economic Analysis of Law, Public and International Economics, Sociology of Law, Political Science, Administrative Science, Social Psychology, Legislative Science, History of Political Ideas, etc.

At FDUNL, access to other fields of knowledge is seen as a way of providing different contextual frameworks for lawyers, enabling students to gain a broader understanding of the social and intellectual world of which law is (just) a part.

**2.3.** After finishing the *licenciatura* with an average mark of not less than 14/20, one can apply to study for a second degree, the *mestrado em Direito* (Master's in Law). The Master's takes two full academic years or four semesters.

In the first year the student must attend seminars on different subjects and deliver a paper at the end of each seminar (around 100 pages). The second year is fully dedicated to the dissertation: an essay on an original subject (around 300 pages). Some comparative law research in foreign countries is expected. The dissertation is argued before a panel of examiners composed of three to five professors. The dissertation is discussed by one or two of the panel's members, for half an hour each. The candidate has the same amount of time in which to reply.

**2.4.** Applications to join a PhD programme (*doutoramento*) may take one of two forms.

Following the Portuguese tradition in the field of law, one applies directly to a law school, under the patronage of a law professor. This is possible only if the candidate obtained no less than 16/20 in the first law degree or in the Master's. The candidate must then prepare an original dissertation, without any time limitation (around 600 pages).

Strong knowledge of both historical issues and comparative law is expected. Since candidates generally perform major research abroad, knowledge of foreign languages is encouraged and is considered useful.

When a candidate considers a dissertation to be complete it is brought before a panel of examiners, usually composed of five to eight professors, for a public debate.

If the candidate already has a Master's degree, the dissertation is discussed by two of the panel's members, for half an hour each. The candidate has the same amount of time in which to reply. If the candidate skipped the Master's degree, he/she must attend two supplementary debates, one on his/her academic CV, and the other on a subject chosen by the candidate from amongst a certain number of subjects selected by the panel.

If the candidate is approved, he/she is entitled to a PhD – usually *summa distintio* or *summa cum laude*.

There is, however, an alternative path to obtain a PhD in law. This new path was for the very first time set up by the law school of the *Universidade Nova de Lisboa*. Due to its success, it was later adopted by two other law schools, those of the *Universidade de Coimbra* and the *Universidade Católica Portuguesa*.

After obtaining a first degree in law a candidate applies to study for a PhD. Applications are submitted to a committee composed of three professors. The committee selects a certain number of candidates – usually around fifteen – who are accepted to attend different seminars for a period of two semesters (first stage). If the candidate is approved in all seminars, with an average mark of not less than 16/20, he/she must then attend two other seminars for the following semester. Then, once again, if he/she achieves a mark of not less than 16/20 in these seminars, preparation of a PhD dissertation begins, which may not take longer than five years. Once completed, the dissertation is subject to the above-mentioned process of examination and public debate.

## 3. Innovation in the FDUNL

The FDUNL was set up by authority of a Government Order 164/ME/96, dated 17 July 1996. The founder's objective for the new school was to create "a dynamic new centre for developing knowledge and teaching of law in Portugal, by pioneering research in new disciplines and responding to the new demands of professional and occupational training". These words – quoted from the Government Order which set up the Establishment Committee – reflected the sense that, regardless of quality, the current teaching of law in Portuguese universities needed to be more attuned to the context of the legal professions, both in Portugal and in Europe.

Legal professions have become increasingly diverse, demanding more flexible and dynamic career paths. Internationalization requires greater competence in European, international and comparative law, as well as closer attention to the international equivalence of study programmes. The development of teaching and research models assumes that periods of study for doctoral degrees will be shorter, and will be combined with post-doctoral cycles. Increasing social exchange means that legal training should pay greater attention to the non-legal contexts within which the law operates, and be more open to cross-disciplinary studies.

Faculty staff was recruited along innovative guidelines, as defined by the Establishment Committee. Only lecturers qualified with a PhD would, in principle, lead classes. All lectures and other types of teaching – practical exercises, debates, moot courts and tutorials – would therefore be oriented by professors. In the new, non-legal, subjects it was decided to recruit professors with an expertise in those fields. At the same time, it was decided that non-university lawyers should be in charge of a limited number of subjects, which have a clearly practical nature, as a way of allowing students to benefit from their experience outside the academic world.

# CHAPTER 4

# EU Law and Portuguese Law

MIGUEL POIARES MADURO
FRANCISCO PEREIRA COUTINHO

SUMMARY: *1. Introduction 2. Law in the books 3. Law in action*

## 1. Introduction

This article deals with the incorporation and application of European Union (EU) law[1] in Portugal since the accession in 1986. The purpose is to provide an overview of the impact that EU law has had on the Portuguese legal order. As we will try to demonstrate, the legal implications of the accession can be characterized as dual--natured. On the one hand, in terms of law in the books Portugal can almost be described as a paragon of virtue, symbolized in the recent Constitutional revision (2004), which recognizes in broad terms the principle of the supremacy of EU law (subject to a systemic compatibility with the basic values of the rule of law, democracy and fundamental rights), and shown in an overall reasonable level of transposition of EU Directives. On the other hand, regarding law in action, the reality is quite different. The Portuguese courts, as revealed by the

---

[1] Throughout the text and for the sake of simplicity and clarity we will use the expression EU law even if, in certain cases, it would be more correct to use the expression Community law (notably because in certain cases EU norms do not benefit from the authority traditionally granted to Community norms).

numbers of preliminary references made to the European Court of Justice, represent one of the least EU-enthusiastic judicial systems.

The framework we have chosen for this article reflects this dual perspective of law in the books and law in action. We will start by briefly discussing the major structuring principles of the relationship between EU law and Portuguese law, focusing on the doctrinal and judicial perspectives that represent the current state of the Portuguese-European constitutional discourse. Our purpose in this first section is to describe potential problems related to the incorporation of EU law in the Portuguese legal order, bearing in mind the difficulties embraced in other Member States, especially in that which concerns the relationship between EU law and the national constitutions. In the subsequent section, we intend to review the application of EU law in the Portuguese legal order by focusing on both the preliminary references made by Portuguese judges and the actions for failure to fulfil obligations instigated against Portugal by the Commission. Both procedures, we argue, can provide an excellent barometer of the effective incorporation of EU law within the national legal realm.

## 2. Law in the books

### 2.1 *Doctrinal perspectives on EU supremacy*

In Portugal, the vast majority of national constitutional scholars tend to cite Article 8 of the Constitution in referring to the incorporation of the EU legal order, including the constitutional principles of supremacy and direct effect. The history of the changes brought in this Article since the accession is in itself revealing of the efforts made to prevent conflicts between national constitutional law and EU law.

The Portuguese Constitution has several times adapted itself to Portuguese membership of the European Union. Although the Constitution already included a norm incorporating international law within the national legal order, even that provision was specifically revised prior to Portuguese accession to the European Community, so that it covered Community secondary law. Such norm is Article 8/3, which, in its latest version, states: "Any rules enacted by the competent institutions of the International Organizations of which Portugal is a member apply directly in the domestic order so long as that is established in the founding Treaties of such International Organizations". On the other hand, the general rule applicable to international treaties is set out in Article 8/2: "The norms of the international conventions, which have been regularly ratified or approved, are directly applicable in the domestic legal order after their official publication and as long as they remain binding for the Portuguese State in the international order".

Based on this configuration of Article 8 both doctrine and the Portuguese courts agreed that the hierarchical position of EU law in the Portuguese legal order was superior to that of ordinary national law (i.e. all other legal acts of the Portuguese legal order). This reasoning, however, at the same time that it accepts the supremacy of EU law limits it in two ways: first, the supremacy of EU law, contrary to the conception of the European Court of Justice (ECJ), does not derive from its own independent claim of authority but from the authority given to it by the national constitution; and second, this reasoning also assumes that such supremacy only extends insofar as it is determined by national constitutional law and, therefore, it does not extend to national constitutional norms themselves.

Although the above would appear to be the normal conclusions to be drawn from the described constructs, there are very few Portuguese authors that still defend the supremacy of any norm of the Constitution over any EU act. Instead, the growing trend has been towards recognizing a limited constitutional supremacy on the part of EU law. This position reflected the dominant legal approach in other Member States, in particular as expressed by some national constitutional courts; they accept the supremacy of EU law over the national constitution except where it infringes the core values of such constitution (i.e. those that could be said to define the national constitutional identity).

Such recognition of limited constitutional supremacy for EU law has found expression in two main versions. The first corresponds to the approach developed by the German Constitutional Court in the second of the famous *Solange* decisions, where this Court stated that so long as the European Court of Justice guarantees a sufficient level of protection of fundamental rights *vis-à-vis* Community acts it would no longer exercise its jurisdiction in reviewing those acts[2]. Some national constitutional courts have, however, embraced a more aggressive doctrine. They still admit the possibility of national constitutional review of EU acts on a case-by-case basis and not simply by a systemic control. This is the traditional doctrine espoused by the Italian Constitutional Court (*Granital* and *Fragd* decisions), the Belgian *Cour d'arbitrage* (*Ecoles euroéeennes* decision*)*, and, to a more limited degree, the Danish Constitutional Supreme Court (*Carlsen and others v. Paul Nyrup Rasmussen* decision). Nevertheless, even in these cases, the national courts accept a partial supremacy of EU law over the national Constitution; they will only review EU acts that conflict with fundamental principles of the Constitution and not with any specific national constitutional norm. This is confirmed by the fact that an EU act has never been struck down under this doctrine.

The latter appears to be the position that, albeit without any textual support in the Constitution or in the case law of the Portuguese Constitutional Court, is increasingly dominant among Portuguese scholars in considering the relationship between EU law and the national Constitution. On the one hand they identify the national Constitution as the ultimate authority and refer to the authority that it grants to EU law. On the other hand, they limit the circumstances in which EU norms should be subject to national constitutional review.

This means that there is no real acceptance of constitutional pluralism in Portugal, with the supremacy of EU law admitted only via legal reasoning that is internal to the Portuguese constitutional legal system. Therein lays the origin of potential conflicts between national constitutional law and EU law: once the reference point becomes the national Constitution it is difficult to incorporate within the national legal order the full extent of the claim to constitutional supremacy that is made by EU law. Accordingly the extent to which incorporation occurs becomes highly fluid and arbitrary. It becomes difficult to separate and to recognize the autonomy of the EU legal

---

[2] Judgment of 22 October 1986 of the Bundesverfassungsgericht (available in english in *CMLR*, 3, 1987, at 258). This approach was reinstated in the Maastricht decision (Judgment of 12 October 1993 of the Bundesverfassungsgericht, available in english in *CMLR*, 57, Vol. 1, 1994, at 1).

order, and its interpretation and application at the national level runs the risk of becoming entangled in national constitutional traps. In this respect, if one argues that the Portuguese Constitution recognizes the autonomy of the EU legal order (even whilst not accepting its absolute supremacy over the Constitution) then questions of interpretation and application of EU law should be decided in light of the criteria set forward by the EU legal order and not according to the Portuguese Constitution. Following this reasoning, the hermeneutic paradigm is shifted in the way EU law is incorporated and implemented in the Portuguese legal system.

The constitutional revision of 2004 seems to have chosen the *Solange* path. The new Article 8(4) of the Portuguese Constitution recognizes that the legal authority of EU norms in the Portuguese legal order must the defined according to the parameters laid out by the EU legal order. This recognition is not, however, unconditional, as it must comply with the fundamental principles of a democratic rule of law. As the above-mentioned constitutional norm states: "The norms of the EU Treaties and the norms enacted by its institutions, in the exercise of their competences, are directly applicable in the domestic legal order, in the terms of EU law, with respect for the fundamental principles of a democratic rule of law".

In other words, the Portuguese Constitution recognizes the primacy of EU law *as long as* both legal systems are compatible in systemic terms. Such compatibility can be identified in the mutual respect for the fundamental principles of a democratic rule of law. This means that the recognition of the supremacy of EU law enshrined in this Article is not a national constitutional capitulation, as it is limited by respect for the fundamental values of the Portuguese constitutional order. It is precisely this systemic identification between these two legal orders that will ultimately prevent the existence of any conflicts of normative authority.

## 2.2 *Constitutional Case Law on EU law*

The Portuguese Constitutional Court has never challenged the ECJ and EU law in the manner that it has, for example, been challenged by the German and Italian Constitutional Courts or, more recently, by the Belgian *Cour d'Arbitrage* and the Irish Supreme Court (*Grogan* decision). Portugal's Constitutional Court has, so far, only made marginal references to EU law. Notwithstanding, these limited references already hint at some of the risks inherent in the absence of a clear recognition of the autonomy of the EU legal order. The Court has not addressed the fundamental question of the review of EU norms in light of the national Constitution, but it has recognized its supremacy over infra-constitutional law. However, it is clear, first of all, that such supremacy is drawn from and delineated by Article 8 of the Constitution. In its first decision addressing issues of Community law, the Constitutional Court appeared to be ready to deny the direct effect to Directives, following the wording of Article 8/3 of the Constitution, which at the time only recognized the direct effect of international norms where expressly stated in their founding treaties.[3] And, based upon the same reasoning, it appears clear that the Court did not extend, at least at that time, the recognition of supremacy to constitutional norms.

The Portuguese Constitutional Court has already taken a position regarding two aspects of the relationship between EU law and the national constitution: the degree to which the national constitutional order still retains its sovereignty in defining the conditions for the implementation of EU law and the role of the Constitutional Court in applying EU law; and, secondly, the possibility of referring cases to the ECJ.

The first issue was addressed by the Constitutional Court, precisely in the above-mentioned initial decision of 1989. In its decision the Court appears to determine that it is for the constitutional order of each Member State to determine the conditions and the means for implementing EU law. However, whilst as regards the specific issue at hand (the national legal form of the act) there is no doubt that EU law does not affect the determinations of the national constitution, it is also recognized today that EU law may, in some cases, impose important deviations from the national constitutional order if deemed necessary to guarantee the effective protection of rights awarded by EU norms.

---

[3] Judgment 184/89, Diário da República – I Série, n.º 57, of 9 March 1989, at 1051. The Constitutional amendments adopted that same year ended up eliminating this possible constitutional conflict by deleting the reference to "expressly".

The clearest position taken so far by the national Constitutional Court with regard to EU law was adopted in a decision of 1990. The decision appears, at least at face value, to be friendly towards the ECJ; the Portuguese Court admits the possibility of referring a case to the ECJ under what is now Article 234 of the EC Treaty, though it did not consider such a referral relevant to the case at hand.[4] Moreover, it has never, in effect, made a referral.

As we have shown in this section, Portuguese doctrine and constitutional case law have peacefully recognized the supremacy and incorporation of EU norms into the national legal order based on Article 8 of the Constitution. This recognition made it possible for other EU constitutional principles, such as the direct effect, to be swiftly and promptly integrated. The process of adoption and integration in other Member States was often more difficult.

In spite of the challenge that the above-described constitutional perception entails for EU law, there is an overall optimism in Portuguese constitutional scholarship regarding a peaceful incorporation of EU law into the Portuguese legal realm. We can find several explanations for both the optimism of Portuguese constitutional scholarship and the restraint of the Portuguese Constitutional Court. First, there is a generalized perception that the core legal values of the Portuguese Constitution are shared by the EU legal order and that, therefore, it is unlikely for an EU act to go against a national constitutional provision. Second, there is a tendency to see the compatibility between the Portuguese Constitution and EU law as something that is dealt with and secured at the moment of ratifying the relevant treaties (including revision treaties). It is as though a form of systemic control is seen to exist, which prevents any future specific collisions. Thirdly, the Portuguese Constitution was amended several times to prevent any risks of constitutional collision with the successive EU treaties. This was effected without recourse being made to the Constitutional Court, which, moreover, was never asked to expound its position on the relationship between European integration and national constitutional law in a high profile case. The final

---

[4] Judgment 163/90, *Acórdãos do Tribunal Constitucional*, vol. 16, 1990, at 301. See, in the same sense: judgment 606/94 of 22 November 1994, *Acórdãos do Tribunal Constitucional*, Vol. 29, 1994, at 161.

reason is linked to the general attitude of the Portuguese legal community towards EU law and will be developed in the next section. As we will see, although traditionally open to international law, the Portuguese legal system is one of the national legal systems within the EU with a lower degree of incorporation of EU law in its judicial proceedings. In other words, the true extent of its openness towards EU law has never in practice been challenged.

## 3. Law in action

Two decades after Portugal's accession to the EU and at a time when there seems to be an absence of normative conflicts with national law, especially after the 2004 constitutional revision, we will try to assess the real level of implementation of EU law in Portugal.

There are several ways in which implementation may be measured: through the application of EU law by national courts; through the degree of EU law's transposition into national law (when required); or, finally, though the implementation of EU law by the national administrative organs. Since it is impossible to study all these realities within the confines of this text, we have chosen as our yardstick the judicial process. It not only has pivotal importance in the legal system of the EU, but also represents a decentralized model, in which national administrations and courts work simultaneously as European entities.

In this section we will present a comprehensive range of statistics/data referring to the number of preliminary references made by Portuguese judges (Article 234 of TEC) and to the actions for failure to fulfil obligations proposed against Portugal by the Commission (Article 226 of the TEC). The choice of these measurement mechanisms is justified by the fact that they can work as a barometer of the effective application of EU law: the preliminary references allow us to estimate the day-to-day influence of EU law in the national courts and the actions for failure to fulfil obligations provide a register of the compliance of the Member States with their EU law duties.

## 3.1 *Preliminary references*

The preliminary reference mechanism has been put to very limited use in Portugal since its accession to the EU.

In Table I we compare the number of preliminary references made by the courts of the different Member States in the last twenty years[5].

| Table I – Preliminary References | | | | | | | | | | | | | | | | |
|---|---|---|---|---|---|---|---|---|---|---|---|---|---|---|---|---|
| **1986-2005#** | | | | | | | | | | | | | | | | |
| | **BE** | **DEN** | **FR** | **GER** | **GR** | **HOL** | **IT** | **IRL** | **LUX** | **PT** | **SPA** | **UK** | **AUS\*** | **FIN\*** | **SWE\*** | **Total** |
| **1986** | 13 | 4 | 19 | 18 | 2 | 16 | 5 | 4 | 1 | 0 | 1 | 8 | - | - | - | 91 |
| **1987** | 15 | 5 | 36 | 32 | 17 | 19 | 5 | 2 | 3 | 0 | 1 | 9 | - | - | - | 144 |
| **1988** | 30 | 4 | 38 | 34 | 0 | 26 | 28 | 0 | 2 | 0 | 1 | 16 | - | - | - | 179 |
| **1989** | 13 | 2 | 28 | 47 | 2 | 18 | 10 | 1 | 1 | 1 | 2 | 14 | - | - | - | 139 |
| **1990** | 17 | 5 | 21 | 34 | 2 | 9 | 25 | 4 | 4 | 2 | 6 | 12 | - | - | - | 141 |
| **1991** | 19 | 2 | 29 | 54 | 3 | 17 | 36 | 2 | 2 | 3 | 5 | 14 | - | - | - | 186 |
| **1992** | 16 | 3 | 15 | 62 | 1 | 18 | 22 | 0 | 1 | 1 | 5 | 18 | - | - | - | 162 |
| **1993** | 22 | 7 | 22 | 57 | 5 | 43 | 24 | 1 | 1 | 3 | 7 | 12 | - | - | - | 204 |
| **1994** | 19 | 4 | 36 | 44 | 0 | 13 | 46 | 2 | 1 | 1 | 13 | 24 | - | - | - | 203 |
| **1995** | 14 | 8 | 43 | 51 | 10 | 19 | 58 | 3 | 2 | 5 | 10 | 20 | 2 | 0 | 6 | 251 |
| **1996** | 30 | 4 | 24 | 66 | 4 | 10 | 70 | 0 | 2 | 6 | 6 | 21 | 6 | 3 | 4 | 256 |
| **1997** | 19 | 7 | 10 | 46 | 2 | 24 | 50 | 1 | 3 | 2 | 9 | 18 | 35 | 6 | 7 | 239 |
| **1998** | 12 | 7 | 16 | 49 | 5 | 21 | 39 | 3 | 2 | 7 | 55 | 24 | 16 | 2 | 6 | 264 |
| **1999** | 13 | 3 | 17 | 49 | 3 | 23 | 43 | 2 | 4 | 7 | 4 | 22 | 56 | 4 | 5 | 255 |
| **2000** | 15 | 3 | 12 | 47 | 3 | 12 | 50 | 2 | 0 | 8 | 5 | 26 | 31 | 5 | 4 | 224 |
| **2001** | 10 | 5 | 15 | 53 | 4 | 14 | 40 | 1 | 2 | 4 | 4 | 21 | 57 | 3 | 4 | 237 |
| **2002** | 18 | 8 | 8 | 59 | 7 | 12 | 37 | 0 | 4 | 3 | 3 | 14 | 31 | 7 | 5 | 216 |
| **2003** | 18 | 3 | 9 | 43 | 4 | 28 | 45 | 2 | 4 | 1 | 8 | 22 | 15 | 4 | 4 | 210 |
| **2004** | 24 | 4 | 21 | 50 | 18 | 28 | 48 | 1 | 1 | 1 | 8 | 22 | 12 | 4 | 5 | 249 |
| **2005** | 13 | 3 | 11 | 36 | 8 | 29 | 12 | 2 | 2 | 1 | 9 | 11 | 12 | 4 | 9 | 166 |
| **Total** | 350 | 91 | 430 | 931 | 100 | 399 | 693 | 33 | 42 | 56 | 162 | 348 | 273 | 42 | 59 | 4016 |

\# Data until 1 September 2005.
\* States that joined the EU in 1995.

---

[5] There is no reference to the number of preliminary references made by the new Member States. Their recent accession (2004) does not allow for any kind of useful comparative analysis to be made. In any event, it should be mentioned that the Hungarian (2 in 2004 and 3 in 2005) and Polish judges (1 in 2005) have already had the opportunity of questioning the ECJ though a preliminary proceeding.

BE – Belgium; DEN – Denmark; FR – France; GER – Germany; GR – Greece; HOL – Holland; IRL – Ireland; IT – Italy; LUX – Luxemburg; PT – Portugal; SPA – Spain; UK – United Kingdom; AUS – Austria; FIN – Finland; SWE – Sweden.

Considering the data for all Member States, Portugal is 12th in the number of preliminary questions presented (56), only ahead of Ireland (33), Luxembourg (42) and Finland (42), although it should be noted that this latter country only joined the EU in 1995. Portuguese judges have only presented about 1/8th of the questions referred by Dutch judges (400), 1/7th of the questions referred by Belgian judges (350), 1/3rd of the questions presented by Spanish judges (162) and 1/2rd of the questions made by the Greek judges (100). Portuguese preliminary references accounted for only 1.39% of the total number of preliminary references presented in the last twenty years (56 out of a total 4,016).

Another interesting element brought to the fore by Table I is the fact that the evolution of Portuguese preliminary references has not been uniform. After the presentation of the first preliminary references in the late 1980s there was a steady rise, which peaked in 2000 (8). The millennium, however, brought a sudden fall in the number of preliminary references. In the last three years the average has been one question a year. This evolution contradicts, at least in the Portuguese case, the opinion of authors Sweet and Brunnel (2004, p. 63), who associate the evolution of gross domestic product and the commercial trade between the Member States with the presentation of preliminary references by national judges.

One of the possible explanations for the low number of preliminary references made by Portuguese judges could be the relatively small population of Portugal, especially when compared with other Member States. For this reason we have decided to introduce the population factor (Table II).

| Table II – Preliminary References and Population of the Member –States 1986-2005* | | | |
|---|---|---|---|
| | N.º of References | Population (in millions)# | Ratio References/Population |
| AUSTRIA | 273 | 8.2 | 33.29 |
| BELGIUM | 350 | 10.4 | 33.65 |
| DENMARK | 91 | 5.4 | 16.85 |
| FINLAND | 42 | 5.2 | 8.08 |
| FRANCE | 430 | 60.5 | 7.11 |
| GERMANY | 931 | 82.5 | 11.28 |
| GREECE | 100 | 11.1 | 9.01 |
| HOLAND | 399 | 16.3 | 24.48 |
| IRELAND | 42 | 4.1 | 10.23 |
| ITALY | 693 | 58.5 | 11.85 |
| LUXEMBURG | 33 | 0.46 | 71.74 |
| PORTUGAL | 56 | 10.5 | 5.33 |
| SPAIN | 162 | 43.0 | 3.78 |
| UNITED KINGDOM | 348 | 60.0 | 5.80 |
| SWEDEN | 59 | 9.0 | 6.55 |

\* Data until 1 September 2005.
\# Source: Eurostat, 2005.

After the introduction of the population factor we can verify that the Portuguese courts have one of the lowest ratios of population/ references (5. 33), which is higher than the figure for Spain (3.78), but well behind the Dutch (24.48), Austrian (33. 29) and Belgian judges (33.65). One should mention, however, that the population factor should not have an excessive influence, since the number of judicial processes can vary according to population, but the number of processes that give rise to interpretative doubts about EU law depends, to a large extent, on the different potentials for conflict between national and EU norms. Since the regulatory activity tends to be the same between all the Member States, the population factor is less important in this context.

A more thorough study of the Portuguese preliminary references allows us to discover some interesting trends. Below we consider their origin (Table III), the subject they refer to (Chart I), the EU norms they mention (Chart II), and the respective answer given by the ECJ (Chart III).

We will begin by showing the origin of the preliminary references presented by Portuguese judges since the accession of Portugal to the EU (Table III).

| Table III – Origin of the Preliminary References* | | |
|---|---|---|
| 1986-2005# | | |
| Courts | N.º References | % |
| Constitutional Court | 0 | 0 |
| Supreme Court of Justice | 0 | 0 |
| Supreme Administrative and Tax Court | 32 | 57 |
| 2nd Instance Administrative and Tax Courts | 3 | 5 |
| Court of Appeal (civil) | 2 | 4 |
| 1st Instance Administrative and Tax Courts | 11 | 20 |
| 1st Instance Civil Courts | 8 | 14 |
| Total | 56 | 100 |

# Data until the 1st September 2005.

The data presented in Table III reveals that the Supreme Administrative and Tax Court is solely responsible for 57% of the total of preliminary references presented (32). In contrast, the Constitutional Court and the Supreme Court of Justice, also jurisdictions of last instance forced to make preliminary references according to Article 234(3) of the EC Treaty, have never made any references to the ECJ.

Another interesting conclusion to be drawn from Table III concerns the huge disproportion between the number of references made by administrative jurisdictions (82%) and civil jurisdictions (18%) and also the fact that only 1/3rd of the preliminary references were made by courts of first instance. This last statement is very surprising, as according to the thesis of the judicial empowerment sustained by Joseph H. H. Weiler (1991, p. 2426), these judges have the strongest incentive to cooperate with the ECJ, namely because they could be expected to use the preliminary reference procedure to overcome the case law of superior courts (thereby, according to Weiler and other authors, empowering themselves through EU law).

The subject matter of the preliminary references reflects their origin (Chart I).

### Chart I – Subject matter of preliminary references*
#### 1986-2005#

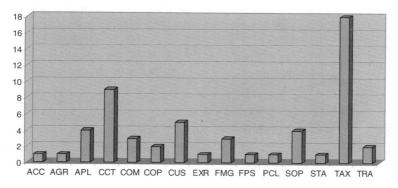

\* Due to the fact that some preliminary references concern more than one subject matter we have chosen the dominant subject matter.
\# Data until 1 September 2005.

ACC – Accession of new States; AGR - Agriculture; APL – Approximation of Laws; CCT – Common Customs Tariff; COM – Competition; COP – Commercial Policy; CUS – Customs Union; EXR – External Relations; FMG – Free Movement of Goods; FPS – Freedom to Provide Services; PCL – Principles of Community Law; SOP – Social Policy; STA – State Aid; TAX – Taxation; TRA – Transports.

The Portuguese preliminary references are concentrated in the areas of tax (18) and customs (14), which taken together are responsible for 57% of all references. Curiously, very important EU areas, such as agriculture or the freedom to provide services, have each only given rise to one question.

In addition to subject matter, the type of EU rules that were object of Portuguese preliminary references (Chart II) provide interesting material for analysis.

### Chart II – EU norms object of preliminary references
**1986-2005***

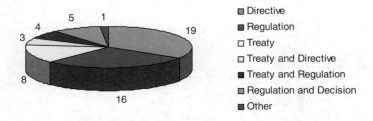

* Data until the 1st September 2005

According to Chart II, there is a clear predominance of secondary EU law, especially Directives and regulations, which represent almost 2/3rds of the total number of preliminary references. Surprisingly, primary EU norms only account for 14% of all preliminary references presented, which is symptomatic of the limited scope of the Portuguese references. It seems that the Portuguese courts have not yet adopted the treaties as a "constitutional charter"[6].

Finally, in order to determine their quality, it is important to consider the way the ECJ has decided the preliminary references made by Portuguese judges.

---

[6] Expression used by the ECJ in the Case n.º 294/83, *Parti écologiste "Les Verts" vs. Parlement européen*, Rec., 1986, p. 1365, par. 23.

### Chart III – Decisions and Orders of the ECJ regarding preliminary references 1986-2005*

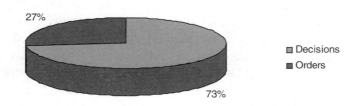

* Data until 1 September 2005.

Chart IV is a very eloquent indicator of the high level of orders resulting from preliminary references that originated from Portugal (27%). In other words, a high percentage of the references made by Portuguese courts are summarily dismissed by the Court of Justice (normally as inadmissible for several procedural reasons). If one considers that the number of references is already, in itself, quite low, the conjugation of the two elements appears to suggest that there is a problem in the functioning of the preliminary mechanism with regard to Portuguese courts.

Several conclusions can be drawn from the statistics presented above. Primarily, and in contrast to the success that legal integration has had throughout the majority of the Member States, it seems obvious that there is a problem regarding the judicial application of EU law in Portugal. Even considering the necessity of further and more complete studies in this matter, which could eventually cover all the national decisions that do not give rise to a preliminary reference, one can attempt to provide some possible explanations for this phenomenon.

First of all, the low number of preliminary references may in part result from the general lack of knowledge and training in EU law of the Portuguese judges and lawyers. This can also explain the high percentage of ECJ orders resulting from Portuguese preliminary references.

Another factor that may have inhibited Portuguese judges could be the length of the preliminary procedure, nowadays an average of 18 to 20 months. This length of time, within the context of the already significant delays in the Portuguese domestic judicial system, may explain some reluctance on the part of national judges to question the ECJ more frequently. Moreover, the organization of the Portuguese judiciary, which is divided into specialized jurisdictions, may have made it more difficult for a learning process to exist that could have led to a spill-over effect (as visible in the steady increases of preliminary references in other judicial systems). This is well evidenced by the huge concentration of preliminary references in the Administrative Supreme Court, especially in its Tax section, and their complete absence in the Supreme Court of Justice.

This brief, even impressionistic, description of Portuguese preliminary references suggests a diffused and fragmented implementation of EU law, which is reflected in the subject matters of the preliminary references presented and in the predominance of secondary over primary EU law issues. Portuguese judges appear not to have effectively incorporated EU law as part of their domestic law and also appear to ignore the constitutional approach to primary rules adopted by the ECJ. This, in turn, limits the europeanization of the national legal questions and the absorption of EU law into the mainstream of national legal discourse.

### 3.2 *Actions for failure to fulfil obligations*

Following the presentation of the preliminary reference data, our analysis will now turn to the actions for failure to fulfil obligations presented against six Member-States, including Portugal. This will allow us to verify if the Portuguese State complies with its EU law duties and therefore can be considered as a "good student" when compared with the four largest Member States of the EU (Germany, France, Italy and the United Kingdom) and Spain, who also acceded in 1986. With this purpose we will examine the number of actions for failure to fulfil obligations (Table IV) and their subject matters (Chart IV). In contrast to our preliminary references analysis we will not introduce any scale element, because EU legal duties are the same in every Member State, regardless of their different dimensions.

Table IV – Actions for failure to fulfil obligations presented against six Member States

1986-2005*

|  | FRA | GER | ITA | PT | SPA | UK |
|---|---|---|---|---|---|---|
| 1986 | 8 | 11 | 18 | 0 | 0 | 1 |
| 1987 | 8 | 3 | 22 | 0 | 1 | 2 |
| 1988 | 10 | 8 | 14 | 0 | 1 | 0 |
| 1989 | 8 | 5 | 36 | 1 | 5 | 5 |
| 1990 | 6 | 5 | 19 | 2 | 3 | 2 |
| 1991 | 4 | 1 | 19 | 2 | 2 | 0 |
| 1992 | 1 | 5 | 9 | 1 | 5 | 4# |
| 1993 | 2 | 3 | 9 | 0 | 5 | 0 |
| 1994 | 8 | 5 | 12 | 5 | 9 | 1 |
| 1995 | 6 | 10 | 17 | 4 | 7# | 2 |
| 1996 | 11 | 9 | 9 | 6 | 9 | 1 |
| 1997 | 15 | 20 | 20 | 15 | 7 | 1 |
| 1998 | 22 | 9 | 12 | 5 | 6 | 1 |
| 1999 | 35 | 9 | 29 | 13 | 7 | 6 |
| 2000 | 25 | 12 | 22 | 10 | 9 | 4 |
| 2001 | 20 | 13 | 21 | 7 | 15 | 11 |
| 2002 | 22 | 16 | 24 | 10 | 11 | 15 |
| 2003 | 22 | 18 | 20 | 10 | 28 | 8 |
| 2004 | 23 | 14 | 27 | 7 | 11 | 12# |
| 2005 | 8 | 10 | 28 | 6 | 6 | 6 |
| **Total** | 264 | 186 | 387 | 104 | 147 | 82 |

\* Data until 1 September 2005.

# Includes one action brought under Art. 227.º of the EC Treaty by Spain against the UK (1992), Belgium against Spain (1995) and Spain against the UK (2004).

FRA – France; Ger – Germany; ITA – Italy; PT – Portugal; SPA – Spain; UK – United Kingdom.

As Table IV shows, Portugal's record (104) is worse than that of the United Kingdom, but, in any event, is better than that of Germany (186), Spain (147), France (264) or Italy (387). Another interesting aspect relates to the fact that 86% of all actions for failure to fulfil obligations presented against Portugal were instigated in the last ten years. This however has happened, albeit with less intensity, in all the other Member States analysed and it is probably due to an increased effort by the Commission to bring infringement actions against Member States.

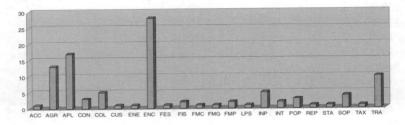

Chart IV – Subject matters of actions for failure to fulfil obligations presented against Portugal*

**1986-2005#**

* Due to the fact that some preliminary references concern more than one subject matter we have chosen the dominant subject matter.
# Data until 1 September 2005.
ACC – Accession of new States; AGR – Agriculture; APL – Approximation of Laws; CON – Competition; COL – Company Law; CUS – Customs Union; ENE – Energy; ENC – Environment and Consumers; FES – Freedom of Establishment; FIS – Fisheries Policy; FMC – Free Movement of Capitals; FMG – Free Movement of Goods; FMP – Free Movement for Persons; FPS - Freedom to Provide Services; INP– Industrial Policy; INT – Intellectual Property; POP – Population Protection; REP – Regional Policy; STA – State Aid; SOP – Social Policy; TAX – Taxation; TRA – Transports;

As regards the subject matters of the actions for failure to fulfil obligations presented against Portugal there is, as in the case of the preliminary references, a notable concentration (63%) in a short range of domains: transport (10), agriculture (13), environment and consumer law (27) and approximation of legislation (17).

The data related to the actions for failure to fulfil obligations shows us that Portugal can be regarded as a complying State, at least when compared with some of the other Member States considered in this study. This conclusion is, however, challenged by the growing number of actions presented in the last decade, which, as stated above, is probably due to the more active role of the Commission in the detection of irregularities coupled with the enlargement of the EU's competences and legislation (as the increasing number of actions in such domains as the environment or consumer law clearly demonstrates).

### 3.3 *Preliminary references vs. actions for failure do fulfil obligations*

In one final chart (V) we compare the number of preliminary references and actions for failure to fulfil obligations, in a bid to trace their different evolutions.

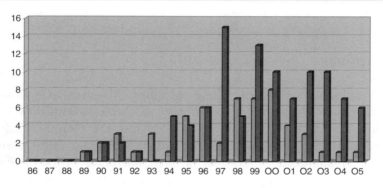

Chart V – Evolution of Portuguese Preliminary References and actions for failure to fulfil obligations presented against Portugal
1986-2005*

# Data until 1 September 2005.

Twenty years after Portugal's accession to the EU we can confirm that only in four years (1991, 1993, 1995 and 1998) was the number of preliminary references higher than number of actions for failure to fulfil obligations. Moreover, in the last five years, there has been a growing disparity between questions presented by Portuguese courts and actions brought against Portugal by the Commission.

In this section we have presented a very large range of statistical data, with the aim of identifying the real degree of EU law incorporation in Portugal. We stated earlier that both the preliminary references as well as the actions for failure to fulfil obligations could be seen as barometers of the effective application of EU law. The reading of the statistical data presented is, we think, a very clear sign that in action EU law incorporation and application is still very far removed from its written conception. There seem to be problems in the way Portuguese courts apply EU law but also an increasing number of actions for failure to fulfil obligations presented against Portugal. Although we have advanced some justifications for the current state of the art, it is difficult to draw definitive conclusions without a further study that involves all legal national actors.

EU law is increasingly embraced in Portuguese doctrinal and legislative discourse but appears to be held at a distance by the courts.


**Bibliography**

CARDOSO DA COSTA, José Manuel Moreira, *O Tribunal Constitucional Português e o Tribunal de Justiça das Comunidades Europeias*, Ab Vno Ad Omnes – 75 Anos Da Coimbra Editora, Coimbra, 1998,1363. BRITO, Maria Helena, *Relações entre a ordem jurídica comunitária e a ordem jurídica nacional: desenvolvimentos recentes em direito português*, Estudos em homenagem ao Conselheiro José Manuel Cardoso da Costa, Coimbra, 2003, 301. MADURO, Miguel Poiares; *The State of Portuguese European constitutional discourse*, F.I.D.E, XX Congress London, Vol. II, 2003, 387. MEDEIROS, Rui, *Relações entre Normas Constantes de Convenções Internacionais e Normas Legislativas da Constituição de 1976*, O Direito, 1990, II, 355. MIRANDA, Jorge, *A Constituição Europeia e a Ordem Jurídica Portuguesa*, Colóquio Ibérico – Constituição Europeia: Homenagem ao Doutor Francisco Lucas Pires, Studia Iuridica, 84, Coimbra, 2005, 537. ID, *O Tratado de Maastricht e a Constituição Portuguesa*, A União Europeia na Encruzilhada, Coimbra, 1996, 46. MOTA DE CAMPOS, João, *A ordem constitucional portuguesa e o Direito Comunitário*, Braga, 1981. MOURA RAMOS,

Rui, *Das Comunidades Europeias à União Europeia: Estudos de Direito Comunitário,* 2ª Edição, Coimbra, 1999. Piçarra, Nuno, *O Tribunal de Justiça das Comunidades Europeias Como Juiz Legal e o Processo do Artigo 177° do Tratado CEE – As relações entre a ordem jurídica comunitária e as ordens jurídicas dos Estados--membros da perspectiva dos tribunais constitucionais,* Lisbon, 1991. Pitta e Cunha, Paulo and Nuno Ruiz, *O Ordenamento Comunitário e o Direito Interno Português,* Revista da Ordem dos Advogados, Ano 55, 1995, 341. Sweet, Alec Stone and Thomas Brunnell, *Constructing a Supranational Constitution,* The Judicial Construction of Europe, Alec Stone Sweet (ed.), Oxford, 2004. Joseph H. H. Weiler, Joseph H. H., *The Transformation of Europe,* Yale Law Journal, 100, 1991.

# II
# PUBLIC LAW

# CHAPTER 5

# Constitutional Law

JORGE BACELAR GOUVEIA

SUMMARY: *1. The Portuguese State and the historical development of its constitutional law 2. The shaping and evolution of the Portuguese Constitution 3. The republican, democratic and semi-presidential political system 4. The unitarian structure of the Portuguese State and the minor political entities 5. The guarantee of the constitution and the Constitutional Court*

## 1. The Portuguese State and the historical development of its Constitutional Law

**1.1** Within a European and even a world context, Portugal is one of the oldest existing States. It was founded in the 12th century when a conjunction of historical facts gave birth to a new state community: 1139, the date of the Battle of Ourique, D. Afonso Henriques takes the title of King of Portugal; 1143, the date of the Treaty of Zamora, D. Afonso Henriques is recognized as king by D. Afonso VII, King of Castille; 1179, the date of the *Manifestus probatum* edict, whereby Pope Alexander III acknowledges D. Afonso Henriques as king, who until then had been addressed as duke.

**1.2** Since that founding moment and until the present time, Portuguese history has experienced many vicissitudes, which can be summarized as follows:

a) 1st period, 12th -14th centuries: territorial consolidation thanks to a succession of conquests and the creation of institutions according to mediaeval feudal schemes;
b) 2nd period – 15th and 16th centuries: the apogee of the Portuguese discoveries: Bartolomeu Dias rounds the Cape of Good Hope (1488), the discovery of the sea route to India by Vasco de Gama (1498) and the discovery of Brazil by Pedro Álvares Cabral (1500);
c) 3rd period – 16th and 17th centuries: political submission to Spain between 1580 and 1640, with the crown of Portugal being worn by the Spanish kings;
d) 4th period – 17th and 18th centuries: system of absolute monarchy and decline of the overseas empire as a result of strong competition on the part of other seafaring powers such as the Netherlands, the United Kingdom and France;
e) 5th period – 19th and 20th centuries: introduction and development of constitutional ideals within the framework of the contemporary State.

**1.3** From the 19th century onwards, constitutionalism makes its appearance in Portugal. The country is subject to the influences of the European and American liberal revolutions. Four different stages may be identified:

a) 1820-1910: the period of monarchic and liberal constitutionalism, with three constitutional texts - the first Constitution in 1822, the constitutional Charter of 1826, and the Constitution of 1838;
b) 1910-1926: the period of republican and liberal constitutionalism, with only one constitutional text, the Constitution of 1911 (First Republic);
c) 1926-1974: the period of authoritarian and corporative constitutionalism, also with only one constitution, that of 1933 (Second Republic or *Estado Novo*);
d) 1974 to the present time: the period of democratic and social constitutionalism, which began in 1974 with the 25 April Revolution and was formalized by the Constitution of the Portuguese Republic (CRP) of 2 April 1976, which has been

in force since then and has been subject to seven revisions (Third Republic).

**1.4** The present period belongs to the Third Portuguese Republic, which began in 1974, and during which various meaningful economic and social reforms have been undertaken: the enactment of legislation to ensure political democracy through the democratic election of the different ruling bodies and to enable, concomitantly, the dismantling of the former authoritarian structures; the granting, in 1975, of independence to those territories that had until then been colonies of Portugal (Angola, on 11 November; Cape Verde, on 5 July; Guinea-Bissau, granted on 24 September 1973, but entering into force only in 1975; Mozambique, on 25 June; and São Tomé and Principe, on 12 July); Portugal's entry into the European Communities on 1 January 1986, at the same time as Spain (it thus became 1 of 12 Member States); in 1989, a process of privatization of the many enterprises that had been nationalized in the aftermath of the revolution began; and in 1999 and 2002, two former Portuguese territories in Asia ceased to belong to Portugal (Macao was integrated into China on December 20, 1999, and East Timor became independent on 20 May 2002).

**1.5** Nowadays, Portugal comprises both mainland (it occupies an area of 88,797 sq km in the western part of the Iberian Peninsula), and islands (the archipelago of the Azores and Madeira, in the Atlantic Ocean, with areas of 2,333 sq km and 797 sq km respectively). The capital is Lisbon.

According to the 2004 census, the resident population is 10,536,000 and the active population 5,523,000. This results in a population density of 14 inhabitants/sq km.

The predominant religion is Roman Catholicism, professed by approximately 80% of the population, although many other religions co-exist in the country in a context of total religious freedom.

## 2. The shaping and evolution of the Portuguese Constitution

**2.1** Present Portuguese constitutional law rests on the Constitution of the Portuguese Republic (CPR) adopted on 2 April 1976, which came into force on 25 April 1976.

This supreme constitutional law of the Portuguese State is a corollary of the April 1974 Revolution – known as the revolution of the carnations – which put an end to the nationalist, corporative, fascist-leaning, right-wing authoritarian regime known as the "Estado Novo", which had been strongly influenced by the Italian fascist regime.

Prior to the adoption of the CPR, during the 2-year interim period in which the democratically elected constituent assembly drafted the new constitution, a series of urgent measures were simultaneously put in place in order to achieve (i) decolonization; (ii) democratization; and (iii) development.

**2.2** The CPR text currently contains 296 articles distributed over 4 parts, some of which include chapters. It is preceded by an introduction and brought to a conclusion by a final part.
- General principles (Articles 1-11);
- Part I – Fundamental rights and duties (Articles 12-79);
- Part II – Economic organization (Articles 80-107);
- Part III – Organization of political power (Articles 108-276);
- Part IV – Revision of the constitution (Articles 277-289);
- Final and transitional provisions (Articles 290-296).

**2.3** The CPR has already undergone seven revisions since it came into force, although the scope and extent of the revisions have varied considerably.

The first constitutional revision of 1982 – Constitution amendment act n° 1/1982 – attempted to stabilize the political system. It suppressed the Revolution Council, a body composed of military officers, which had been preserved by the constitution as a tribute to the role played by the armed forces in the revolution of the carnations. However, the continued existence of an organ of this type – whilst favoured by its members – gave rise to well-founded doubts about the truly democratic character of the Portuguese State.

The second constitutional revision of 1989 – Constitution amendment act n° 1/1989 – opened up the economic system to the large-scale movement towards privatization, which was deemed necessary following Portugal's 1986 entry into the European Communities. The revision repealed the principle of the irreversibility of nationalizations and established the mechanism of political referendum, thus promoting a more participative democracy.

The third constitutional revision of 1992 – Constitution amendment act n° 1/1992 – specifically focused on the constitutional provisions concerning European integration. It ensured that the Maastricht treaty could be ratified without incurring the risk of being ruled unconstitutional. Provisions were made for an enlargement of European integration, allowing for the new common foreign and security policy, the justice and home affairs pillar and the adoption of an economic and monetary union.

The fourth constitutional revision of 1997 – Constitution amendment act n° 1/1997 – was less specific in its scope, establishing various provisions concerning new fundamental rights, the granting of voting rights in the presidential election to Portuguese citizens living abroad, and the suppression, in peace times, of military courts, as well as the reinforcement of some of Parliament's legislative powers at the cost of the government's legislative powers.

The fifth constitutional revision of 2001 – Constitution amendment act n° 1/2001 – prepared the CPR for the ratification of the Rome Statute of the International Criminal Court, although it also concerned itself with other matters, including allowing police forces to create trade unions whilst excluding their right to strike, and defining Portuguese as the official State language.

The sixth constitutional revision of 2004 – Constitution amendment act n° 1/2004 – modified the regulatory body in charge of the media, enlarged the legislative competencies of the autonomous regions of Azores and Madeira vis-à-vis the State's legislative competencies, and provided for the possibility of setting maximum limits to the number and length of terms in public office, thus bestowing more consistency on the republican principle.

The seventh constitutional revision of 2005 – Constitution amendment act n° 1/2005 – concerned itself exclusively with providing for direct referenda on international treaties relating to European integration.

**2.4** The CPR is indeed a good example of a highly rigid constitution. The procedure for amendment sets out numerous limitations, protecting the stability of the constitution in view of its legitimizing function within the Portuguese juridical system:

    a) Organic limits: among the legislative bodies, only Parliament can initiate a constitutional revision;

    b) Time limits: the constitutional amendment procedure can only take place once every five years (ordinary revision), although a constitutional amendment procedure can be initiated at any time as long as it is supported in Parliament by a majority of four-fifths of its total number of members;

    c) Procedural limits: the legislative procedure for constitutional revision is subject to some special requirements, such as the fact that it can only be initiated by Parliament, that it must be adopted by a majority of two-thirds of its members entitled to vote, and that the President of the Republic may not refuse to promulgate the revision;

    d) Material limits: a considerable number of matters defined in the original version of the CPR cannot be amended; these are considered to be the identifying traits that characterize the CRP's notion of law;

    e) Circumstantial limits: constitutional revision cannot be initiated during exceptional circumstances, that is during a state of war or a state of emergency declared in accordance with the CRP.

## 3. The republican, democratic and semi-presidential political system

**3.1** The republican system was introduced in Portugal in the 20th century by the Revolution of the 5 October 1910. Since then Portugal has always been a republic, which means that a President, who is elected to a five-year term of office and who can only be re-elected to a single consecutive term, heads the State.

Similarly, public office is generally held on the basis of democratic legitimacy – direct legitimacy in the case of Parliament, and indirect legitimacy in the case of the government. The Constitution does not recognize any aristocratic privileges and sets out the principle of reappointment to public office, which can never be held for life.

The fact that the State system is a republic also implies that the principle of the separation of State and church is set out in the constitution. Thus, there is no official religion and all religious practices must be equally treated; as a result, across the various fields of activity, such as for example the State-held media, State-run education sector or taxation, religion must be respected in a context of cooperation and not of persecution.

**3.2** Another substantial change directly brought about by the Third Republic has been the development of a democratic system, within which different devices for the expression of the people's will co-exist at the three levels of public intervention:

a) Representative democracy, asserted in the election by direct universal suffrage of the President of the Republic (5-year term of office), of the Members of Parliament (4-year term), of the Members of the European Parliament (5-year term), of the Members of the regional assemblies (4-year term) and of local authorities (4-year term);

b) Referendum democracy, which consists in the possibility of holding referenda at the national, regional and local levels on the most relevant issues to be decided upon by their respective governing bodies;

c) Participative democracy, which characterizes the exercise of the various fundamental rights and freedoms of a political nature, conducive to the free expression of public opinion not only via the media, but also via the formation of associations and political parties.

**3.3** The political organs of the Portuguese State comprise the President of the Republic, Parliament (*Assembleia da República*) and the Government, all of which are separate from the judiciary. These political organs share some common powers.

The relationship between these three political organs has been defined according to the semi-presidential model, whereby each has effective powers of intervention in political action, based on the separation and interdependence of powers.

The President, who is elected by the people, does not hold executive power, and does not even preside over the Cabinet (*Conselho de Ministros*), but has the right to interfere in political action, using the inherent political powers of his office, when deemed necessary. These powers include: (i) power of political veto over legislative acts; (ii) the final power to call political and legislative referenda; (iii) the power to dismiss the government when the democratic institutions are not functioning properly; and (iv) the power to dissolve Parliament (*Assembleia da República*).

Parliament is unicameral. It has 230 members, elected to a 4-year term in accordance with the system of proportional representation using the Hondt method of highest average. There are 20 constituencies within the national territory (18 districts and 2 autonomous regions) and 2 for Portuguese citizens residing in foreign countries (one for Europe and one for outside Europe). Parliament exercises the most important legislative powers, including that of amending the constitution. The formation of government originates in Parliament since the government is accountable to it.

The government is appointed by the Head of State following the results of a general election. It is the organ that conducts the general government of the country, endowed with some legislative and political powers, and above all, with very wide administrative powers. The government comprises the Prime Minister and a variable number of ministers depending on the departments represented in it, as well as secretaries of State. It is the supreme organ of the State's civil service.

Despite those traits that characterize the Portuguese political system as being semi-presidential, practice has led to emphasis on the predominance of parliament. This is very much the result of the same ideology having held both a majority in parliament and the office of head of State for the last ten years. It should also be pointed out that the composition of parliament, even in 2002-2005, when there was a period of political cohabitation, always enabled the formation of stable government majorities: an important political factor in emphasizing the parliamentary side of any semi-presidential regime.

## 4. The unitarian structure of the Portuguese State and the minor political entities

**4.1** The territorial organization of the Portuguese State is not fully centralized, despite the fact that Portugal is a unitarian State, where no other State political structures exist apart from the ones mentioned above. This is has been a feature of Portuguese constitutionalism practically from the first, and has certainly been influenced by the exiguity of its territory.

Within its territory, the State recognizes decentralized political structures with the ensuing related powers: political and legislative powers in the case of the autonomous regions of the Azores and Madeira; and administrative powers in the case of administrative bodies, chiefly local authorities.

**4.2** The autonomous regions of the Azores and Madeira – one region for each of these groups of islands in the North Atlantic – are bodies that are defined in the CPR. In addition to administrative powers, they also hold political and legislative powers for reasons that stem from the need to overcome the difficulties of collective organization on the islands. Their insular position requires a larger degree of political and legislative self-government, albeit with due respect to the unity of the Portuguese Republic.

From the legislative viewpoint, the powers of the autonomous regions are quite extensive. They are entitled to issue regional legislative decrees for their territories, unless the subject matter does not fall within their powers or falls within the exclusive powers of Parliament (in some cases, however, these may be delegated).

The organization of the autonomous regions comprises their own organs, which are the legislative assemblies elected in the regional territory by direct universal suffrage of the Portuguese citizens who inhabit it, and the regional governments, appointed in the wake of the electoral results, who form the regional executive, accountable to the legislative assemblies.

The State's representation in each of the autonomous regions rests with the Representative of the Republic, a single-member body appointed by the President of the Republic, with limited powers of intervention in the regional government system, amounting to little more than the signing of regional decrees and the power to bring them before the Constitutional Court for judicial review.

**4.3** Another significant dimension of the territorial organization of the Portuguese State is found in local government. Local authorities are bodies of local self-government with administrative powers, exercised at two different levels.

There are 308 municipalities on the mainland and in the islands. Their organs are the municipal assembly and the municipal executive (*câmara municipal*), both democratically elected by the citizens who reside within the area of each municipality (*conselho*).

At the parish level, there are 4,260 parishes, similarly scattered throughout the entire territory. Their organs are the parish assembly and the parish executive (*junta de freguesia*), the first being also democratically elected by the citizens who reside within the area of each parish.

# 5. The guarantee of the Constitution and the Constitutional Court

**5.1.** The effectiveness of the constitutional text demands that devices are laid down in order to guarantee its protection against unconstitutional acts, otherwise the hierarchical supremacy of its provisions could not be upheld.

The CPR accordingly establishes the general principle that any acts that violate its provisions and principles are void. Simultaneously, it lays down the general principle of civil liability for acts committed against the CPR.

However, there are also other specific defence mechanisms that apply to specific unconstitutional situations, such as:

a) The state of constitutional exception, when the State, in response to institutional and political disturbances, suspends a certain number of rights and freedoms, and reinforces its administrative powers with a view to re-establishing constitutional normality;

b) The prohibition of fascist and racist associations, in which case freedom of association is not recognized on the grounds that these organizations infringe the fundamental values of the democratic constitutional order;

c) The right to resist, which recognizes the possibility for citizens not to obey orders by public authorities that infringe their rights and freedoms, albeit as a subsidiary means and only when other legal means are unavailable.

**5.2** However, the main defence mechanism of the CPR is judicial review, in particular the scrutiny conducted by the Constitutional Court.

The Constitutional Court makes up part of the judiciary, together with the other courts. It comprises 13 judges, 10 elected by Parliament by a majority of two-thirds of its members, and 3 who are co-opted by the elected judges, for a 9-year non-renewable term of office.

The result of a judicial review of constitutionality is a juridical and judicial judgement on the conformity with the CPR of all laws, procedures or actions by public bodies.

There are 4 different types of review:

a) Preventive scrutiny by the Constitutional Court, carried out upon the request of the President of the Republic, of the more relevant legislation. It takes place before the legislation is complete, when it is awaiting the President's signature or promulgation;

b) In concreto review conducted in its first stage by any ordinary court and, later, on appeal, by the Constitutional Court; it assesses the conformity with the constitution of provisions applied in court decisions. Those that are ruled to be unconstitutional must be quashed and those that comply with the Constitution must be applied. This type of review may be initiated by the Constitutional Court itself or upon request from one of the interested parties in the case;

c) In abstracto review, exclusively carried out by the Constitutional Court, which assesses the conformity with the Constitution of legal provisions or actions by public bodies. Should the court decide that the provision is contrary to the Constitution, the unconstitutional provision is declared void and, therefore, it disappears from the juridical order with general effects. The ruling of the Constitutional Court is binding and has an *erga omnes* effect, even though there may be a few exceptions in the case of already-produced effects;

d) Unconstitutionality by omission, which review is also exclusively carried out by the Constitutional Court. The court verifies whether there has been a breach of the CPR, not on the grounds of acts contrary to its provisions, but as a result of the omission of enactment of legislative measures demanded by the Constitution. There is, therefore, a violation by inertia or failure to act. In such case the Constitutional Court is called upon to bring the omission to the attention of the relevant body, in order that it may enact the necessary legislative provisions.

**5.3** The notion of constitutional justice encompasses more than that which has been described here. Indeed, the enforcement of the CPR is not restricted to the mechanism of judicial review.

In addition to the monitoring and scrutinizing activities outlined above, other powers, most of which vested on the Constitutional Court, are interesting from the standpoint of the enforcement of constitutional law:

a) Electoral disputes: the review of elections at their different stages, from the moment that candidates are announced to the proclamation of results;

b) Institutional disputes: the scrutiny of the exercise of public office, namely ascertaining the vacancy of the office of President of the Republic and the loss of parliamentary mandate of Members;

c) Referenda disputes: the *ex ante* review of the constitutionality and legality of national, regional and local referenda;

d) Partisan disputes: the review of the legality of elections and other ballots held within political parties, and of the establishment of parties.

## Bibliography

BACELAR GOUVEIA, Jorge, *Manual de Direito Constitucional*, vol. I and II, Coimbra, 2005. GOMES CANOTILHO, José Joaquim, *Direito Constitucional e Teoria da Constituição*, 7th ed., Coimbra, 2003. MIRANDA, Jorge, *Manual de Direito Constitucional*, vol. I-VI, Coimbra, 2000 to 2005.

# CHAPTER 6

# Fundamental Rights

JORGE BACELAR GOUVEIA

SUMMARY: *1. The relevance of fundamental rights in Portuguese constitutional law 2. Fundamental rights in the Portuguese Constitution of 1976 3. The general system of fundamental rights 4. Rights and freedoms 5. Economic, social and cultural rights*

## 1. The relevance of fundamental rights in Portuguese Constitutional Law

**1.1** The constitutional protection of fundamental rights has been one of the most dynamic parts of constitutional law and has experienced far-reaching developments since the liberal revolutions that began in the 18th century, in the United States of America and in France, and spread to other parts of the world throughout the 19th century, bringing with them the emergence of fundamental rights that have steadily grown in number.

Accordingly the constitutional law of any State governed by the rule of law (as contemporary political history clearly testifies) cannot but pay careful attention to the protection of fundamental human rights, starting with the relevant constitutional texts and evolving from there.

Portugal, in this respect, is no exception. Through the evolution of its Constitutions the various stages in the recognition of fundamental rights may be traced.

**1.2** In the 19th century, the first fundamental rights made their appearance in constitutional texts, closely linked to liberal political thought. These rights were either the subject of autonomous declarations or mentioned in the texts themselves, always within the context of the natural law theory largely developed by the Enlightenment philosophy.

This first generation of fundamental civil and political rights would, however, rapidly be joined by a second generation of fundamental social rights, which were to be dramatically asserted during the last quarter of the 19th century, at the time of the so-called Social Question. The fundamental social rights protected the workers' and trade unions' interests and helped build the welfare state that would only fully come into being in Europe after the 2nd World War.

More recently, since the 1960s, a third and fourth generation of fundamental rights have emerged. These latter rights are not linked by a single guiding thread but rather give vent to new concerns related to multiple issues, such as the environment, the protection of the individual against its misuse, the protection of man against genetic manipulation, or the right of peoples and nations to safeguard their cultural autonomy.

The evolution of Portuguese constitutional law partly reflects this chronology, with the first four constitutional texts – dating from 1822, 1826, 1838 and 1911 – evidencing a predominantly liberal view on fundamental rights. The Constitution of 1933, on the other hand, although drafted in the context of an authoritarian State, already enshrined some social rights. It was, however, only under the Constitution of 1976 that fundamental rights found their fullest expression, in a global concept that covered all the various generations of rights and freedoms emerged in the course of the evolution of the contemporary state.

**1.3** It should also be pointed out that constitutional law is definitively not the only branch of law concerned with protecting the fundamental rights of human beings. On the contrary, this protection is afforded by interaction with various other branches of law.

Civil law, since its origins, has turned to the protection of personal rights. The first codifications, in the 19th century, already offered schemes for the protection of an individual's privacy and personal inviolability. Such was the case in Portugal with the first Civil Code of 1867, setting a pattern that was again followed by the current Civil Code of 1966.

Likewise, in the 20th century, international public law has seen the development of various systems of human rights protection. First at the universal level, within the framework of the United Nations Organization, but later at the regional level, in the Council of Europe, the European Union, the Organization of American States and the African Union. Portugal is fully bound by both the universal and the European systems for the protection of human rights.

## 2. Fundamental rights in the Portuguese Constitution of 1976

**2.1** In current Portuguese constitutional law, fundamental rights feature prominently in Part I of the Constitution of the Portuguese Republic (CPR). These rights are enshrined in a range of articles, from Articles 12 to 79, which means that the majority are enumerated and characterized.

In Part I of the Constitution, fundamental rights are divided into two separate groups: in section II, "Rights, freedoms and guaranties"; and in section III, "Economic, social and cultural rights and duties".

The difference between the two categories is not very clear, notwithstanding the variety of criteria that have been put forward in order to distinguish them, ranging from the autonomous constitutional density of the first, which is not found in the second, to respective structures of protection in the first case and of service in the second.

Notwithstanding, and in the absence of a totally secure substantial criterion, the two categories are differentiated by their respective legal force within the juridical order. Hence, rights and freedoms belong to the category of provisions with direct and immediate effect, whilst economic, social and cultural rights have a merely programmatic nature.

**2.2** Nevertheless, this does not mean that the constitutional sources of fundamental rights are uniquely concentrated in the above-mentioned sections of the Constitution. It is possible to identify other sets of fundamental rights, for instance the non-enumerated fundamental rights set out in: section I of Part I of the CPR, under "General principles" of the "Fundamental rights and duties"; section I of Part II of the CPR, under "General principles" of the "Economic organization"; Section IX of Part III of the CPR, under "Civil service", which is part of the general topic of the "Organization of political power".

**2.3** It is also possible to identify fundamental rights outside the Constitution. These acquire constitutional force under the so-called open clause of article 16, §1 of the CPR, which states: "Fundamental rights enshrined in the Constitution do not exclude any other fundamental rights contained in statutes or in applicable international law rules".

In accordance with this wording, the set of fundamental rights with constitutional force is widened to encompass other rights that have not been defined in the Constitution. Boundaries are however provided by the following three parameters: the material breadth of the incorporated rights (their compatibility with the basic values of the Portuguese system of fundamental rights); the sources from which they stem (internal law and applicable international rules, meaning that the rights must be preceded by a formal recognition); the applicable regime (they share the same degree of protection granted by the constitution's supremacy and the rigour that goes with it; therefore, the notion that these rights might be secondary with regard to the fundamental rights asserted in the constitutional text is not acceptable).

## 3. The general system of fundamental rights

**3.1** From a formal standpoint, it is easy to argue that the fundamental rights proclaimed in the CPR are there because of a clear intention to bestow on them formal recognition within a text endowed with the value of a constitution, conferring on them in this way the highest legal force that a state can grant.

However, the legal and constitutional recognition given to fundamental rights has another, no less important, rationale, which also emphasizes their relevance, namely that this recognition was accompanied by an autonomous definition and enumeration of the various types of fundamental rights.

Furthermore, owing to the so-called open clause of article 16, the constitutional catalogue of fundamental rights is at all times ready to incorporate further types of fundamental rights, adapting to new needs or modifying existing rights.

**3.2** From the standpoint of a substantial rationale, fundamental rights enshrined in the Constitution may be seen as the composite outcome of various criteria that have been filtered by constitutionalism over the years – from the liberal State to the welfare State. Nowadays, it is possible to say that there are several thematic poles around which fundamental rights gravitate and find their own explanation, based on a pluralist notion, on the influences to which they have been exposed and on their historical chronology.

It is also interesting to note that the Portuguese Constitution is a good example of the harmonious composition of various existing trends with regard to the recognition of fundamental rights, namely liberal fundamental rights, which are rooted in liberal theory. They present themselves as areas of protection and autonomy vis-à-vis the State (rights and freedoms), social fundamental rights imposed by social theory and provided to citizens by the State and other public bodies, and finally democratic fundamental rights, which pay tribute to democratic theory. According to the latter, certain rights play an integral role in political participation, by enabling citizens to be active players in political society.

**3.3** Concerning the rules that govern these fundamental rights in general, three issues should be addressed. Other related questions appear to be specific to the respective rights and freedoms and economic, social and cultural rights.

Firstly, the issue of subjective granting. The principle of universality implies that fundamental rights must be held in general, extending to each and every natural person, whether national or non-national, with the exception of a few rights reserved to Portuguese citizens. Corporations may also hold fundamental rights if these are compatible with their structure; the principle of equality determines that fundamental rights must always abide by the rules dictated by the principle of equal treatment, in terms of both their equalizing and differentiating effects, with discrimination being prohibited and some forms of positive discrimination being accepted as long as they are found to be materially justified.

Secondly, the issue of juridical exercise. The regulation of fundamental rights is conducted by Parliament. A higher standard of rationality and democracy is thereby ensured. Any limitations laid down to their exercise are dictated solely by the need to protect other fundamental rights or constitutional values worthy of protection.

Finally, effective protection. The protection of fundamental rights is broad. In its non-jurisdictional form, attention should be drawn to the expanding role of the ombudsman (*Provedor de Justiça*), while in its jurisdictional form protection is provided by the courts, which can invalidate unconstitutional legal provisions, as well as apply mechanisms of civil and criminal responsibility against the infringement of fundamental rights.

## 4. Rights and freedoms

**4.1** The first broad category of fundamental rights comprises the so-called rights and freedoms, consisting of three even more specific sets of rights, namely:

a) Personal rights and freedoms: those rights that relate to an individual's personal life; not only civil rights, but also rights pertaining to the enforcement of criminal law and of criminal procedural law;

b) Rights and freedoms of political participation: those rights that are connected to the intervention of Portuguese citizens in political decisions, by way of elections, referenda or merely by shaping public opinion;

c) Workers' rights and freedoms: those rights that concern the protection of workers' interests within the context of the enforcement of labour laws. They grant protection to the socially and economically weaker position of the employee in relation to the position of the employer.

The dividing line between each of the above sets of rights and freedoms is not always clearly demarcated, but in broad terms it is possible to say that each concentrates on a field of human activity, *i. e.* personal life, political life and working life.

**4.2** The relevance of the specific rights and freedoms can be basically assessed by the special legal force they carry, in acknowledgement of the higher effectiveness of their enforcement, due not only to the fact that their commands become immediately operative but also because they represent demands that citizens make on the State that can be immediately answered.

There is no doubt that the provisions governing the rights and freedoms apply to all fundamental rights, recognized as such and set out in the Constitution under section II of Part I, since that is their function within the constitutional organization.

However, the constitutional text itself also mentions and extends protection to other fundamental rights, which it identifies as being similar to the rights and freedoms enshrined.

**4.3** The force of law is greater in the protection of rights and freedoms than economic, social and cultural rights, as is evident from the following characteristics:

a) Direct and immediate applicability: the rights and freedoms, by virtue of their legal nature, are directly and immediately applicable in the legal order and do not depend upon the existence of favourable economic and social conditions. In addition, with very few exceptions, they are directly applicable without further enactment;

b) Binding effect on public and private bodies: the rights and freedoms bind public bodies that emanate from the corresponding legislative, administrative and jurisdictional powers. To a lesser extent, they can also be applied to legal relationships between private individuals, depending on the degree of legal and social assymetry that is present;

c) Limited possibility of being restricted under non-constitutional law: the legislature is entitled to restrict rights and freedoms, but only to a very limited extent. Limitations must be both formal – provided for under the CPR - as well as material. The restrictions must be of a general and abstract nature, proportionate to achieve their legitimate ends, non-retroactive and should never infringe the essential core of the rights.

d) Suspension in exceptional circumstances: rights and freedoms may be suspended if a situation of constitutional crisis arises, during the states of war or emergency, in order that political and social upheaval may be minimized. However, the suspension is always limited to a maximum of 15 days at a time.

## 5. Economical, social and cultural rights

**5.1** Economic, social and cultural rights complete the global vision of fundamental rights enshrined in the CPR. These rights may, in turn, be divided into three more specific sets of rights:

a) Economic rights and duties: the rights that pertain to the organization of the economy, namely economic initiatives and the rules governing private property, as well as the rights of consumers;

b) Social rights and duties: the rights that concern the integration of citizens within various social age groups, from childhood to old age, and that cover medical care, social security and housing;

c) Cultural rights and duties: the rights that pertain to the instruction and education of individuals, under which it is the State's duty to provide a public service of education at the various levels, to protect Portuguese culture and to further the practice of sports.

**5.2** Compared with rights and freedoms, the legal protection afforded to economic, social and cultural rights is less intense, due to the fact that they are enshrined in programmatic provisions and, as a result, cannot give rise to the same obligations of fulfilment.

This reality is a general one. However, it also makes itself felt in various aspects of the specific regime that governs the above-mentioned rights, which certainly offers much less protection than the regime applicable to right and freedoms. For instance, economic, social and cultural rights are not immediately enforceable and their fulfilment depends on the availability of favourable social and economic conditions. Moreover economic, social and cultural rights are not generically enforceable, as they are essentially addressed to public authorities, binding them to the realization of the existing constitutional programme on economic and social matters.

## Bibliography

BACELAR GOUVEIA, Jorge, *Manual de Direito Constitucional*, vol. II, Coimbra, 2005, pp. 1005 and ff.. GOMES CANOTILHO, José Joaquim, *Direito Constitucional e Teoria da Constituição*, 7th ed., Coimbra, 2003, pp. 393 and ff.. MIRANDA, Jorge, *Manual de Direito Constitucional*, vol. IV, 3rd ed., Coimbra, 2000, pp. 7 and ff.. VIEIRA DE ANDRADE, José Carlos, *Os direitos fundamentais na Constituição Portuguesa de 1976*, 3rd ed., Coimbra, 2001.

# CHAPTER 7
# Administrative Law

DIOGO FREITAS DO AMARAL
JOÃO CAUPERS

SUMMARY: *1. Historical precedents 2. Administrative codes 3. Structure of the Administration 4. Administrative procedure 5. Administrative rules and regulations ("regulamentos administrativos") 6. Administrative decisions ("actos administrativos") 7. Administrative contracts ("contratos administrativos") 8. Public Administration liability 9. Administrative remedies 10. Judicial structure 11. Judicial remedies.*

## 1. Historical precedents

Portugal was an absolute monarchy until 1820, when a liberal revolution put an end to absolutism and implanted a constitutional monarchy. The first two Portuguese Constitutions – established in 1822 and 1826 – proclaimed the individual rights of man and the separation of powers.

However it was only in 1832, after several coups and civil wars, that the Government of King Pedro IV, through its Home Secretary, Mouzinho da Silveira, approved legislation that, on the one hand, separated the judiciary from the executive power and, on the other hand, imported the French administrative system – a system that gave a strong power to administrative bodies and submitted their decisions, not to judicial review by the ordinary courts of law, but to a limited jurisdiction of a few special administrative tribunals[1], more inclined than the former to understand the need for the general interest – as interpreted by the central Government – to be prevalent over private, individual interests of the common citizens.

This scenario, with some minor exceptions, lasted until well after the democratic revolution of 1974 (see below §8).

## 2. Administrative codes

Portugal has had, since the above-mentioned liberal revolution, a tradition of Administrative codes, which have experienced three stages of evolution.

The first stage lasted for about one hundred and fifty years (1836 to 1976). There were then several laws called Administrative codes, which dealt, however, only with the legal status of the local authorities. Nowadays, only a small part of the last Administrative Code (1936) is still in force.

Then, in 1991, a second stage began: Portugal adopted its first Administrative Procedure Code (*Código do Procedimento Administrativo*), which still remains in force. It brought about an extensive and profound reform of the due process of law before public bodies and public agencies, including both central Government and local authorities. Despite its title, this Code is in fact much more than a mere law regulating administrative procedure: besides procedural rules and regulations, the Code also establishes the legal regime of the three main tools of administrative action: administrative regulations (*regulamentos administrativos*), administrative decisions (*actos administrativos*), and administrative contracts (*contratos administrativos*). This Code has inspired the publication of numerous studies and commentaries by legal scholars and marked the beginning of a new era in the general theory of administrative law.

---

[1] The word *tribunal* is, in Portuguese, a synonym of the expressions *court of justice* or *court of law*. Unlike in English, every court of justice is a tribunal and vice versa. So, administrative tribunals are courts of law ("jurisdição administrativa") with jurisdiction in the field of administrative matters.

Finally, in 2002, the third stage took place: Portugal enacted a new Administrative Courts Statute (*Estatuto dos Tribunais Administrativos e Fiscais*) and, for the very first time, a detailed Administrative Courts Procedure Code (*Código de Processo nos Tribunais Administrativos*), which departs from the old French tradition of the *recours pour excès de pouvoir* (*ultra vires* appeal) and approaches the German model of a full jurisdictional control of administrative activities, based on the model of the civil actions in the ordinary courts of law. Significantly enough, administrative tribunals, which during almost two centuries (1832-2002) could not punish or issue injunctions against public bodies, received full powers of punishment and injunction, with the sole limitation that tribunals cannot invade the area of administrative discretion, so that the separation of powers can be preserved and fully respected. In other words, administrative tribunals can now command the Administration to perform a legal duty, but they are not allowed to give instructions on how the Administration shall use a legal power or exercise a legal right.

In summary, Portugal nowadays has three important codes in the field of administrative law: one – albeit substantially modified by several statutes – deals with local authorities (1940), another regulates administrative procedure (1991), and a third regulates judicial procedure before administrative tribunals (2002). The only important field of administrative law that remains uncodified is the organization and operation of central government: this specific area is regulated by a large number of separate statutes (Ministries' organization, public agencies' statute, public companies' statute, and so on).


## 3. Structure of the Administration

The Portuguese Public Administration (*organização administrativa portuguesa*) encompasses the following types of public bodies:
- The State;
- Public agencies (*institutos públicos*);
- Public associations (*associações públicas*);
- Autonomous regions (*regiões autónomas*, that is, Azores and Madeira);

- Local authorities (*autarquias locais*);
- State-owned companies (*empresas públicas*);
- Some private companies and charities submitted to an administrative legal regime or subjected to Government supervision (*entidades particulares de interesse público*).

Public Administration involves a huge machinery, engaging about 750,000 civil servants and employees (17.5 per cent of the total working population). The civil service is ruled by special administrative statutes, according to the French model, and not by general labour law, as in the UK or the USA. Only the employees of the Public Administration are subject to general labour law.

## 4. Administrative procedure

Administrative procedure – that is, legal procedure concerning administrative activities – is ruled by the Administrative Procedure Code, as mentioned above in §2.

The major principles of law which govern Portuguese administrative procedure are:

a) Rule of law (*princípio da legalidade*): the Public Administration must always act in accordance with the rules of law, equality, proportionality, justice, impartiality and good faith (Administrative Procedure Code, Articles 3 to 6-A);

b) Cooperation with individuals and their right to be heard (*princípio da colaboração da Administração com os particulares* and *direito de audiência prévia*): the Public Administration must always act in full cooperation with individuals. These individuals have, as a rule, the right to be heard before a final decision of an administrative procedure is taken by a public body or agency; this important right to be heard exists whenever the planned administrative decision is, in its content, unfavourable to the individual's interests or requirements (Administrative Procedure Act, Articles 7, 8 and 100 to 105);

c) Power of coercive enforcement (*privilégio da execução prévia,* corresponding to the French *privilège du préalable*):

once a final decision is taken by the Public Administration against an individual, and he does not comply with his obligations or duties thereof, the public body or agency concerned is allowed by law to use its power of coercion and enforce the decision, without having to request any kind of previous permission or authorization from the courts (Administrative Procedure Code, Articles 149 to 157).

## 5. Administrative rules and regulations
### (*regulamentos administrativos*)

These are defined as legal rules or regulations, issued by an administrative body or agency empowered by law, and enforced within the limits of its powers. Four major principles apply to administrative rules and regulations:

a) Respect of law (*subordinação à lei*): all administrative rules and regulations must be issued on the basis of a specific legal authorization (*lei de habilitação*) and cannot contradict or violate the laws of the country. Should they do so, they will be considered as illegal, and therefore declared void or annulled by an Administrative Court (Administrative Courts Procedure Code, Articles 72 to 77);

b) Popular initiative (*petições de iniciativa particular*): all individuals or associations with *locus standi* (*legitimidade procedimental*) are entitled to submit individual or collective petitions to any public body or agency, requesting the drawing up, modification or revocation of a certain administrative rule or regulation. Those petitions must be accompanied by an explanation of the legal and social reasons that justify the need for the new rule. The petition cannot be refused by the public body or agency without the disclosure of the reasons justifying such refusal (Administrative Procedure Code, Article 115);

c) Right to be heard (*direito de audiência prévia*): as a rule, and only with a few exceptions, the competent public body or agency must hear, before the final approval of a new administrative rule or regulation, all private associations and organizations which legally represent the collective interests of those affected by the new rules, e.g. trade unions, employers' associations, non-governmental organisations, lobbies, etc. (Administrative Procedure Code, Article 117);

d) Public hearing (*discussão pública*): as a rule, subject to a few exceptions, a thirty-day public hearing will take place on the draft of the regulation (same Code, Article 118).

## 6. Administrative decisions (*actos administrativos*)

These are defined as unilateral decisions taken by public bodies or agencies, under a specific provision of law, which allows a decision to be taken that is binding upon the individual concerned (Administrative Procedure Code, Article 120). Major principles applying to administrative decisions are:

a) All administrative decisions must be taken in strict accordance with the applicable law (*princípio da legalidade*). Should there be any violation of the law, the consequences are the same as stated above in §5.a);

b) Written form (*forma escrita*): as a rule, with a few exceptions, all administrative decisions must be issued or registered in writing in a public document (*documento oficial*) (Administrative Procedure Code, Article 122);

c) Right to be heard (*direito de audiência prévia*): as a general rule, and with a few exceptions, before an administrative decision is taken, the individual or individuals to whom it is applicable have the right to be heard and are allowed to produce any factual or legal argument to try to convince the public body or agency concerned not to go ahead with its planned decision or, at least, to change it as required to bring about less damages to the individual or individuals concerned. This kind of individual hearing can be held in oral or written form. The individual concerned has, as a general rule, eight to ten days to present his case. If his or her reasons are not accepted by the public body or agency, the motives for the rejection must be clearly stated and may be subject to a subsequent judicial review (Administrative Procedure Code, Articles 100 to 105);

d) Administrative silence (*silêncio administrativo, inércia*): if a written request presented in due form to the appropriate administrative body or agency is not formally answered and decided within 90 days, Portuguese administrative law states that the absence of a decision shall always have a legal consequence, which is in some cases positive (*deferimento tácito*), and in other cases negative (*indeferimento tácito*) (Administrative Procedure Code, Articles 108 and 109). Whenever the legal consequence of administrative silence is a negative one, the individual concerned or damaged by it can refer the case to an administrative court, which may, according to the circumstances, decide: (a) to accept the silence as justified; (b) to command the appropriate body or agency to produce a written answer or decision within a fixed term set by the court; or (c) to declare that the silence implies a violation of a legal duty and, therefore, to condemn that body or agency to issue a decision in favour of the individual within a fixed term set by the court (Administrative Courts Procedure Code, Articles 66 to 71). The Court may condemn the administrative body or agency to issue a decision, but – observing the principle of separation of powers, as interpreted by the French legal tradition – may not take the decision itself. As a matter of fact, administrative courts exist in this country to handle judicial control, not to take administrative decisions that belong solely to the executive power, even if the latter fails to accomplish its duties (the Portuguese Constitution does not support any kind of judges' government);

e) Justification (*fundamentação*): in almost every case, administrative decisions must include a full explanation of their content. In a very few cases this justification may be avoided – namely when the decision grants that which the citizen has requested. In addition to these cases, disclosure of all the true grounds for any decision must be evident, coherent and sufficient. If, on the contrary, the justification is ambiguous, contradictory or insufficient, the decision shall be considered illegal. The Code sets out those cases in which administrative illegal decisions are void or may be annulled by an administrative court (Administrative Procedure Code, Articles 124 to 126);

f) Revocation of administrative decisions (*revogação de actos administrativos*): an administrative decision that is illegal shall be revoked by the administrative body or agency that has produced it; however, if that decision is the source of any rights or other relevant interests granted to an individual, the revocation is only possible up to the end of the time limit to refer the case to an administrative court (Administrative Procedure Code, Article 141);

g) Power of coercive enforcement (*privilégio da execução prévia*): see above §4.c).

## 7. Administrative contracts (*contratos administrativos*)

These are defined as contracts between an administrative body or agency and an individual, or company, which are not ruled by civil law, but instead by administrative law, according to the needs of the public interest. These are the major principles that apply to administrative contracts:

a) Written form: they must all be entered into in writing (Administrative Procedure Code, Article 184);

b) Main administrative contracts: the main categories regulated by law are the following (same Code, Article 178):
  – Public works contract (*empreitada de obras públicas*);
  – Public works concession contract (*concessão de obras públicas*);
  – Public services concession contract (*concessão de serviços públicos*);
  – Public domain contract (*concessão de utilização* and *concessão de exploração do domínio público*);
  – Concession of casinos (*concessão de exploração de jogos de fortuna e azar*);
  – Public supply contract (*contrato de fornecimento contínuo*);

- Provision of services contract (*contrato de prestação de serviços*): these contracts only have an administrative nature when they are entered into by a public body or agency, for the pursuit of a task in the immediate public interest. If this public aim does not exist, the contract will be considered as regulated by, and belonging to, civil law (Administrative Procedure Code, Article 182/2);

c) Use of administrative contracts: in so far as the Public Administration remains within the limits of its legal powers, it can freely choose whether the performance of a specific task in cooperation with private individuals or companies will be legally formalized through a unilateral administrative decision – subject to further acceptance by the private entity – or through an administrative contract (Administrative Procedure Code, Article 179);

d) Public powers of the Administration: the great majority of the typical administrative contracts mentioned above are contracts associating a private individual or company to the performance of a public task. Therefore, on behalf of the public interest, the administrative body or agency receives from the law some powers over the private contractor, who remains for the duration of the contract in a subordinate position (Administrative Procedure Code, Article 180).

In addition to two powers that are not alien to private relations based on civil law contracts – the power to command the execution of the contract and the power to impose sanctions for the breach of the contract – two other powers are strongly linked to the public interest:

- The power to introduce modifications in the contract, in order to adapt its content to the changing public interest – a power balanced with the duty of compensating the private part for losses or increases in charges resulting from those modifications; and
- The power to terminate unilaterally the contract, based on reasons of public interest.

e) Choice of the private contractor: notwithstanding some important exceptions, the general rule is that the administrative bodies and agencies may only choose their private contractors through a process of public tender (Administrative Procedure Code, Article 182).

Final observation: all litigious cases arising from the interpretation, validity or execution of an administrative contract shall be referred to an administrative court.

## 8. Public Administration liability

Portuguese public bodies and agencies are liable for their administrative decisions. This is a general principle, stated in the Portuguese Constitution, Articles 22 and 271. Legal rules concerning this liability are included in two different statutes: the Civil Code and Decree-Law 48051, of 21 November 1967.

The first statute applies to relations between public bodies and citizens whenever those relations are under private law; the second one applies to the same relations whenever they are under public law. When the source of liability is a material behaviour, instead of an administrative decision – *e.g.* a death due to medical malpractice in a military hospital or caused by a police car engaged in a pursuit after a bank robbery - which happens often, this distinction is controversial and very hard to establish.

Nevertheless, the distinction was crucial when the correct qualification was necessary to determine the kind of court able to handle the dispute: a civil court or an administrative one. However, from 1 January 2004, this is no longer the case. Now all statutes concerning public administration liability are to be enforced by administrative courts.

There are two major types of liability: the subjective type is based on a relation of damage > guilt > punishment (compensation); the other, the objective type, is based on a special relation of economic advantage > damage > compensation. While the former is a general principle, the latter is an exception, and has to be based upon a particular statute. The major objective is, in both cases, the transfer of the material loss caused to the victim by the public agent, to the community, through the allocation of a pecuniary compensation from taxpayers' money.

## 9. Administrative remedies

The Portuguese Public Administration must respect several constitutional principles, namely, the rule of law, equality, impartiality, neutrality, proportionality and *bona fides*. Should public bodies violate these principles, the legal system allows citizens, damaged by such violation, the use of both administrative and judicial remedies.

Administrative remedies operate within public bodies, mainly taking advantage of the existence of internal administrative controls. Such is the case with administrative review, usually handled by the superior of the author of the administrative decision. In most situations, administrative review may result in the confirmation, the substitution, the revocation or the modification of the administrative decision.

In some cases, administrative review may be handled by someone other than the author's superior. This happens when an administrative decision taken by an independent public body – e.g. a public agency – is submitted to the administrative control of a minister.

A complaint to the *Provedor de Justiça* (the Portuguese Ombudsman) is, perhaps, the most popular and relevant administrative remedy.

Drawing upon Scandinavian influence, the figure of the Ombudsman appeared in Portugal in 1975 and earned constitutional recognition in 1976. The Portuguese Ombudsman is an independent officer elected by Parliament for a four-year term, although he is allowed to run for a second term.

The Ombudsman is free to monitor every administrative decision, either at the request of a citizen or a company, or upon his own initiative. He has the power to criticize any decision – or even any lack of decision – whether he believes the decision is unlawful or if he simply finds it to be inappropriate. However, the Ombudsman does not have any power to change, replace or revoke an administrative decision.

As a matter of fact, the Ombudsman's actions are based on his ability to persuade administrative officers to do «the right thing». In order to fulfil that aim: he can inspect any public body; he must deliver, every year, a report to Parliament; he has the power to recommend any administrative decisions or actions; and he is entitled to use the media to increase pressure on administrative authorities.

Besides these tasks, the Ombudsman is also one of the few public authorities who has the power to file requests to the Constitutional Court in order to obtain a decision that declares null and void any law which the court considers to be against the Constitution, or even to constrain the Parliament or the Government to produce new legislation needed to enforce any constitutional rule or principle.

## 10. Judicial structure

According to the new Administrative Courts Statute and the new Administrative Courts Procedure Code, both dating from 2002 and enforced since 1 January 2004, the tradition, derived from the French model, of a dual jurisdiction is maintained. Nevertheless, the system evolved from its roots – the *contentieux d'annulation* – to a system more able to insure effective protection of citizens' rights affected or threatened by any public body or agency.

According to the Portuguese Constitution, disputes concerning relations between public authorities and citizens or companies fall within the jurisdiction of administrative courts. However this does not apply to all of those relations. As a matter of fact, administrative courts are the ordinary jurisdiction for those disputes, but not the exclusive jurisdiction. Some conflicts – namely those concerning private property and public notaries' activities – fall within the jurisdiction of the civil courts.

Administrative courts are organized on three levels. The lower level is composed of fourteen administrative and tax courts, the medium level has two administrative central courts. At the top level is the Supreme Administrative Court.

In spite of these three levels of tribunals, there are usually only two degrees of jurisdiction. In the majority of cases only one level of judicial review is granted, generally by an administrative central court, sometimes by the Supreme Administrative Court (*per saltum* appeal). Very seldom will there be a third degree of jurisdiction.

## 11. Judicial remedies

Since 2004 the administrative courts have dealt with three kinds of remedies: main remedies; urgent remedies; and provisional remedies.

Main remedies are used to decide common disputes between an administrative authority and a citizen or a company. There are two main remedies: the ordinary administrative action and the special administrative action.

The ordinary administrative action should be chosen whenever the conflict concerns a relationship between an administrative authority and a citizen or a company that is similar to any other relationship between citizens or companies themselves, namely a relationship based on contract or tort.

The special administrative action should be chosen whenever the conflict concerns a relationship originated by an administrative decision or omission. Similar to the old French *recours pour excès de pouvoir*, the special administrative action is indeed the heir of the old judicial review, whose only purpose was to refute an administrative decision in order to have it declared void or annulled by the court. This action is also appropriate to obtain from the court an order given to a public authority to take a decision to which a citizen or a company is entitled. It is a brand new tool, which copies the German *Verpflichtungsklage*.

Urgent remedies are used to refute two types of administrative decisions, both of which demand a swift judicial decision: decisions concerning elections and decisions concerning contract negotiation. Urgent remedies are also used to demand from the court two different types of injunctions: the injunction to obtain information or a certification from an administrative authority or to be allowed to consult a file kept by it, and the injunction to obtain court protection against an administrative decision which damages, or will probably damage, a citizen's fundamental right.

Provisional remedies have two major characteristics: on the one hand, they should be attached to a main remedy; on the other hand, they demand a court assessment based on two major concepts, both of Roman origin: *fumus boni juris* and *periculum in mora*. The judge performs a provisional evaluation based on a prognosis and decides in favour of the plaintiff whenever he believes that a court decision is needed to avoid either the occurrence of a future damage or the escalation of an existing one.

## Bibliography

ALMEIDA, Mário Aroso de, *O novo regime do processo nos tribunais administrativos*, 4rd ed., Coimbra, 2005. CADILHA, Carlos Alberto Fernandes, *Dicionário de Contencioso Administrativo*, Coimbra, 2006. CAUPERS, João, *Introdução ao Direito Administrativo*, 8th ed., Lisbon, 2005. FREITAS DO AMARAL, Diogo, *Curso de Direito Administrativo*, Vol. I, 2nd ed., Coimbra, 1994, and Vol. II; Coimbra, 2001. REBELO DE SOUSA, Marcelo, and André Salgado Matos, *Direito Administrativo Geral, Introdução e Princípios Fundamentais*, 2.ª edição, Lisbon, 2006; VIEIRA DE ANDRADE, José Carlos, *A justiça administrativa (Lições)*, 7th ed., Coimbra, 2005.

# CHAPTER 8
# Competition Law

JOSÉ LUÍS DA CRUZ VILAÇA
DOROTHÉE CHOUSSY SERZEDELO

SUMMARY: *1. Introduction 2. Restrictive practices
3. Merger control 4. State aid 5. Revision of existing provisions*

## 1. Introduction

The year 2003 brought profound changes in the enforcement of Portuguese competition law. First, Decree-Law No. 10/2003 of 18 January 2003 (O.J. No. 15 of the same date) set up a new independent Competition Authority (*Autoridade da Concorrência*) (hereinafter the CA, the Competition Authority or the Authority). It took over the powers formerly entrusted to the Directorate General for Trade and Competition (*Direcção Geral do Comércio e da Concorrência*) and the Competition Council (*Conselho da Concorrência*). Second, a new Portuguese Competition Act, Law No. 18/2003 of 11 June 2003 (O.J. No. 134 of the same date) (hereinafter the Competition Act or the Act) was adopted.

The landmark reform of EC competition rules, which occurred from early 2003 onwards, also had significant implications for Portuguese competition law. Reference should be made, in this context, to Council Regulation (EC) No. 1/2003 of 16 December 2002 on the implementation of the rules on competition laid down in Articles 81 and 82 of the Treaty (*O.J. L 1, 4.1.03, p. 1-25*), Council Regulation (EC) No. 139/2004 of 20 January 2004 on the control of concentrations between undertakings (the "EC Merger Regulation" – O.J. *L 24, 29.1.04, p 1-22)* and Commission Regulation No. 772/2004 of 27 April, on the application of Article 81/3 to some categories of Agreements of Transfer of Technology (O.J. L123, 27.4.04, p. 11-17).

The reform of Portuguese competition law has given the Competition Authority stronger and more effective powers to prosecute anti-competitive practices, allowing for a period of activism in the enforcement of competition law in Portugal. It remains to be seen how judicial control will delineate the boundaries of such activism.

The purpose of this paper is to analyse the content of national competition law in light of the decision-making practice of the Competition Authority (see its website: www.autoridadedaconcorrencia.pt) and of the former Competition Council – *Conselho da Concorrência* (see its Annual Reports until 2002).

## 2. Restrictive practices

Along the lines of Article 81/1 EC, Article 4/1 of the Competition Act prohibits agreements between undertakings, decisions by associations of undertakings and concerted practices between undertakings, in whatever form, which have as their object or effect the appreciable prevention, distortion or restriction of competition in the national market or in a part thereof.

Similarly to Article 81/3 EC, Article 5 of the Act contains a set of justification provisions that may, if the conditions are fulfilled, confer legality upon agreements relating to such restrictive practices.

In the Portuguese Competition Act abuses of market power encompass abuses of dominant position (Article 6) and abuses of economic dependence (Article 7).

### 2.1 *Anti-competitive agreements and practices between undertakings*

Article 2/1 of the Act defines "undertakings" as "any entity exercising an economic activity that consists in the supply of goods and services in a particular market, irrespective of its legal status or the way in which it functions".

Pursuant to Article 2/2, a group of undertakings that form an economic unit or maintain relations of interdependence or subordination among them is deemed a single undertaking, therefore excluding application of Article 4 to intra-group agreements in compliance with the *Viho* case law os the Court of First Instance (hereinafter "CFI").

Article 3 submits public undertakings, undertakings enjoying exclusive or special rights, and undertakings entrusted with the operation of services of general economic interest, to a regime similar to that of Article 86 EC.

The concepts of "agreement", "decision by association of undertakings" and "concerted practice" have the same broad meaning as under Article 81 EC, the essential element being the existence of a "concurrence of wills" of the undertakings in question.

The prohibited practices listed in Article 4 are similar to those provided for in Article 81/1 EC.

A common distinction is made between horizontal and vertical agreements and practices, depending on whether they are entered into between competitors (horizontal cooperation) or between non-competing undertakings (vertical agreements).

Article 4 of the Act covers both types of arrangements when they have as their object or effect significant prevention, distortion or restriction of competition in the national market or in a part thereof. It thus makes clear that the prohibition provision only applies to agreements and practices that appreciably restrict competition.

Horizontal agreements include typical infringements also covered by EC law, such as: price fixing (e.g. by professional associations representing liberal professions) and agreements fixing other trade conditions; price discrimination; output restrictions, including covenants not to compete; market allocation and exclusive customer allocation; group boycotts; tying; and detailed information exchange.

Article 4/1 of the Competition Act applies also to joint ventures that are not "full function joint ventures", within the meaning of EC Merger Regulation, i.e. that do not perform all the functions of an autonomous economic entity on a lasting basis. Otherwise, they shall constitute a concentration within the meaning of Article 8/2 of the Act.

Vertical agreements and practices shall also be assessed according to the criteria set forth in Article 4/1 of the Act. Resale price maintenance, exclusive dealing, restrictions in selective distribution agreements, tying, requirements contracts and other territorial and customer restrictions are among the practices covered by that provision.

Pursuant to Article 5/3 of the Act (see below), analysis shall however take into account the provisions of Commission Regulation (EC) No. 2790/1999 of 22.12.1999 on the application of Article 81/3 of the Treaty to categories of vertical agreements and concerted practices – O.J. L 336, 29.12.99, pp. 21-25.

## 2.2 *Justification of restrictive practices*

The practices referred to in Article 4 of the Act may be justified if they contribute to improve the production or distribution of the goods or services in question, or if they promote technical or economic development and satisfy the other three cumulative criteria set out in Article 5, the text of which corresponds to Article 81/3 of the EC Treaty. Accordingly they shall:

a) Grant the users of such goods or services a fair part of the benefits arising from the improvement of production or distribution or promotion of technical or economic development;

b) Not impose on the undertakings in question any restrictions that are not indispensable to attain such objectives;

c) Not grant to such undertakings the opportunity to suppress competition in a substantial part of the market for the goods or services in question.

In this context, Article 5/3 of the Act states that agreements or practices prohibited by Article 4, which do not affect trade between Member States but fulfil the remaining conditions of application of an EC Regulation adopted under Article 81/3 EC, shall be considered justified.

The above-mentioned conditions listed in Article 5 also allow for the benefit of an individual exemption.

Indeed, under Portuguese law, companies fearing that their agreements or concerted practices not covered by EC law may be anti-competitive still have the possibility, under Article 5/2 – contrary to the system under EC Regulation 1/2003 – to notify the CA in order to obtain certainty as to their legality as regards Article 4 or Article 5/1. The procedural rules, information and other requirements for prior notification, as well as the effects of the notification and of the CA decisions, are laid down in Regulation No. 9/2005 of 3.2.05 (O.J. II-24 p. 1746-1749).

At the time of writing, only two prior notifications had been made on the basis of Regulation No 9/2005. Only one decision had been rendered, which was not yet publicly available.

### 2.3 *Abuse of dominance*

The Competition Act prohibits two types of abuses of dominance (or of market power): abuse of a dominant position (Article 6) and abuse of economic dependence (Article 7).

According to Article 6/2 of the Act, a dominant market position for specific goods or services is considered to exist where an undertaking (or two or more undertakings) operates in a market in which it is not exposed to significant competition or in which the undertaking (or undertakings) predominates in relation to competitors.

It should be noted that the market share-based presumptions of dominance set forth in Article 3/3 of the former Competition Act (Decree-Law No. 371/93 of 29 October) have been abandoned in the new Act.

Article 6/3/a, states that the restrictive practices mentioned in Article 4/1 constitute abusive behaviour. This applies, for example, to excessive and predatory pricing (since the latter implies sale or resale at a loss, Article 3 of Decree-law 370/93 also prohibits such practice), refusal to deal (also prohibited by Article 4/1 of the same Decree-Law), exclusivity clauses or discriminatory or disproportionate trade conditions.

Any other forms of conduct not explicitly listed in Article 4/1 but found abusive by the Commission or the Community courts shall also be prohibited.

Article 6/3/b considers abusive the refusal by an undertaking to give to any other undertaking, for adequate remuneration, access to a network or to other essential facilities that the former controls, provided that, without such access, the latter is unable, for factual or legal reasons, to operate as a competitor of the dominant undertaking in the upstream or downstream market. This does not apply if the dominant undertaking demonstrates that, for operative or other reasons, such access is reasonably impossible to grant. Article 19/4 § 4 of the German Competition Act provided the source of inspiration for this new provision.

Article 7 of the Act prohibits, insofar as it may affect the functioning of the market or the structure of competition, the abusive exploitation by one or more undertakings of the economic dependence on it or them by any supplier or client on account of the absence of an equivalent alternative. In particular, the unjustified partial or total cessation of an established commercial relationship may be considered as abusive, taking into account prior commercial relations, the recognized usage in that area of economic activity and the contractual conditions established.

This concept has only twice been applied by the Competition Authorities.

### 2.4 *Enforcement and procedure*

The enforcement of the Act rests mainly with the Competition Authority created by Decree-Law No. 10/2003 of 18 January, which also approved its Statutes. Any service of the State or administrative authority also has a duty to inform the CA if it becomes aware of any potentially prohibited practices.

The jurisdiction of the Authority extends to any conduct that takes place or has an effect within the Portuguese territory (see Article 1/2 of the Act).

According to its Statutes the CA is a public entity, which has been granted financial and administrative autonomy. It shall be an independent authority, free to pursue its objectives within the limits of the Constitution, the law and the competition policy principles approved by the Government.

The Authority is composed of two bodies: the Council (*Conselho*) and the Sole Supervisor (*Fiscal Único*).

The Council is the Authority's highest body. It is responsible for the enforcement of competition law and for the management of the Authority's services. Further to Article 12 of the Statutes, it is composed of one Chairman and two or four other members, appointed by the council of Ministers, upon proposal by the Minister of Economy and after consultation with the Ministers of Finance and Justice. Their normal term of office is five years. Renewal is possible once, for another term of five years. According to Article 20 of the Statutes, the Council's Chairperson schedules, chairs and directs the Council's meetings and assures the external representation of the Authority.

The Sole Supervisor is responsible for the control of the legality and economic aspects of the Authority's financial and asset management (Article 23 of the Statutes).

The CA is further divided into three main departments: restrictive practices, operations of concentrations and regulated markets. Each department is composed of both lawyers and economists.

The CA's main functions, aside from ensuring the enforcement of competition rules in Portugal, include (i) encouraging implementation of practices that promote competition and help to spread a competition culture in the economy; (ii) publishing guidelines within the area of competition; (iii) following the activity of other competition authorities and establishing with them, along with the European Commission and other international agencies of the same kind, any appropriate form of cooperation (namely within the framework of the "European Competition Network" set up by Regulation No. 1/2003); (iv) promoting research in the area of competition; (v) improving the Portuguese legal system in the areas that may be affected by competition law; and (vi) providing representation of the Portuguese State in EC or international bodies in the area of competition (Article 6 of the Statutes).

With the purpose of enforcing competition law, the Authority is given extensive investigation, evidence collection and decision-making powers, including the powers to order interim measures, accept commitments and impose sanctions including fines (see Article 7 of the Statutes).

Article 6 of Decree-Law No. 10/2003 and Article 39 of the Competition Act provide for rules governing the cooperation between the Authority and the regulatory authorities for different sectors of the economy (energy, telecommunications, banking, insurance, transport by rail, etc).

The Competition Authority shall investigate any possible prohibited practice it becomes aware of, either on its own initiative or in response to a complaint (Article 24 of the Act). The limitation period to conduct such procedures is five years (Article 48/1/b of the Act).

In conducting its investigations, the CA is entrusted with the same rights and powers and is subject to the same duties as criminal police institutions. According to Article 17/1 of the Act, the Authority may question the legal representatives of the undertakings involved, execute dawn raids in the undertakings' or their associations' premises to search for, examine, seize copies or extracts of the relevant written documents and seal the premises of the undertakings in which elements of relevant information are found or may be found. In the performance of its tasks, the Authority may request the collaboration of the police. In conducting such investigations the Authority's employees shall possess credentials from the Authority stating the purpose of the investigations. The exercise of such powers is in general subject to the issuance of a warrant by a judicial authority (Article 17/2).

The Authority has organized several dawn raids so far, concerning the telecoms, copper and pharmaceutical sectors. The courts have already had the opportunity to set some limits to the powers of the CA when investigating restrictive practices (see the judgment of the Lisbon Commercial Court of 31 January 2005, concerning electronic and other correspondence apprehended during a dawn raid organized by the CA in Portugal Telecom's premises).

The Authority may request any information or documentation in the possession of any person or entity. The formal requirements of that request are set forth in Article 18 of the Competition Act.

The refusal to provide documents or information requested by the Authority, the provision of incomplete information, the refusal to collaborate with the Authority and the obstruction of its investigation/ inspection powers may be fined up to 1% of the turnover of the infringing company (Article 43/3/b/c).

The procedure before the CA is composed of two phases – the inquiry and the contentious phase. Within the inquiry phase the CA may carry out all investigations it deems necessary for the identification of the infringement and of the agents involved (Article 24). The contentious phase is activated by the issuance of a Statement of Objections (Article 23 of the Act).

According to Article 26 of the Act, the undertakings involved shall have the opportunity to state their position in writing and orally and may request supplementary investigations where appropriate (such request may be dismissed where it is clear that the evidence requested is irrelevant or it is aimed simply at delaying the proceedings).

The Act provides for the protection of procedural rights of third parties, such as complainants in infringement procedures (Article 25/2).

Article 26/5 of the Act establishes that the Competition Authority shall protect the legitimate interests of the undertakings involved by not disclosing their business secrets.

The Competition Authority decides cases by means of decisions. It may thus close a file or declare that a restriction to competition exists and in that case order preventive measures and apply fines and other penalties (Article 28 of the Act). Before adopting its decision and if the operation affects a market that is subject to sector regulations, the CA will always consult the respective sector regulator before adopting its decision (Article 28/2 and Article 29 of the Act ).

Jurisdiction to hear appeals against a decision of the Competition Authority lies with the Lisbon Commercial Court. Such appeal has a suspensive effect when it concerns the CA's decisions to apply fines or other penalties (Article 50 of the Act).

Pursuant to Article 59 of the General Regime for Administrative Offences (Decree-Law No. 433/82 of 27October as amended by Decree-Law No. 244/95 of 14 September), which is applicable on a subsidiary basis to infringement proceedings (see Article 22 of the Act), the time limit to file an appeal against a CA decision on prohibited practices is 20 working days from its notification to the undertaking(s) concerned, which, given its brevity, is open to criticism as regards the protection of the rights of defence.

## 2.5 Penalties and remedies

According to Article 43/1/a of the Act, the Competition Authority may impose fines for breach of the provisions on anti-competitive agreements and abuse of dominance, which may amount to as much as 10% of the total turnover of the undertaking concerned in the Portuguese market during the previous financial year.

Such infringements may involve the responsibility of individuals, legal persons or any entities without legal status. Directors may also incur penalties when they knew or should have known of the infringement and failed to take the appropriate measures to terminate it immediately (Article 47 of the Act).

The amounts of the fines are set taking into account various factors, in particular: the gravity of the infringement, the advantages that the offending undertakings have enjoyed as a result of the infringement, the repeated or occasional nature of the infringement, the extent of participation in the infringement, the cooperation with the Authority until the close of the proceedings, and the offender's behaviour in eliminating the prohibited practices (Article 44 of the Act).

The CA imposed its highest fines ever by Decisions of 13 October 2005 (Communication No. 10/2005) (public tenders in hospitals) and of 20 October 2005 (Communication No. 11/2005) (milling sector). Appeals are pending against these two decisions.

In the case of multiple infringements to Articles 4 and 6 of the Act, Article 19 of the General Regime of Administrative Offences shall apply, limiting the maximum applicable fine to 20% of the total turnover of the undertaking concerned in the Portuguese market in the previous financial year.

Pursuant to Article 45 of the Act, the Authority may order publication of its decisions in a newspaper at the expense of the infringing party(-ies).

A new law establishing a leniency programme was approved by the Portuguese Parliament on May 2006.

It provides for immunity and reduction of fines, as foreseen in the Commission Notice on Immunity from Fines and Reduction of Fines in Cartel Cases (2002/C 45/03 - OJ C 45 2002, p. 3).

Article 42 of the Act provides that the imposition of fines is without prejudice to any criminal liability that may arise in accordance with the general rules set forth in the Portuguese Criminal Code. However, it is not foreseen that criminal penalties, such as imprisonment, apply specifically to the violation of competition rules. Therefore, Article 42 applies to infringements such as fraud, forgery or false declarations.

According to Article 27/1 of the Act, where the investigation shows that the practice under examination may create an imminent, serious and irreparable damage to competition or to third parties' interests, the Authority may, at any stage, order the immediate suspension of the practice concerned or set out any interim measures it may deem either necessary to the immediate re-establishment of competition or indispensable to preserve the useful effect of the decision to be adopted. The duration of such protective measures cannot exceed 90 days, unless an extension is justified.

Finally, it should be pointed out that agreements and concerted practices adopted in breach of Article 4/1 of the Act are null and void. Nullity may be invoked at any time by any interested party, and may be confirmed by a court of law in pursuance of Article 286 of the Portuguese Civil Code.


## 3. Merger control

Merger control has been significantly amended by the introduction of the new Act. First, it has been made applicable to the banking and insurance sectors. Second, a turnover threshold for the target company has been created. Third, undertakings now enjoy a one-week period after signing to notify the deal, but they cannot, unless duly authorized, close the transaction before clearance is given.


### 3.1 *Types of transactions covered*

According to Article 8/1 of the Act, the rules on merger control are applicable where: two or more previously independent undertakings merge; or one or more persons already controlling at least one undertaking, or more than one undertaking, acquires direct or indirect control of the whole or part of one or more undertakings.

The creation of a joint venture constitutes a concentration provided that the joint venture performs the functions of an autonomous economic entity on a lasting basis.

The concept of control is defined in paragraph 3 of the same provision, as any act, of whatever form, which, having regard to the factual and legal circumstances involved, confers the possibility of exercising, whether separately or jointly, a decisive influence on the activities of an undertaking. Such acts include: the acquisition of all or the majority of the share capital; the acquisition of ownership or the right to use or enjoy all or part of the assets of an undertaking; or the acquisition of rights, or conclusion of agreements, which confer a decisive influence on the composition or the decision-making of the governing body of an undertaking.

The provisions on concentrations do not apply to: the acquisition of shares or assets within the framework of a special procedure for rescuing or failing undertakings; the acquisition of shares for the purposes of guaranteeing or satisfying credits; and the acquisition by credit institutions of participations in non-financial undertakings, when not covered by the prohibition in Article 101 of the Statute on Credit Institutions and Financial Companies.


### 3.2 *Test of jurisdiction*

Pursuant to Article 9/1 of the Act, where the concentration does not have a Community dimension the parties proposing the concentration must obtain prior approval of the Competition Authority before implementation whenever one of the following conditions is fulfilled: (a) the parties will enjoy after the merger a combined market share of more than 30% of the national market for a particular good or service, or of a substantial part thereof; (b) the combined turnover of the participating undertakings in Portugal exceeded € 150 million in the preceding financial year, after deduction of taxes directly related to turnover, provided that the turnover individually achieved in Portugal by at least two of such undertakings has exceeded € 2 million.

Transactions in which an undertaking that has achieved no turnover in Portugal in the preceding financial year (and, thus, has no share of the relevant market) acquires control of an undertaking with a market share greater than 30% are subject to compulsory prior notification (see CA's decision *Otto Sauer Achsenfabrick / Deutsche Beteiligungs*, Case 07/2004).

Detailed instructions are given in Article 10 of the Act for the calculation of market share and turnover.

### 3.3 *Substantive treatment*

The creation or reinforcement of a dominant position in such a way that it is likely significantly to prevent competition in the national market or in a substantial part thereof remains the key substantive criterion according to which any given concentration may not be cleared (Article 12/4 of the Act).

Article 12/1 of the Act states that concentrations shall be assessed with the objective of determining their effects on the structure of competition, bearing in mind the need to preserve and develop, in the interest of customers and final consumers, effective competition in the relevant market.

In order to carry out such assessment, the following factors shall, inter alia, be taken into account: (i) the structure of the relevant market and the position of the participating undertakings in said market; (ii) the existence of potential competition and of barriers to entry; (iii) the choices available to suppliers and users; (iv) access to sources of supply and to distribution channels; (v) the evolution of supply and demand for the products or services in question; (vi) the existence of special or exclusive rights; (vii) the control of essential facilities by the participating undertakings; (viii) the evolution of technical and economic progress; and (ix) the contribution the concentration will make to the international competitiveness of the national economy.

### 3.4 *Enforcement and procedure*

Enforcement lies with the CA, which is responsible for assessing notifications and making the relevant decisions.

Article 9/2 of the Act provides that notification is to be filed within seven working days after execution of the agreement or, in the case of a public bid, within seven working days after the date of publication of the preliminary announcement of a public offer to acquire control of another undertaking.

The notification shall be served in the case of a merger by all the participating undertakings jointly, through a common representative, and in the case of an acquisition of control, by the undertaking or by the persons intending to acquire control (Article 31/1 and 2 of the Act].

The notification shall be filed in accordance with the "Form for the notification of operations of concentrations between companies" (Regulation 2/E/2003, *Aviso* 8044/2003 – O.J. II 170, of 25/07/03, p. 11148-11151). The documents and data to be included in the notification broadly correspond to the requirements of EC merger notifications stated in the Form CO.

The notification is effective upon the date of payment of a fee that ranges from € 7,500 to € 25,000 depending on the turnover realized in Portugal for the preceding financial year by all the participating undertakings (Regulation No. 1/E/2003 on the fees applicable to the analysis of concentration operations between undertakings, *Aviso* 8044/2003 O.J. II 170, of 25/07/03, p. 11148-11151). If the notification is incomplete, the Authority may grant an additional period of seven working days for completion of the notification.

For more than two years the CA did not agree to hold pre-notification meetings even in transactions involving complex legal or economic issues or creating or reinforcing substantial market shares. However, Article 4 of Decree-Law n.º 219/2006 of 2 November added a paragraph 3 to Article 9 of the Act allowing for the possibility of submitting an intended concentration to a prior assessment by the CA according to a procedure to be established by the latter.

Article 11/1 of the Act establishes that a concentration subject to notification may not be implemented before it has been notified and before it has been the object of an express or tacit decision of authorization. However, paragraph 4 of the same provision provides that the Competition Authority may, upon request, waive the standstill obligation when the implementation of the merger will not have a detrimental impact on competition. Similarly, a public bid or an exchange offer that has been notified may be implemented before the decision is made, provided that the acquirer does not exercise the new voting rights.

Further to Article 40/1 of the Act, the Authority may initiate ex-officio proceedings in case of failure to notify a concentration or when the parties provided false or inaccurate information that led to a decision of non-opposition, or in case of disregard for the obligations or conditions imposed by a decision of non-opposition.

The procedure for the appraisal of operations of concentration comprises two stages and will be closed by a decision of the Authority.

During the first stage, the CA shall first publish the essential elements of the notification in two national newspapers, so that any interested third party may present its observations within the prescribed time (Article 33 of the Act) Within 30 working days from the date on which the notification is effective, the CA shall complete the investigation and adopt its decision. The CA may request additional information or documentation from the notifying party or other public or private bodies. The request addressed to the notifying parties will suspend the time limit for adoption of the CA decision (see Article 34 of the Act).

At the end of the first stage, the Authority may decide (i) that the concentration did not have to be subject to prior notification, (ii) not to oppose the concentration, with or without conditions and obligations, or (iii) to open an in-depth investigation (second stage proceedings) – see Article 35/1 of the Act.

Where no decision has been issued upon the expiry of the time limit for assessment of the concentration, the latter is deemed tacitly approved in accordance with Article 35/4 of the Act.

If the CA decides to initiate second stage proceedings and thus opens an in-depth investigation, it will have to adopt its decision within 90 days from the date on which the notification is effective (see Articles 35 and 36 of the Act). In accordance with Article 36/3 as amended by Decret-Law n.º 219/2006, suspensions of the proceedings for gathering additional information cannot exceed a total of 10 working days.

Article 37 determines that, at the end of the in-depth investigation, the Competition Authority may decide either: (i) not to oppose the concentration, with or without imposing conditions and obligations appropriate for the maintenance of effective competition; or (ii) to prohibit the concentration and, where it has already been put into effect, order appropriate measures to re-establish competition, in particular the separation of the undertakings or of the combined assets or cessation of control.

So far, the new Competition Authority has adopted three negative decisions.

Rules concerning, in particular, the Authority's evidence gathering powers, rights of defence and of third parties, protection of business secrets and cooperation with other regulatory authorities in merger control proceedings are provided for in the Competition Act (Articles 34, 38, 39 of the Act) and in the Administrative Procedure Code, applicable as subsidiary law pursuant to Articles 20 and 30 of the Act.

### 3.5 Penalties and sanctions

In pursuance of Article 43/3 of the Act, failure to notify a concentration is punishable with a fine of up to one percent of the total turnover of the undertakings involved in the preceding financial year.

The Competition Authority may, furthermore, apply a periodic penalty payment that will not exceed five percent of the daily average turnover in the preceding financial year for each day of delay when the undertakings concerned do not comply with an order to notify or to provide information (Article 46).

Article 11/2 determines that the validity of any concentration implemented in breach of the standstill obligation depends on the express or tacit authorization of the concentration. Nevertheless, regardless of the potential illegality of the concentration, pursuant to Article 43/1/b, failure to suspend the transaction is punishable with a fine of up to 10% of the total turnover of the undertakings involved in the preceding financial year.

Article 41 states that any agreements relating to a concentration are null and void when they are entered into in breach of a decision of the Competition Authority prohibiting the concentration, imposing conditions on its implementation or ordering appropriate measures to re-establish effective competition.

Should the participating undertakings put the concentration into effect before a clearance has been obtained, the Competition Authority may, in pursuance of Article 84 of the Administrative Procedure Code, order the necessary interim measures for the maintenance of effective competition.

### 3.6 *Appeals*

Article 34 of the Statutes of the Competition Authority provides for a mechanism of "extraordinary administrative appeal" by which the Minister for Economy may, upon request by the notifying party, and by means of a reasoned decision, authorize a concentration prohibited by the Competition Authority "where the benefits resulting from the operation for the fundamental interests of the national economy exceed the disadvantages for competition". This mechanism was used once (case Brisa/AEA).

According to Article 54 of the Act, the Lisbon Commercial Court shall hear appeals against merger review decisions.

The Administrative Courts Procedure Code applies, on a subsidiary basis, to the procedure to be followed in the merger control area (Article 53 of the Act).

Judicial appeal against the Lisbon Commercial Court's decisions shall be lodged with the Lisbon Court of Appeal. An appeal to the Supreme Court of Justice, limited to matters of law, is also possible.

## 4. State aid

As regards State aid, Article 13 of the Competition Act states that the CA shall make sure that these aids do not significantly restrict or affect competition within the relevant Portuguese market. The CA may issue recommendations to the Government to such effect.

## 5. Revision of existing provisions

According to Article 60 of the Competition Act, the current provisions in the Act and in the Statutes of the Authority shall be amended in order to keep pace with the evolution of EC competition law, particularly with regard to the enforcement of Articles 81 and 82 EC and merger control.

## Bibliography

BELLAMY and Child, *European Community Law of Competition*, 5th ed., London, 2001. COOK, C. J., and C. S. Kerse, *EC Merger Control*, 4th ed, London, 2005. FAULL and Nikpay, *The EC Law of Competition*, Oxford, 1999. FERREIRA, J. Pinto, and A. Bangy *Guia Prático do Direito da Concorrência*, Lisbon, 1988. NAVARRO, Edurne, Andrés Font, Jaime Folguera and Juan Briones, *Merger Control in the European Union (Law, Economics and Practice)*, Oxford, 2002. VAN BAEL and J.-F. Bellis, *Competition Law of the European Community*, 4th ed., The Hague, 2005. VILAÇA, José Luís da Cruz, and Dorothée Choussy, *Modernisation in Europe – Portugal*, Global Competition Review, 2004. VILAÇA, José Luís da Cruz, and Miguel Gorjão-Henriques, *Código da Concorrência*, Coimbra, 2004. VILAÇA, José Luís da Cruz, and Ricardo Oliveira, *Dealing with Dominance – Portugal*, Nauta Duthil (eds.), The Hague, 2004. VILAÇA, José Luís da Cruz, and Teresa Pessoa Brandão, *Private Antitrust Litigation – Portugal*, Global Competition Review, 2004. WISH, Richard, *EC Competition Law*, 5th ed., London, 2003.

# CHAPTER 9
# Tax Law

FRANCISCO DE SOUSA DA CÂMARA

SUMMARY: *1. History 2. Sources of tax law 3. Interpretation of tax law 4. Basic structure of Portuguese tax system 5. Conclusions*

## 1. History

Whilst it would be anachronistic to apply the umbrella term "tax" to all the different types of obligations or compulsory unrequited payments imposed by the crown in the Middle Ages, there are specific payments that may be qualified as such [for instance *as terças* (levied by the town halls for the purpose of building fortifications), *as dízimas* (customs duties), or *as portagens, alcaidarias*, etc. (consumption taxes)]. Following the restoration of the Portuguese monarchy in 1640 (i.e. the reconquest of independence following Spain's occupation of Portugal between 1580-1640, which also intensified the taxes borne by all social classes), Portugal adopted a tax that may be characterized as a global income tax (*a décima militar*) in which the principle of equality already played an important role.

The liberalism period (19th century – in particular after 1832) and the Republic, founded in 1910, were also responsible for significant tax reforms, reflecting new ideas and serving as instruments to transform economic and social structures.

In 1922 a new tax reform was initiated, abolishing old taxes and creating new taxes (including a new individual income tax applied in accordance with a schedular system) but a new reform would take place from 1929 onwards, with a clear agenda of simplification, pragmatism – considering the economic and social background – and administrative feasibility and efficiency. Basically, the reform of 1929 adopted a system of taxes that functioned on the basis of presumptive or notional assessment methods.

The system was completely substituted by a new reform (1958 – 1965), which adopted a dualistic or composite system resulting from the superimposition of a global-type tax on overall net income (*imposto complementar*) upon a set of schedular taxes which were levied in each category of income. The main goal was again to introduce taxes that would tax real income instead of taxing so-called normal income, in spite of allowing SMEs to continue to be taxed under a type of indirect method.

The new Constitution adopted in 1976 (after the revolution that occurred in 1974), the adhesion of Portugal to the EEC and the economic and social changes meanwhile underway in Portugal led to a complete tax reform that was introduced in several phases, as Table 1 shows below.

## 1. TABLE 1

| TAXES/TAX LEGISLATION | | DATE OF ENTRY INTO FORCE | MAIN LEGAL BASE |
|---|---|---|---|
| **DIRECT** | | | |
| | CORPORATE INCOME TAX | 1989 | Domestic[1] |
| | INDIVIDUAL INCOME TAX | 1989 | Domestic[2] |
| | VAT | 1986 | EC Law/Directives |
| **INDIRECT** | | | |
| | CUSTOMS DUTIES | 1986 | EC Law/Regulation |
| | STAMP DUTIES[3] | 2000 | Domestic[4] |
| | EXCISE DUTIES | 2000 | EC Law/Directives |
| | MUNICIPAL TRANSFER TAX | 2004 | Domestic |
| | MUNICIPAL REAL ESTATE TAX | 2003 | Domestic |

---

[1] In a few areas (e.g. distributions of profits and payments of interest & royalties between subsidiaries and parent companies as well as in the course of reorganization operations such as mergers, divisions, transfers of assets and exchanges of shares) an EC base already exists (Directives). Elimination of double taxation in connection with adjustments of profits of associated enterprises is also ensured by an EC multilateral Convention.

[2] No positive and direct EC harmonization exists apart from a Directive that seeks to make savings, in the form of interest paid to individuals resident in another Member State, subject to effective taxation.

[3] Stamp duties also apply on gifts, including bequests, although specific exemptions apply, allowing, for instance, inter-generational and familial transfers (i.e. gifts from parents to children or between spouses).

[4] An EC Directive on capital duties concerning indirect taxes on the raising of capital is also the basis for some harmonization at this level.

**TABLE 1 cont.**

| TAXES/TAX LEGISLATION | | DATE OF ENTRY INTO FORCE | MAIN LEGAL BASE |
|---|---|---|---|
| | MUNICIPAL TRANSFER TAX | 2004 | Domestic |
| | MUNICIPAL REAL ESTATE TAX | 2003 | Domestic |
| **PROCEDURES** | GENERAL TAX LAW | 1999 | Domestic |
| | ADMINISTRATIVE/JUDICIAL TAX PROCEDURES | 2000 | Domestic |
| | ADMINISTRATIVES AND TAX COURTS STATUTE | 2004 | |
| **TAX INFRACTIONS** | GENERAL REGIME OF TAX INFRACTIONS (CRIMES & ADMINISTRATIVE INFRACTIONS) | 2001 | Domestic |

# 2. Sources of tax law

## 2.1 *Introduction*

The sources of tax law in Portugal do not differ from the vast majority of other civil law countries. The classical main sources of tax laws are as follows: the Constitution, treaties, laws, regulations, jurisprudence and doctrine.

In practice, one should also refer to the internal administrative regulations (e.g. *Circulares* or *Ofícios-Circulares*), which provide clarification as to how the tax authorities will approach and treat a specific case or will interpret a specific legal provision, and to the binding rulings issued by the tax authorities upon request from taxpayers.

Taxpayers (contrary to the tax authorities themselves) are not obliged to accept such views, but prudence dictates that their analysis and appraisal is at least considered before action is taken.

## 2.2 *Constitution*

The Constitution broadly defines the Portuguese tax structure and imposes several types of limits on tax legislation. The Constitutional Court may even determine whether a particular law infringes any constitutional provision prior to its enactment. Some of the most important tax principles are expressly enshrined in the Constitution, such as: (i) the principle of legality (i.e. taxes must be imposed by laws created by the Portuguese Parliament or, if consented to by the latter, by the Government); (ii) the principle of non retroactivity (taxes cannot be imposed retroactively, i.e., they should only apply from the time of their enactment onwards); and (iii) the principle of equality (i.e. taxpayers should pay an equal amount of tax if their circumstances are equal, based on the ability-to-pay principle).

Apart from these, other Constitutional principles exist and are often invoked by taxpayers before the courts.

The Constitution is, on the other hand, quite programmatic. The majority of taxes must have a redistributive effect, as one may see below [items (i) (iii) and (iv)]. Currently the wording of the Constitution specifically states that: (i) individual income tax should have a global nature (a schedular system would not comply with such requirement), and be progressive (in case a flat rate were to be introduced it would be necessary to create tax exclusions, abatements or tax credits in order to maintain the progressive system) and "should consider the needs and the income of the family"; (ii) the corporate income tax should be predominantly levied on real income determined in accordance with standard accountancy rules, unless otherwise provided in the Tax Code (as opposed to "normal income" or income determined by indirect methods); (iii) the "wealth taxes" (in particular, immovable or stamp duties, considering that Portugal never adopted a net wealth tax) must also contribute towards equality between citizens; (iv) consumption taxes may adapt the consumption structure to further the evolution of the economy and justice, and should be heavier in relation to luxury products.

## 2.3 *Main sources of legislation*

Three levels of legislative sources are especially relevant: international treaties, EC tax law and domestic law.

There are several bilateral and multilateral treaties signed by Portugal, which specifically deal with tax issues or which are relevant for tax purposes. The most relevant ones are, however, the so-called "double tax treaties" (DTTs) drawn up along the lines of the UN and OECD Model Tax Treaties. Within this context one may say that Portugal is a party to 50 DTTs, one Convention concerning inheritance and gift tax, a number of treaties on mutual legal assistance and on information exchange, the EC Arbitration Convention, and Social Security treaties, etc. Moreover, many other relevant multilateral treaties such as the EC Treaty, the WTO agreement, the ECHR, and the Vienna Convention on treaties, also play an important role in completing the fiscal picture.

Portugal has been a member of the EU since 1986. Notwithstanding the existence of a unanimity rule to approve tax measures, the fact is that there are already several important limits imposed upon the national Parliaments and governments, derived from the EC Treaty and from legislation passed by the organs of the European Community, namely Regulations and EC Directives.

This clearly applies in the case of customs duties, turnover taxes (VAT) and excise duties. However, the limits also apply in specific areas concerning the concentration of capital, direct taxes related with reorganizations of companies (e.g. mergers, divisions, transfers of assets and exchanges of shares), as well as the distribution of dividends, interest or royalties between subsidiary and parent companies.

Moreover, considering the relative lack of positive integration in the field of direct tax matters, the ECJ has been increasingly called upon to interpret whether Member States' domestic tax rules are contrary to EU law. In an important movement initiated during the 1980s, the ECJ declared as contrary to EC law many domestic tax provisions, found to be discriminatory on the grounds of nationality, mainly in the area of the four fundamental freedoms. To date ECJ rulings have found specific Portuguese tax rules not to be in compliance with EU rules, namely with the Treaty of Rome (e.g. C – 345/93 related with the applicability of Car Tax to the importation of second-hand vehicles), the Parent-Subsidiary Directive (e.g. C-375/98, the *Epson* case concerning the limits of withholding tax on dividends during the derogation period and the inheritance and gift tax applied on the dividends), the Sixth Directive on VAT (e.g. C-276/98 related with the application of reduced rates of VAT to the importation and supply of certain goods and services) and the Capital Duties Directive (e.g. C-56/98 concerning the application of notary and registration fees) amongst others.

Therefore, in the absence of new harmonization measures, the European Court of Justice is obliging the Member States, including Portugal, to dismantle several domestic regimes as a result of their non-compliance with EC law.

The essence of the right to impose taxation (covering four specific elements, notably the object of taxes, tax rates, tax incentives and the taxpayers' guarantees) is protected by the legality principle, with a two-fold meaning: first, that taxes must be imposed by law; and second, that such law should be enacted by the Parliament, unless the latter grants the Government the possibility to create such rule by itself. In such case, the authorization law should expressly indicate the matters covered (i.e. the object of such authorization), the meaning (i.e. the purpose intended), the extension (i.e. the definition of such magnitude, namely stipulating the tax rates of a specific tax) and the time limit that applies to the exercising of such right.

These days, the Government takes the lead in terms of creating new tax laws as the vast majority of Tax Codes and legislation approved by Decree-laws of the Government shows. However, apart from the four areas reserved to the Parliament, the Government may freely legislate upon all other matters, normally concerning the assessment and collection of taxes or the development of principles or rules defined by the Parliament.

Nowadays, the most important act approved by the Parliament, including tax measures, continues to be the Budget Bill. This is passed before the end of the civil year, to become effective from January 1 of the following year. Any new taxes, however, have to respect an important constitutional rule, which prevents tax provisions from having retroactive effect.

Either by way of law or Decree-law the tax regime is constantly being modified and fine-tuned, in order to close gaps, to combat tax fraud and evasion, to implement EC rules or ECJ rulings, and overall to assist in the achievement of economic, social, environmental and political results that not only change, but which are seen from different perspectives depending upon the political forces in power. Obviously, tax provisions often lack the requisite degree of precision and accuracy, undermining stability and certainty, which increases the number of tax disputes.

## 3. Interpretation of tax law

### 3.1 *General approach*

The General Tax Law (GTL) expressly prescribes a set of rules to be applied in interpreting tax provisions. Firstly, it states that in determining the meaning of a specific provision and in the process of qualification of facts submitted under those provisions, one should apply the rules and the general principles of interpretation and application of the law, which follow an objective and actualist approach towards interpretation. According to these principles, the tax authorities and judges have had the possibility to requalify agreements and re-characterize categories of income (see the Administrative Supreme Court decision of 8 July 1998, on the Four Seasons Country Club case).

Furthermore, although controversially, it is also indicated in the law that where doubts arise concerning the object of the tax provision being interpreted, following those principles, one should take into consideration the economic substance of the tax. This rule, introduced few years ago in the GTL, raises some perplexity as to the value attributed to the former rule. Moreover, the tax courts have reserved extensive rights of interpretation, notwithstanding the prohibition upon the use of analogy in order to close loopholes.

Nevertheless, there is an express command stipulating that the terms of other branches of law referred to in tax law should be interpreted in accordance with their original meaning, except if otherwise provided in the law.

In spite of possible disputes arising under different principles of interpretation, practice shows that the traditional approach of the tax courts has been to make literal interpretations in defence of certainty and security principles. However, the scenario is changing with the recent introduction of the rule that, in specific cases, requires the consideration of the economic substance, and moreover with the emphasis given to constitutional and other EC legal principles as limits to the interpretation of anti-avoidance tax rules.


### 3.2 *Anti-avoidance rules*

As a general rule, an entity is free to organize its business in the way it deems appropriate. However, the tax authorities have been empowered for some time (the first legal provision was still introduced in the old Industrial Tax Code – Article 51-A) to adjust certain transactions according to the arm's length principle, making the necessary tax assessments when the operations between related parties do not respect that principle. Basically, this reallocation of profits among related (resident or non resident) companies occurred under the transfer pricing rules.

However, from the mid 1990s onwards, anti-avoidance measures have become very popular in Portugal. First, several specific provisions were introduced in the Corporate Income Tax Code dealing with such various matters as the non-deductibility of expenses paid to entities located in low tax jurisdictions, thin capitalization and CFC rules and, more recently, another anti-avoidance rule to prevent the application of the exemption method on dividends received by parent companies when profits were not effectively taxed or when income was recharacterized into dividends with a specific purpose of benefiting from the exemption.

Thereafter, in 1999, it was decided that a general anti-avoidance rule should be introduced, allowing the tax authorities to re-characterize a transaction if it is shown that the sole or the principle objective was the reduction or elimination of tax which would otherwise be due. The wording of the GAAR has already been amended and today reads approximately as follows: juridical acts or agreements do not produce effects for tax purposes, when it is evidenced that they were performed by artificial or fraudulent means and abuse legal forms, with the sole or principle objective of reducing, eliminating or deferring the taxes that would have been payable if juridical acts or agreements of equivalent economic result had been pursued, or with the purposes of obtaining tax advantages that would not be achieved, totally or partially, with the use of those means; in such cases, the taxes will apply as if those means and forms were not used and no advantage would also apply.

The introduction of all these rules follows a certain European trend, not to say a trend which is observable in the majority of OECD countries, drawing inspiration from other legislation that featured those precise specific anti-avoidance rules (SAARs) and a general anti-avoidance rule (GAAR).

The wording of the GAAR is very imprecise and has been responsible for the introduction of a significant degree of uncertainty, although the SAARs probably raised still more problems considering that they can apply automatically, provided some criteria (blind tests) are met. Accordingly, and from this perspective, several other criticisms may be pinpointed. These rules, it may be argued: (i) deter investments, particularly when one intends to use a tax competitive structure; (ii) create complacency (their very existence threatens to lower the standards of precision applied in drafting legislation), shifting the legislator's task to the tax authorities and often, at the end of the day, into the judiciary's hands; (iii) foment disputes with unpredictable results due to the inherent lack of precision; and (iv) are not well adapted to a civil law jurisdiction such as Portugal, with no tradition in implementing these types of rules and with a system that, on one hand, does not follow the precedence rule and, on the other hand, is not as sophisticated as the systems of the states where those rules were originally introduced.

Whilst two of three cases are still subject to appeal, the fact is that to date not a single case has been concluded (to the best of our knowledge) in which the tax authorities have used the GAAR with success. A transparent policy in this domain would probably increase the efficacy of the rule.

On the other hand, the specific anti-avoidance rules, although more precise and more effective, are often contrary to the EC Treaty, and arguably, to specific DTTs, which means that they cannot be applied in particular cases.

### 3.3 *Tax courts' interpretation*

The interpretation of legal provisions made by the tax courts has enormous importance because their decisions represent the last word upon a case. Once they interpret and apply the law, without an additional right of appeal, the decision becomes *res judicata*, *i.e.* final.

As mentioned above, the administrative and tax courts [with specialized judges dealing with fiscal and para-fiscal matters (defined, however, so broadly as to encompass income taxes, consumption taxes, social security, municipal taxes, stamp duties, DTT issues, etc.)] tended to interpret tax law based on the literal meaning of the legal provision, using classic methods of interpretation that require the analysis of several elements such as the grammatical, the systematic, the historical and teleological methods.

This is to say that, as a rule, the general principles *in dubio pro fisco* or *in dubio contra fiscum* are not followed by courts, although the economic result of specific transactions is considered, as described above. Moreover, and apart from cases where taxes are determined by indirect methods, it is important to stress that if a relevant doubt arises as to whether something is subject to tax or not, or as to the respective value of such tax, any previous tax assessment should be considered void by the court.

Following tax assessments, taxpayers may lodge administrative claims or dispute the assessment immediately in court. As a rule, any court decision may also be reviewed, at least a second time, either by the Court of Second Instance (*Tribunal Central Administrativo*) or by the Administrative Supreme Court in case the appeal is restricted in its scope to legal terms. Taxpayers are not obliged to pay these taxes but they are obliged to render a guarantee to suspend the relevant foreclosure file and to avoid pledges, mortgages or other claims against their assets.

As a rule, written judgments are not very lengthy (between 6 and 8 pages). After the presentation of a succinct summary of the parties' views and the arguments exchanged by them, the facts considered proven are expressly mentioned and then the decision is taken, mentioning the legal grounds in a concise manner. The second and third instance decisions are in general published.

As mentioned above, the precedence rule does not apply in Portugal, but lower courts tend to follow the position held by the courts of higher jurisdiction, which is comprehensible given the possibility of appeal existing in the system.

## 4. Basic structure of Portuguese tax system

### 4.1 *Structure and composition of the present tax system*

The current Portuguese tax structure is relatively recent. Income taxation is based on two taxes (the individual and the corporate income taxes – recognized in Portugal as IRS and IRC, respectively) that entered into force on 1 January 1989.

Although the corporate income tax increased in terms of revenue in the last years, (notwithstanding the existence of a high percentage of companies that register tax losses consecutively over a number of years) in terms of efficiency, it is important to point out that VAT remains the undisputed champion of the Portuguese tax coffers.

The consumption taxes (mainly VAT and excise duties) were immediately introduced when Portugal adhered to the EEC on 1 January 1986. The normal VAT rate is currently 21%. In the islands of Madeira and Azores, part of Portuguese territory, the normal rate is 15% – which (together with Luxembourg's) represents the lowest VAT rate in Europe. The clear benefit of this lower rate has been used in some structures related with E – Commerce transactions.

The current general wealth taxes were all approved in the new millennium including the stamp duties applied on bequests (maximum 10%), the immovable property taxes (IMI – tax rates vary between 0.2% and 0.8%, unless the immovable is owned by an "offshore entity", which is then subject to 1% or 2%, in case of a vacant immovable), and the transfer tax on immovables (IMT – apart from specific exemptions, the tax rates vary between 0.2% and 6.5%, unless the immovable is acquired by an offshore entity which is then subject to 8%), which were all revised or introduced in 2003/2004. It is obvious that these types of taxes already existed prior to their enactment, but were construed from a different perspective or even under another name. In spite of possible discussions concerning stamp duties, there is a general consensus that the tax reform on immovables reduced significantly the inequality that characterized previous taxes. Apart from those wealth taxes, the most important tax in this area is the tax on motor vehicles, considering that Portugal did not adopt a net wealth tax.

### 4.2 *Income taxes*

Following an international trend, with the 1989 tax reform the tax bases were broadened and the rates lowered.

Apart from IRS (currently imposing progressive tax rates up to 42%), individuals are, in general, obliged to pay social security contributions [11% for employees, 10% for members of corporate boards, but the base of their contribution is subject to a ceiling (€ 4.836), and 25.4% or 32% for self-employed individuals, but also with the possibility to select the base for contributions between 1.5 and 12 times the national minimum monthly salary (€ 403 in 2007)].

Individual income tax represented an important progress in terms of modern taxation and was designed as a global personal tax (in spite of doctrinal disputes based on the fact that some items of income were subject to specific rules and tax rates), adopting a broad income concept (wealth accretion income method) considering the series of changes and allowances of an individual and family nature. Currently Portugal applies a partial exemption system

Corporate income tax is the only tax on the profits (taxed at a rate of 25%) of corporate entities, apart from the possible municipal surcharge on the IRC levied by municipalities (up to 1.5% on the taxable profits), wich may elevate the tax burden to 26.5%. Employers, as already mentioned, are also subject to contributions towards social security (23.75% in relation to employees and 21.25% in relation to members of corporate bodies). A total or partial exemption system also applies for inter-company distributions of dividends.

These taxes (IRS and IRC) have been subject to several amendments since their enactment.

## 5. Conclusions

The Portuguese tax system has developed significantly in the past fifteen years. The international trend towards broadening the tax basis and reducing the nominal tax rates has played an important role, but the revision of each specific tax and serious efforts to combat against tax evasion have also contributed towards the reduction of inequity.

However, the reshaping of all taxes along the lines of the most advanced tax systems together with the introduction of an immense arsenal of anti-avoidance measures was probably over ambitious and at times inappropriate, having been to some extent responsible for the growth of uncertainty.

Certain regimes and legal provisions are so difficult to implement (i.e. to tax small and medium-sized companies under the direct methods, to apply the current transfer pricing provisions, some SAARs, the GAAR, etc...) that administrative, feasibility and efficiency principles may require a review of those regimes or rules, or at least their applicability to all situations. In this context improvement of the tax authorities' capabilities should be treated as a priority.

Overall, it is difficult to accept that the GAAR's "dissuasive effect" compensates for the embedded hidden costs, requiring that an astute and perspicacious appraisal is made from time to time, based on empirical data and statistics and free of "tax pre-judgments".

Moreover, in the author's opinion, more emphasis needs to be given to the competitive, investment-friendly, aspects of Portugal's tax system. Whilst continuing to enshrine and espouse the guiding principles of the 1989 reform (equity, simplicity, efficiency) the tax system must be reshaped, with targeted measures to contribute further to maintaining current, and attracting new, national and foreign investment.

## Bibliography

A.A..V.V., *Problemas Fundamentais do Direito Tributário*, Lisbon, 1999. BRONCHI, Chiara and José C. Gomes dos Santos, *Reforming the tax system in Portugal*, OECD, Economics Department Working Papers, n.º 302, ECO/WKP (2001)28, 10.7.01. *Cahiers de Droit Fiscale Internationale*, IFA, ed. Kluwer (Portuguese Chapters). LEITE DE CAMPOS, Diogo e Mónica Leite de Campos, *Direito Tributário*, 2ª ed., Coimbra 2000. *IBFD publications* (Portuguese chapters of all existing loose-leaf and comparative publications). PITTA E CUNHA, Paulo, *A Reforma Fiscal*, Lisbon, 1989. SALDANHA SANCHES, José Luís, *Manual de Direito Fiscal*, 2nd ed., Coimbra, 2002. SOARES MARTÍNEZ, Pedro, *Direito Fiscal*, 7th ed., Coimbra 1993. NABAIS, José Casalta, Direito Fiscal, 2ª ed., Coimbra 2003; TEIXEIRA, Glória and David Williams, *The Portuguese Tax System and Double Tax Agreements Network*, Intertax, n.º 4, 1994. XAVIER, Alberto, *Direito Tributário Internacional*, 2nd ed., Coimbra 2007.

# CHAPTER 10
# Criminal Law

TERESA PIZARRO BELEZA
FREDERICO DE LACERDA DA COSTA PINTO[1]

> SUMMARY: *1. Brief history 2. Sources of criminal law 3. The Criminal Code and the general rules of criminal responsibility 4. Specific offences 5. Criminal sanctions 6. Perspectives on evolution*

## 1. Brief history

**1.1** The scattered legislation enacted by Portuguese monarchs after 1143 (when Portugal was officially recognized as a kingdom) aimed at progressively centralizing punitive power, as well as circumventing and repressing private vengeance and customary practices. From the 15th century onwards, legislation was included in the *Ordenações*, a collection of five books compiling various clusters of legislation. Both criminal law and procedure were included in the fifth book of the *Ordenações Afonsinas* (1447), later revised and replaced by the *Ordenações Manuelinas* (1521). During the period of Spanish rule (1580-1640), this body of law formed part of the *Ordenações Filipinas* (1603) and stayed in force until the implementation of the first Criminal Code (1852). It can thus be said that, unlike other European kingdoms, Portugal has had a written *corpus*

---

[1] English version *Raquel van der Wijk*.

of criminal law, uniformly applied throughout the whole territory, since medieval times.

Judged against present criteria, the *Ordenações* contained a detailed, case-by-case and asymmetric description of criminal offences. Religion and the monarchy were converted into symbols of the highest significance *(e.g.* by creating multiple heresy and high treason offences, which were severely punishable), and the text featured a number of minor offences (for instance, gambling, excessive noise and weapon possession), which were socially relevant at the time. Some of the penalties were disproportionately severe and, in many cases, the offences were defined in vague terms. Much was left to the arbitrary opinion of the judge. Justice tended to vary according to the social status of the perpetrator. One of the most effective available penalties was the perpetrator's banishment to a distant land.

Following the social, economic and political changes that occurred in the 18th century, such offences, as well as the severity of their penalties and the discriminatory criteria for their application, became both politically and socially intolerable. Enlightenment criminalists such as Pascoal de Mello Freire, Professor at Coimbra University and an eminent jurist during the second half of the 18th century, highlighted the negative aspects of old regime's criminal law: its imprecision, the irrationality of its incriminatory choices, the violence and arbitrariness of its penalties and its procedural ambiguity. Their comments, albeit justified in part, were exaggerated. However they helped to legitimize the criminal reforms under way, particularly Pascoal de Mello Freire's draft Criminal Code. This draft was presented to the Queen, D. Maria I, in 1786 but was never sanctioned (probably for political reasons), despite its popularity in subsequent decades as a reference text in Portugal and in several Latin American countries. The main academic text in the field of criminal law during this period was Pascoal de Mello Freire's *Institutiones Juris Criminalis Lusitanis* (1794).

**1.2** The liberal Constitution of 1822 was sanctioned while the fifth book of the *Ordenações Filipinas* was still in force. It contained the fundamental principles of liberal Criminal Law: *nullum crimen* and *nulla poena sine lege* (principle of legality), proportionality of penalties, the *ratione personae* character of criminal responsibility and the prohibition of cruel and defamatory punishment (Articles 10 and 11 of the 1822 Constitution). However, political instability frustrated all attempts to bring forward a new Criminal Code, which was sanctioned only in 1852. Clearly utilitarian at source, it was divided into two parts (a general part and a special part) and was inspired by the 1810 French Criminal Code. Immediately after entering into force, it was profoundly criticized by the most prominent 19th century criminal law commentators: Levy Maria Jordão (*Comentário ao Código Penal Portuguez*, 1853) and Silva Ferrão (*Theoria do Direito Criminal applicada ao Código Penal Português*, 1856). Regarding the teaching of criminal law, the transition from the *Ordenações* to the 1852 Criminal Code was achieved by Basilio Alberto de Sousa Pinto's several written lessons (*Lições de Direito Criminal*, Coimbra, 1845, 1857 and 1861).

In 1861, Levy Maria Jordão presented the first project for the amendment of the Criminal Code, which did not gain the attention of political power. Having been redrawn in 1864, it failed to obtain the favourable political and legislative reception to which it aspired. Nevertheless its retributive and reforming spirit (based on the "Philadelphia System") influenced the 1867 penitentiary reform (which, *inter alia*, abolished the death penalty for civil crimes, although in any case executions had not been carried out since 1846) as well as the 1884 penal reform in which the 1886 Criminal Code originated.

**1.3** Notable criminal legislation was passed during the *Estado Novo* period (1926-1874) and the process of drafting a new Criminal Code, which was approved by a revisory committee and resumed only after the 1974 revolution, was initiated. The following legislation, in particular, should be highlighted: the changes to State security offences (Decree 32832, 1943, and Decree 35015, 1945), the prison organization reform (Decree 26643, 28 May 1936, which established a truly progressive system), and the Criminal Code amendment (Decree 39688, 5 July 1954).

Between 1963 and 1965, a revisory committee of university professors and career judges debated and sanctioned a draft of a new Criminal Code (general part and special part), which was presented by the Coimbra University Professor Eduardo Correia. The immediate legislative realization of this project was prevented, due to the absence of appropriate political conditions. It was thereafter resumed in 1979, within a new political context.

**1.4** The sanctioning of the 1976 Constitution (CPR) brought with it a vast number of programmatic, protective criminal norms, which provided the starting point for reform of the Portuguese penal system. Thus, the new Portuguese criminal law was anticipated in doctrinal terms during the 1960s (with Eduardo Correia's draft Code and the debate it generated) but it was realized only with the entry into force of a "Criminal Constitution" in 1976. A reform of the penal system was effected during the 1980s, with the sanctioning of the 1982 Criminal Code (still in force after two major amendments in 1995 and 1998), the 1987 Criminal Procedure Code and the new Administrative Law Offences Regime (*Regime Geral do Direito de Mera Ordenação Social*, contained in Decree-Law No. 433/82, 27 October, which followed a 1979 statute and was ultimately revoked).

## 2. Sources of criminal law

**2.1** In Portugal, only statute law (or black letter law) may legitimately qualify a fact as an offence and establish a punishment for such a crime. This excludes the incriminating relevance of other sources – namely customary law or judicial precedent – which, nevertheless, may weigh argumentatively *in bonam partem* (as possible exculpatory or mitigating causes).

In order to understand the reach of such a source system, as well as the pivotal role of statute law within criminal law, it is important to describe Portugal's particular brand of separation of powers and its hierarchy of normative acts.

The Portuguese political system is based on the principle of the separation of powers (Article 111 CPR): legislative power is shared by Parliament and Government; executive power is exercised by Government, under parliamentary check; and, finally, the courts are free to perform their judicial role in a completely independent manner, imperatively following statute law and the decisions of higher courts in concrete cases. The Constitution establishes the exclusive authority of Parliament to create criminal law, thus assuring parliamentary predominance over Government in this context.

On another level, the Portuguese legal order is founded upon a formal hierarchy of normative acts (Article 112 CPR) headed by the 1976 Constitution (subject to several amendments), the supreme law of the state, from which all legislation derives and is subordinate. All criminal law must be in accordance with the demands and guidelines of the "Criminal Constitution". Parliamentary and governmental legislative acts occupy the same hierarchical level, but the latter must abide by the "authorization statutes" according to which they are created (Article 112 CPR).

**2.2** The Constitution addresses criminal law and criminal procedure matters extensively, particularly concentrating on the constitutional protection of fundamental rights (Article 24 ff CPR). The existence of a "Criminal Constitution" – composed of norms controlling the creation, contents and limits of criminal law – may be identified. The majority of those norms (referring to the protection of fundamental rights) are directly applicable and are therefore a source of legal solutions in concrete cases.

The Constitution establishes the necessarily statute-based character of criminal law (Article 165/1/c) CPR). This means that both the definition of offences and the establishment of penalties are subject to either a parliamentary statute or a governmental act, following parliamentary authorization (Article 165/2-5 CPR). Government may not create, revoke or modify incriminatory norms or penalties without a previous authorization from Parliament. There is no other legitimate source for incrimination and penalty determination (Article 29/1 CPR). The only exception to this rule occurs in international criminal law, where other sources, such as international custom, may be admissible (*ex vi* Articles 29/2 and 8/1, CPR).

The essentially protective nature of the criminal system is outlined in the Constitution, which establishes the need for a "previously existing and express criminal statute" (in that which regards the facts constituting an offence and the applicable penalties) as the only legitimate source of criminal responsibility (Article 29/1 CPR). This, in turn, may only occur in the context of a "procedure equally established by the law" [Articles 27/1 and 29 CPR, as well as Article 2 of the Criminal Procedure Code (CPP)], within an "independent and legally bound court" (Article 203 CPR). Consequently, only a court ruling resulting from a strictly law-abiding procedure can determine the criminal responsibility of an individual. This excludes the administrative nature of crime-related procedures. Criminal responsibility is non-transmissible (Article 30/3 CPR). The death penalty is forbidden, as is any kind of cruel or defamatory punishment (Articles 24/2 and 25 CPR), and indeed all perpetual, indeterminate or indefinite penalties (Article 30/1 CPR). All incriminations and penalties must be in conformity with the principle of equality (Article 13 CRP) and must also be necessary, adequate and proportionate to the gravity of the facts (Article 18/2 CPR).

**2.3** Criminal law extends from the Criminal Code to complementary legislation and sectoral codifications, which contain crimes specific to the regulated area. Despite the framing and guiding role of the general part of the Criminal Code, all mentioned sources have the same hierarchical dignity.

On the one hand, the Criminal Code contains the general and fundamental norms for the legal sector, the criteria for attributing and excluding responsibility, and penalties and the criteria for their application in concrete cases. On the other hand, it also includes a catalogue of those crimes whose definition has been absorbed and recognized by the legal order.

Unlike Spain, but similarly to Germany, Portugal's Criminal Code does not provide an exhaustive list of criminal offences within the legal order.

The above-mentioned complementary legislation covers new offences which are technically dependent on other areas and whose borders are yet to be fixed. Examples include computer-related offences (Law No. 109/91, 17 August), the criminal regime of cheques (Decree-Law No. 454/91, 28 December, with subsequent amendments), or some anti-economic or anti-public health infractions (Decree-Law No. 24/84, 20 January).

For reasons of congruence and due to the need to identify easily the addressees of certain norms, there are sectoral codifications designed to regulate several different legal aspects of a certain activity. Such is the case in relation to the following offences: illicit deposit reception (Article 200, *Regime das Instituições de Crédito e Sociedades Financeiras*, Decree-Law No. 201/2002, 26 September); insider trading and market manipulation (Articles 378 and 379, *Código dos Valores Mobiliários*, Decree-Law No. 486/99, 13 November, with subsequent amendments); tax crimes (from Article 87, *Regime Geral das Infracções Tributárias,* Law No. 15/2001, 5 June); or labour crimes (Articles 608-613, *Código do Trabalh*o, Law n° 99/ 2003, 27 August).

**2.4** Rightly understood, the minimum intervention principle (emerging from the proportionality, necessity and adequateness demands – regarding norms restrictive of fundamental rights – contained in Article 18/2, CPR) entails that criminal law ought to be considered an *ultima ratio* solution by the legislature. In order to fulfil such a *desideratum*, other sanctioning but non-criminal branches of public law fulfil a complementary role. Examples include offences under administrative law (*Direito de Mera Ordenação Social,* Decree-Law No. 433/82, 27 October, with subsequent amendments, and special administrative infractions are to be found in sectoral legislation), as well as disciplinary law (*Estatuto Disciplinar dos Funcionários e Agentes da Administração Central, Regional e Loca*l, Decree-Law No. 24/84, 16 January).

Administrative law offences (*Direito de Mera Ordenação Social*) refer to illicit facts (*contra-ordenações*), which are socially less serious than criminal offences. Unlike crimes, their punishment is either pecuniary or of a temporarily impeding nature (the agent is temporarily suspended from a certain activity). In any case, the possibility of imprisonment is excluded in this context. If the defendant fails to pay the "administrative" fine (a non-criminal fine), his assets are subject to foreclosure. However in contrast to pecuniary penalties applied to crimes, non-payment of administrative fines cannot result in imprisonment. Additionally, the procedure that is followed is administrative, and penalties are enforced by specialized administrative authorities. A defendant may impugn an administrative decision. There is also the possibility of appealing to a higher court. Presently, this legal branch comprises all sectors of socio-economic life, from traffic infractions to financial markets, from commerce to tax duties, construction licensing, and production and environmental organization. It has outgrown the limited number of minor infractions for which it was originally developed.

Public disciplinary law contains sanctioning mechanisms, which are designed to ensure the proper organization and functioning of Public Administration services. For such purpose, it labels as illicit those acts that violate the duties of zeal, obedience, loyalty, secrecy, correctness, assiduity and punctuality of public officials (Article 3/4 of the above-mentioned *Estatuto Disciplinar*). The same document establishes (Article 11) the following disciplinary sanctions: written reproach, fine, suspension, inactivity, compulsory retirement and dismissal. The gravity of such sanctions justifies the constitutional assurance of public officials' defence rights (Articles 32/10, and 269/3 CPR), as well as the inclusion of its general regime within Parliament's exclusive authority (Article 165/1/d CPR).

Other infractions (of a criminal nature) such as contraventions and transgressions – which ought, according to the gravity of the relevant facts, to have either been revoked or converted into crimes or administrative offences, *contra-ordenações,* in the 1980s – subsisted, despite their questionable constitutionality, until the recent announcement by the Government (September 15 2005) of a proposed Statute, which shall eliminate this type of infraction (*Proposta de Lei* No. 43/ X/1, 26.10.2005, currently under parliamentary analysis).

**2.5** In Portugal, case law is not considered a legal source, *i.e.* it does not generate imperative general and abstract solutions. It only has a binding effect in concrete cases under judicial scrutiny. This is partly a consequence of the principle of legality, but it also reflects a specific form of judicial organization. Courts are, as we have seen, bound by legislation and cannot ascribe criminal responsibility to an individual if the individual's actions have not been qualified as an offence by a previous piece of legislation. Moreover, with the exception of decisions upon appeal, there is such a thing as vertical (lower courts are not obliged to follow the rulings of higher courts, except in the case of an appeal) and horizontal (same-level courts do not determine each other's rulings and a court is not bound by its own previous decisions) independence among the several different kinds of courts. Judicial precedent can be said to have a merely argumentative and persuasive force, which has particular relevance in the case of higher courts. However, a good knowledge of case law is essential in anticipating court decisions, as well as calculating the probability of certain punitive results. Mastering a legal system entails a deep knowledge of its case law, as well as of the interpretive currents that emerge from a case-by-case application of the law.

In connection with the absence of a generic binding force regarding the rulings of higher courts, it is useful to set out the historical background. Until 1995, there was a legal institute called *assento* (Article 2 *Código de Processo Civil*), through which the Portuguese Supreme Court of Justice established *"generally binding doctrines"* for all legal branches, including criminal law and, in particular, criminal procedure. Such a generally binding force, within and outside the ambit of procedure, was initially questioned by the Constitutional Court, which led to the final elimination of the *assentos* by Decree-Law No. 329-A/95, 12 December. Consequently, there was a change in the texts referring to Supreme Court rulings, directed at solving interpretative conflicts within criminal law and procedure, the so-called *recursos extraordinários para fixação de jurisprudência*, (Article 437 ff CPP). After the 1998 penal reform (Law No. 59/98, 25 August), the non-binding character of such uniformization rulings was established by Article 445/3, CPP. There was, however, a specific duty to justify disagreement. Uniformization rulings (*acórdãos de fixação de jurisprudência*) are thus not internally or externally binding. Nevertheless, they do make it necessary for courts lower in the hierarchy to specifically ground their disagreement whenever their ruling diverges from a decision advanced by the Supreme Court.

For an overview of the present system of criminal courts see *Lei de Organização e Funcionamento dos Tribuanis Judiciais* (Law No. 3/99, 13 January), as well as this book's section on criminal procedure.

**2.6** Criminal doctrine is not a source of law in Portugal. Its value is merely argumentative or persuasive. When controversial questions arise, it is common to invoke the legal opinions of lawyers, academics or experts (Article165/3 CPP).

Portuguese literature on criminal law may be divided into four types: general works, monographs, works on specific crimes, commentaries on existing legislation.

During the last twenty years several monographs (often master's and doctoral dissertations) have been published, both on the general part of the Criminal Code and on particular crimes. Even partial enumeration is incompatible with the limitations of the present study. For a perspective on specific crimes, see *Comentário Conimbricense ao Código Penal*, 3 vols., Coimbra, 1999-2003.

The above-mentioned *Comentário Conimbricense* contains a deep analysis of all offences found in the Criminal Code. The analysis is completed by relevant bibliography, case law and references to separate legislation.

A complete commentary on the Criminal Code (a source of vast historical, doctrinal and judicial information) can be found in Manuel Maia Gonçalves's *Código Penal Português, Anotado e Comentado*, 17th edition, Coimbra, 2005, and in Leal Henriques and Simas Santos's *Código Penal Anotado*, 2 vols., 2000 and 2003. All authors are judges who served on the Supreme Court of Justice.

## 3. The Criminal Code and the general rules of criminal responsibility

**3.1** As already stated, the Portuguese Criminal Code is divided into two parts: a general part and a special part. The former includes general rules applicable to any type of criminal offence, and the second contains a catalogue of criminal offences (a description of each crime and the applicable abstract penalties).

The general part of the Criminal Code regulates six different subject areas: (i) rules on the interpretation, validity and application of criminal norms (Articles 1-9); (ii) norms on the ascription of criminal responsibility (punishment prerequisites, forms of offence and exclusion of the causes of responsibility) (Articles 21-39); (iii) an extensive description of penalties, security measures, accessory legal consequences and the conditions for their application (Articles 40-112), (iv) rules on the presentation of complaints, accusations and waivers regarding certain offences (Articles 113-117); (v) justifications for the extinction of criminal responsibility (limitation of prosecution, amnesty, general pardon and exemption) (Articles 118-128);

and (vi) two brief norms on reparation for losses and damages caused by an offence (Articles 129 and 130). This study merely presents a brief overview of some of these topics.

The general part of the Criminal Code plays a role in facilitating the comprehension and application of all criminal law, whether codified or otherwise. The norms it contains are to be jointly applied with those on specific offences, as well as with existing separate criminal legislation. As an example of this, the concepts of *dolo* (criminal intent) (Article 14) and *negligência* (negligence) (Article 15), through which a fact is ascribed to the agent's will (*mens rea*), are shown to be the same throughout the penal system. The role of criminal intent in an offence not included in the Criminal Code follows the criteria described in Article 14 CP. Exceptions to general rules may be created by criminal legislation, but the need for such deviations must be strictly justified. Thus, the general part of the Criminal Code is in itself a source of stability, uniformity and predictability in criminal law.

**3.2** The first rules to be found in the Criminal Code are concerned with the theory of criminal norms. It sets out rules on its application, as well as its temporal and spatial scope. Emblematically, the Code opens with the principle of legality (*nullum crimen sine lege; nulla poena sine lege*): no offence or penalty may legitimately exist without having been established as such by a piece of legislation (Art. 1º). This entails the prohibition of analogy in the context of incrimination, and, according to dominant opinion, also the *praeter* and *contra* literal interpretation of criminal norms. Such prohibition does not apply if the interpretation favours the defendant (*in bonam partem*). Additionally, criminal norms are to be applied to facts occurring whilst they are in force, i.e. retroactivity is excluded. An exception to this rule is the possibility for the retro and ultra-active application of the most favourable norm (Articles 2 and 3 CP).

The Code also contains rules on the spatial scope of criminal norms, following the territoriality principle: criminal norms are applicable to facts occurring within Portuguese territory (Article 4). The place is determined in connection with the agent's conduct or the result of the criminal action (Article 7). In certain cases, Article 5 extends the scope of Portuguese criminal law to facts occurring outside national territory, citing other connections to the Portuguese legal order: crimes against national and global interests or crimes committed abroad by or against Portuguese citizens. The application of foreign criminal law is possible if the trial (based on facts that occurred abroad) takes place in Portugal and if the application of the foreign norms is more favourable to the defendant than the application of Portuguese law (Article 6).

**3.3** The ascription of criminal responsibility is fragmented into a "step-by-step" analysis. In order to determine someone's criminal responsibility, it is necessary to determine if that person has been the author of (Article 26 CP), or merely a participant (accomplice or instigator, Articles 26, *in fine*, and 27) in the practice of a typical, illicit, culpable and punishable fact.

Such a methodological scheme involves the identification of a fact (action or omission) with certain characteristics: it must be imputable to an agent as described in the law (it has to be a typical fact, both objectively and subjectively imputable to the agent); it must be illicit (i.e. violate a legal norm protecting relevant interests in the absence of a permissive norm excluding its illicitness); it must be culpable (i.e. the agent's conduct must be censurable); and, finally, it must be punishable (i.e. all conditions for a penalty to be applied must be met). Only when the presence of each of the above-mentioned elements has been verified and confirmed can the applicable sanction be determined. The determination of the sanction necessarily follows the first step of investigating the agent's responsibility for the criminal facts.

Each stage of analysis has a positive and a negative dimension. It contains both incriminating elements and the corresponding general part data. Regarding culpability, for example, there are positive prerequisites (such as age, understanding and awareness) as well as negative ones, which may lead to the exclusion of responsibility (lack of minimum age requirements, psychological imbalance or non-awareness of the illicitness of the fact).

The above-mentioned methodological scheme has a doctrinal origin and does not derive its legitimacy from criminal law. However, it is congruent with criminal legislation. The general part of the

Penal Code is not the only part of the legal system to mention the categories of fact, type, illicitness, culpability and punishability; procedural law refers to them, by establishing how the criminal ruling ought to be construed (Article 368 CPP) and by distinguishing such considerations from the act of determining a sanction (Article 369 CPP).

**3.4** Relevant for the attribution of criminal responsibility is the action or omission described in the specific type of offence (Article 10). Omission is equivalent to action in resulting crimes if there is a duty to act and if the agent's action would have been adequate to avoid the illicit result (Article 10/2 CP). The agent's behaviour may not correspond to that which the incriminating type expressly describes, but rather to a typical form of participation, i.e. intermediate authorship, co-authorship, instigation or complicity (Articles 26 and 27 CP). Moreover, the agent may, in certain cases, be punished for merely attempting to perform a certain typical action (Articles 22 and 23 CP). Preparatory acts are, in principle, not punishable (Article 21). The only exception to this rule is Article 344 CP, which refers to crimes against the State. Only individuals are capable of criminal responsibility (except where the law expressly allows corporate bodies to be considered responsible for a criminal act – Article 11 CP). All offences within the Criminal Code are thus conceived as crimes of individuals, and corporate criminal responsibility is only possible where expressly authorized.

If an incriminating norm is considered applicable to the case at hand, the fact and its consequences are ascribed to the agent through a causality nexus between the action (or omission) and the result, as well as through a subjective ascription nexus (*mens rea* – criminal intent or negligence – Articles 14 and 15 CP). Most offences require the existence of intent. Punishment for negligence is exceptional and must be established by the law (Article 13 CP). Intent may be excluded in the presence of error (Article 16 CP). In referring to a typical fact ascribable to an agent, one is summing up the essentials of criminal responsibility: an objective and a subjective fact (equivalent to the anglo-american categories of *actus reus* and *mens rea*).

However, an agent's responsibility may be excluded when in the presence of a defence (for instance self-defence, Articles 31 ff CP); exculpatory circumstances (for example duress, Articles 35 ff CP); an element that excludes the possibility of punishment (Article 324/2 CP); or the absence of a condition of punishment (Articles 24 and 25 CP). It is also excluded in the absence of certain pre-requisites such as a minimum age of 16 and mental sanity (Articles 19 and 20 CP). In such cases, the court acquits the defendant (Article 376 CPP).

**3.5** Upon confirmation of the agent's responsibility the appropriate sanction is determined. Minimum and maximum limits are first and foremost established by the incriminating norm. Taking such limits into consideration, the court first considers the possibility of avoiding imprisonment (Article 70 CP) and then calculates the chosen punishment according to the gravity of the facts and the defendant's culpability (Article 71 CP). If the defendant has been accused of several crimes, the ensuing punishment is calculated on the basis of the several different penalties applicable to each of those crimes, but the court will apply a sole penalty (Articles 30 and 77 CP).

## 4. Specific offences

**4.1** The so-called special part of the Criminal Code, together with some complementary legislation, focuses on specific types of offences (Articles 131-386). Following the minimum intervention principle, the universe of specific offences is fragmentary and predicated on two fronts: only certain interests are protected by criminal legislation and only some kinds of behaviour fall within its scope. Criminal law protection is justified by the constitutional dignity of the interest, by the need to make use of the criminal system in that case, and by the preventive and dissuasive potential of such a solution.

**4.2** The several types of offences included in the special part of the Criminal Code are organized into five different groups, according to the protected interests: crimes against persons (Articles 131-201), crimes against property (Articles 202-235), crimes against peace and humanity (Articles 236-246), crimes against society (Articles 247-294), and crimes against public order (Articles 295-386).

The first two groups essentially protect personal interests (life, physical integrity, health, sexual freedom, honour, private life), functionally personal interests (property, ownership and use rights, credit rights, etc.) and legal interests. The third group (crimes against peace and humanity) encompasses offences that, while they may directly or indirectly violate personal interests, are above all offences against universal and transpersonal values. The final two groups of offences apply to facts affecting essentially public interests (the credibility of documents, currency, environment, national territory, the rule of law and the administration of justice) or mixed interests (both public and private, such as religious freedom).

Describing the illicit fact and establishing a penalty for it represent the legislative techniques used to typify offences. The complexity of such descriptions varies according to the nature of the fact to be prevented and at times qualifying or privileged circumstances are added by the legislator to the basic description of the offence (for instance in the case of homicide see Articles 131 and 132, with differing penalties for simple and qualified murder. See also Articles 133-136, where less grave types of homicide are described: manslaughter, homicide at the victim's request, and infanticide in the context of post-natal depression). Punishment in the case of negligence must result from clear legislative permission. Negligent homicide is the object of a specific rule (Article 137 CP).

**4.3** According to the latest official criminal statistics (available at *www.gplp.mj.pt/estjustica*), the majority of offences that came to trial in 2002 were driving offences (14,839 cases of non-licensed driving and 14,796 cases of driving under the influence of alcohol) and physical integrity offences (13,512 cases). The next place in the ranking belongs to offences involving the issuance of bad cheques. (9,456 cases) and theft (7,677 cases). In the same year, 1,103 cases of murder (including attempted murder) and 360 sexual offence cases were brought to trial. The high number of driving offences brought to trial must be placed not only against the background of their statistical frequency, but also in the context of *flagrante delicto* detentions, leading to more numerous and swifter trials.

## 5. Criminal sanctions

**5.1** The Portuguese penal system is based upon a monist conception of criminal reactions despite contemplating two kinds of sanctions; penalties (Arts.41° and subsequent, CP) and *security measures* (Articles 91 ff CP). These sanctions share some application prerequisites and conditions (Articles 40/1 and 90 CP) and the two different sanctions cannot be simultaneously applied to the same person for the same fact (this would constitute a double punishment, which is constitutionally forbidden by Article 29/5). Moreover, the two sanctions apply to distinct contexts; *security measures* (and security measures alone) apply only to those who are not capable of criminal responsibility (*inimputáveis*).

Aspects of the regime are common to both types of sanctions. The first common aspect is their goal: as stated by Article 40/1 CP, they aim at protecting legal interests and contributing to the social reintegration of the perpetrator. They also both conform to the principle of legality and must be clearly stated before they can be enforced (Articles 29/1/3 and 4 and 31/1 CPR). Additionally, they are subject to the principles of proportionality, necessity, adequateness and judicial mediation, and their effects must be of a non-automatic character (Articles 18 and 30 CPR). The Constitution does not allow perpetual or indefinite penalties and security measures (Article 30/1 CRP). The maximum penalty established by the Criminal Code is 25 years, including multiple crime cases (Article 41/2 and 3).

Both types of sanctions are applicable to illicit facts ascribable to a person. No sanction can be applied in the absence of an ascribable illicit fact. Thus, there is no possibility of applying a sanction when only the dangerous character of the agent (but no concrete criminal fact) is cited. Sanctions are conditioned both by the gravity of the fact and by the dangerous character revealed by the agent in the practice of that fact (Articles 40/3 and 91/1 CP).

**5.2** There are two main kinds of penalties in the Portuguese Criminal Code: imprisonment (Articles 41 ff CP) and the payment of fines (Article 47 CP). There are also the so-called substitution penalties: substitute fines (for up to six months of imprisonment, Article 44 CP), imprisonment during weekends (Article 45 CP), semi-detention

(Article 46 CP), community service at the request or with the acceptance of the defendant (Articles 48 and 58 CP), admonition (Article 60 CP), suspension of the enforcement of a prison sentence (Articles 50 ff CP) and subjection to probation (Article 53 CP). When choosing which penalty to enforce, the court should give preference to non-imprisonment penalties, if they prove adequate to the aims of punishment in the respective case (Article 70 CP).

There are also a number of accessory penalties, of a secondary nature and with complementary aims, which presuppose the enforcement of a principal penalty. In such contexts, the following penalties are admitted: prevention from performing a certain professional activity (Article 66 CP), suspension from the exercise of an activity (Article 67 CP), and prohibition from driving motorized vehicles (Article 69 CP). The court can also seize the instruments, products, objects and profits connected with the criminal practice (Articles 109 and 111 CP).

Should the agent show, in the practice of facts pertaining to the offence, a pronounced and current inclination towards criminal behaviour, the court may decide to enforce a relatively indeterminate penalty, which, in any case, cannot exceed the maximum of 25 years (Articles 83 ff CP).

According to the Criminal Code (Articles 91 ff), there are two kinds of security measures: freedom-depriving (in which case the individual is confined to a psychiatric institution, Articles 91 ff CP) or non freedom-depriving measures (when such confinement is suspended (Article 98 CP), certain activities are prohibited (Article 100 CP), licences are taken away or refused (Article 101 CP), and certain rules of conduct are established (Article 102 CP).

The execution of imprisonment penalties is regulated by Articles 477-500 CPP, and by penitentiary legislation (for example Decree-Law No. 265/79, 1 August). There is also special legislation applicable to young delinquents (between 16 and 21 years of age) – Decree-Law No. 401/82, 23 September. The execution of penalties is monitored by a special court (*Tribunal de Execução de Penas*) and by an autonomous entity acting under the auspices of the Ministry of Justice (*Instituto de Reinserção Social*).

**5.3** According to the latest official criminal statistics (_www.gplp. mj.pt/estjustica_), the sanction most frequently applied by Portuguese courts in 2002 was the payment of a fine (approximately 70% of all cases brought to trial), while the sanction of imprisonment was applied in less than 10% of all criminal cases. Furthermore, 50% of the imprisonment penalties did not exceed 3 years, 26% ranged between 3 and 5 years, 16% between 5 and 8 years and only 8% exceeded 8 years. A very significant part of the prison population (approximately 13,000 inmates, in 2005) is remanded in custody before trial.

## 6. Perspectives on evolution

Perspectives on the evolution of the Portuguese penal system tend to vary according to the political paradigm against which it is judged. All things being equal (should the present political system remain intact), and if the principles of the separation of powers, representative democracy and the rule of law continue to frame our legal order, all changes should be directed at reorganizing the catalogue of specific offences, as well as their respective sanctions (coupled with a few procedural changes which will be autonomously addressed in this book).

Instances of neo-criminalization are foreseen (new crimes against persons, offences resulting from recent advances in genetics, some economic crimes and new forms of organized crime), as well as some selective decriminalization (some property and crimes of honour). The penal system should evolve in general terms towards non-detention solutions, with more frequent use of electronic control devices, new victim reparation and mediation mechanisms. Whether as a consequence of trying to avoid the complete socio-professional isolation of defendants, or for strictly economic reasons (the high costs associated with maintaining a prison system), the supra-individual legalist system typical of the 19th century has tended to disappear. The question of how the penal system will cope with variable evolution, according to the social insertion of defendants (integrated citizen/exterior aggressor) cannot be answered at this point, but it is not an issue to be dismissed. Moreover, it is very likely that advancements in new scientific areas (such as genetics and neurobiology) will be reflected in criminal law. Another possible area of evolution concerns the repressive-preventive dichotomy, which has already been the object of important changes in the context of drug abuse (coupled with the decriminalization of acts of mere use). The Portuguese criminal order will have to keep pace with and try to adjust to the frenzy of information society, which is perniciously eroding the liberal inheritance of some penal systems.

## Bibliography

ANTUNES, Maria João, and Pedro CAEIRO, *Criminal Law – Suppl. 6 (May 1995), Portugal,* The Hague, 1995. BELEZA, Teresa Pizarro, *Die Täterschaftsstruktur bei Pflichtdelikten - Pflichtträgerschaft versus Tatherrschaft?,* in "Bausteine des Europäischen Strafrechts". DIAS, J. FIGUEIREDO/SCHÜNEMANN, B.(ed.), Munique, 1995. CORREIA, Eduardo, *Grundgedanken der portugiesischen Strafrechtsreform, in* ZStW 76 (1964), pp. 115 and ff. Idem, *Der Einfluss Franz von Liszts auf die portugiesische Strafrechtsreform, in* ZStW 81 (1969), pp. 723 and ff.. CORTES ROSA, Manuel, *La función de delimitación de injusto e culpabilidad en el sistema del Derecho Penal, in* SCHÜNEMANN, B. / DIAS, J. FIGUEIREDO (coords.) and SILVA SÁNCHEZ (ed.), "Fundamentos de un sistema europeo del Derecho penal", Barcelona, 1995, pp. 247 and ff. (also available in German). COSTA PINTO, Frederico de Lacerda, *L'alternativa delle codificazioni settoriali ed il ruolo degli "illeciti amministrativi" nell'organizzazioni del Diritto Penale secondario. L'esperienza portoghese, in* Massimo DONINI (ed.), "Modelli ed esperienze di riforma del Diritto Penale complementare", Milano, 2003, pp. 141-154. FARIA E COSTA, José, *Les Problèmes Juridiques et Pratiques Posés Par La Difference Entre Droit Criminel et le Droit Administratif Penal,* Coimbra, 1988. FIGUEIREDO DIAS, Jorge, *Der Irrtum als Schuldausschliessungsgrund in Portugiesichen Strafrecht, in* ESER/ PERRON, "Rechtsfertitung und Entschuldigung", Band III, MPI, Freiburg, 1990, pgs. 201-215. Idem, *Schuld und Persönlichkeit, in* ZStW 95 (1983), pp. 220 and ss. HÜNERFELD, Peter, *Strafrechtsdogmatik in Deutschland und Portugal,* Baden-Baden, 1981. Idem, *Die Entwicklung der Kriminalpolitik in Portugal,* Bonn, 1971. SOUSA BRITO, José, *La inserción del sistema de Derecho penal entre una jurisprudencia de conceptos y una (di)solución funcionalista, in* DIAS, J. FIGUEIREDO/SCHÜNEMANN, B.(coords) /SILVA SANCHEZ, J.M.(ed.) – "Fundamentos de un sistema europeo del Derecho Penal". Libro-Homenaje a Claus Roxin, Barcelona, 1995, pp. 99-111 (also available in German).

# CHAPTER 11

# Criminal Procedure

TERESA PIZARRO BELEZA
FREDERICO DE LACERDA DA COSTA PINTO

SUMMARY: *1. History: from an adversarial to an inquisitorial model of criminal proceedings 2. Sources of law: Constitution, statutes, case law 3. As it is now 4. Where the essence lies: coercive measures and rules of evidence 5. What next? Looking to the future*

## 1. History: from an adversarial to an inquisitorial model of criminal proceedings

Before the first collection of Royal Ordinances (*Ordenações do Reino*), Criminal Procedure in Portugal was regulated by custom and local statutes, which amounted to a sort of adversarial system. Complaints had to be brought by the victims in order for a criminal trial to take place.

From the 15th century onwards (the reign of King Afonso V), the system slowly evolved towards an inquisitorial version, although adversarial elements were retained in respect of the trial stage. Confession was by then considered decisive evidence. The ongoing centralization of power – the concentration of power in the hands of the monarch – and the influence of cannon law helped to shape the new rules.

By the end of the 18th century, in line with the Enlightenment reform movement in Europe, the existing model of criminal procedure started to fall from favour, namely because of the extensive use of (legal) torture, the absolute power of the judge, and the various "primitive" ways of gathering evidence. Influential lawyers like Mello Freire, most notably, Ribeiro dos Santos, and Pereira e Sousa, criticized the criminal procedure of the day as antiquated and inhuman. However, absolute monarchy and its fear of the influence of the French Revolution hindered earlier legal reform, and reform had to wait until the advent of Liberalism, in the 1820s, when the Portuguese Liberal Revolution took place.

The first Portuguese Constitution was also the first modern, liberally inspired reform of criminal procedure. Legality and guarantees took their place in the constitutional text, where they have remained until today. Rules were introduced relating to conditions of detention, the remanding in custody of prisoners awaiting trial, the abolition of special privilege courts, the prohibition of torture and criminal expropriation (*confisco*). Trials became public and trial by jury was introduced. Justice was no longer a secret ceremony but something visible.

The constitutional rules in the field of criminal procedure were gradually translated in much greater detail through the ordinary laws of 1832, 1837 and 1841.

Some important reforming steps were taken after the Republican Revolution of 1910. The new Republican Constitution (1911) introduced new time limits for a defendant to be held *incommunicado*. The duration of the period during which suspects could be remanded in custody was also limited. Special criminal courts (criminal political trials, state security) were abolished. The right to remain silent was introduced (1910). So was the preliminary hearing as part of the pre-trial stages, implying the intervention of a *juge d'instruction*.

Between 1910 and 1926 many criminal laws were published, when a new regime, the so-called *Estado Novo*, was established. For political and legal reasons, the need for a new Code of Criminal Procedure was obvious. It was finally published in 1929.

The new Code brought with it the intention to simplify and enlarge the sphere of action of judges, ensuring their active intervention during trial as well as in the course of the investigation. Such a solution mirrors the inquisitorial nature of the 1929 Criminal Code (including a formal accusation presented by the prosecution). Additionally, trials by jury were limited. The political police were reformed in 1933 and acquired specific and exclusive powers of investigation.

Two major legal and judicial reforms occurred in 1945 and 1954. Following the 1945 reform, the prosecution acquired autonomous powers within the preliminary investigation phase; both the judicial police and the political police had their competences widened. From 1954 onwards, the competences of the political police often overlapped with those of the judiciary police.

One of the saddest aspects of the judicial involvement in the dictatorship of the *Estado Novo* was the criminal prosecution of political dissidents. Some of the best practicing lawyers of the day (Abranches Ferrão, Salgado Zenha, Mário Soares) defended such cases in the *Tribunal da Boa Hora*, the Central Criminal Court in Lisbon, often taking considerable risks with their career and liberty. The political police made their physical presence in court felt in a way that amounted to sheer intimidation of both judges and defending lawyers, not to mention the defendants themselves, who often felt it was useless to complain of having been subjected to torture by the very same police. Legislation was eventually enacted allowing for indefinite detention on grounds of *political danger*. Prisons like the Fortress of Peniche and Caxias were allocated to political prisoners. Tarrafal in the Cape Verde islands became a prisoners' camp for political convicts, or merely suspects, who endured extreme harsh conditions and sometimes death. The secret state police (PVE-PIDE-DGS) was in charge of investigation and intimidation, persecuting and torturing the opposition seen as enemies of the State. In some cases (Delgado, Dias Coelho) assassination was the extra-judicial solution to eliminate people who were considered too dangerous or outspoken. Workers were also the victims of police repression during strikes or demonstrations.

The dictatorship moulded criminal law and procedure to serve its narrow political views. Individual liberties were still proclaimed by some laws and the Constitution (1933) but were systematically curtailed either in "special" laws or in practice. This situation would last for almost 50 years, coming to a halt only with the democratic Revolution of 1974, after thirteen years of war in Africa. Military defeat and the political radicalization of young army captains precipitated the end of the political autocracy, with virtually no resistance.

When the Revolution took place on the 25th April 1974, the political regime fell like an over-ripe fruit. The military coup that started it off soon became a general uprising against the Government, the war, the stifling of political liberties. Suddenly, everybody seemed to be engaged in the earnest struggle for democracy.

One of the main points of the "Programme of the Armed Forces Movement", presented to the Portuguese nation on television on the evening of the first days after revolution, concerned criminal procedure. The dignity of criminal procedure was to be restored.

In fact, even before the 1976 Constitution was drafted and enacted, some legislation relating to important topics in criminal prosecution, such as trial by jury that had been abolished by the *Estado Novo*, was changed.

The main legislative changes however only took place some years after the Constitution was adopted. The Constitution itself includes important rules in the area. The Penal Code was replaced in 1982 and the Criminal Procedure Code was replaced in 1987.

## 2. Sources of law: Constitution, statutes, case law

Criminal procedure's legal sources are similar to the described sources of substantive criminal law, although constitutional provisions regarding criminal proceedings are significantly more detailed and judicial precedent carries more weight.

The Portuguese Constitution (1976, with various amendments) contains an important and comprehensive combination of provisions on the structure, contents, and limits of the most essential aspects of criminal procedure.

From among such provisions, the following should be pointed out: accusatorial structure (Article 32/5, whereby the roles of the investigator, the prosecutor and the judge are clearly distinguished), adversarial system (Article 32/5), the right of the defendant to a proper defence (Article 32/1), the participation right of the victim (Article 32/7), the right not to be tried twice for the same offence (Article 29/5), the right to be tried by the legally competent judge

(Article 32/9), limitations to detention and to custody; the judicial basis of freedom deprivation measures (Articles 27, 28 and 32/4); *Habeas Corpus* (Article 31); the nullity of evidence violating fundamental rights (Articles 32/8, and 34/4); the prohibition of special courts (Article 209/4); the opening to the public of criminal trials (Article 206).

The above-mentioned constitutional provisions have a triple role: a guaranteeing role, allowing a direct control of legislation, as well as its enforcement by the courts (through constitutional review); a conforming one, as they determine and impose upon the legislator a certain scope of procedural measures; and, finally, an interpretative role, through which constitutional solutions may be invoked in the process of finding the correct answer to concrete problems. They may even be used to fill in lacunae within procedural legislation.

The procedural system has mostly been codified (*Código de Processo Penal*, 1987 – CPP), but some parts remain regulated in discrete statutes. The CPP regulates the main aspects of this legal branch, such as the different procedural types and phases (Articles 381-398, and Articles 241 ff), the status and powers of the different participants (Articles 8-84), all rules regarding coercive measures (Articles191-228), the process of gathering, producing, and evaluating evidence (Articles 124 ff), or the general regulation of procedural acts (Articles 85 ff).

Scattered legislation may be of various kinds: it either regulates certain matters contained in the CPP (such as the electronic control system applied to coercive measures – Law No. 122/99, of 20 August; trial by jury Decree-Law No. 387-A/87, of 29 December; or it deals with the organization of criminal investigation – Law No. 21/2000, of 12 August); or else it has a special nature according to the specific type of crimes to which it refers to (as is the case with organized, economic and financial crimes – Law No. 36/94, of 29 September; Law No. 5/2002, of January 11). Finally, some legislation focuses on autonomous matters, which, albeit relevant, are too recent or not sufficiently stable to be integrated in the CPP (this applies to victim protection rules – Law No. 93/99, of July 14 as well as undercover investigations- Law No. 101/2001, of August 25).

Court rulings are only effective in concrete cases and legal precedent is merely persuasive. Conclusions concerning the scope of judicial decisions, as well as the nature of legal sources (included in the text on substantive criminal law) apply to the present context. It should be noted, however, that the Constitutional Court's extensive case law has been decisive in determining how to interpret and enforce the provisions of the CPP, as well as in rejecting certain guidelines, which came to the fore during the first years of its "life".

Legal doctrine is not a source of law and its force is merely argumentative. However, specialist opinions may be (and frequently are) called for and included in a legal case (Article 165/3).

The entry into force of new criminal procedure rules is usually immediate, with the exception of cases where the defendant's procedural rights are limited or if there is a rupture in the unity or harmony of procedural acts (Article 5 CPP).

## 3. As it is now

The current criminal procedure legal *corpus* is structurally mixed (it contains both a preliminary inquisitorial investigation phase and a trial phase with many accusatorial elements), albeit essentially accusatorial and completed by an autonomous court investigation principle. Strictly speaking, it is not a system of parties, in that the court retains a complete control of the case and has the duty to take guidance not only from evidence presented by the defence and prosecution, but also from the results of its own search for the truth.

The criminal legal process is framed by the principle of legality of all procedural acts, types and phases (Article 2).

The ordinary type of procedure includes three phases (two preliminary phases and a decision phase), possibly followed by an appeal. The preliminary phases are the following: the inquiry (*inquérito*) phase (which includes an investigation at the end of which either a formal accusation is put forward or the case is filed); and the optional instruction (*instrução*) phase (Articles 262 ff and 286 ff), which may lead to an indictment (in which case there is a trial) or to the closure of the case (where no indictment occurs)

(Articles 307 and 308). The third phase is compulsory and consists of a public, oral and adversarial trial (Articles 311 ff).

There are also three types of special procedure, applicable to less serious offences and therefore swifter and less complex than the ordinary procedure (articles 381 ff).

Criminal trials start with an investigation led by the *Ministério Público* (MP, Public Prosecutors) with substantial help from the various police bodies (most notably the judicial police). As a rule, the MP is under legal obligation to open the investigation ("open inquiries") if it has been notified of a crime in one of a number of ways. A complaint from the victim, a piece of news in the media, or any other source of information, are all legally recognized means of knowing that a crime has possibly been committed (Articles 241 ff do CPP). Before the formal opening of an enquiry by the MP, the police must take the necessary measures so that any available evidence of the crime is not destroyed, but it is up to the prosecutors to steer the proceedings from then onwards.

The prosecution has virtually no discretion as to decide for or against bringing charges against someone. Provided the evidence is relatively solid, the law makes prosecution compulsory (Article 262/2 CPP).

During this investigation, the inquiry phase, a judge (*juge d'instruction*) may be required to intervene. This is the case if the defendant is to be remanded in custody, or, alternatively, subjected to bail or any other coercive measures. Again, if the gathering of evidence involves more delicate interventions, such as house or body searches or telephone tapping the Code requires the permission of the judge (Articles 268 and 269 CPP). The judge will make sure that legal rules are respected and that the MP or the police do not exceed their powers, thus assuming the role of a *Juge des Libertés*.

A judicial stage can follow if either the defendant or the victim (*assistente*) so require (Articles 286 ff CPP). This stage, the so-called instruction, (*instrução*) is presided over by the *Juge d'Instruction*. It is not open to the public, but it is organized in an adversarial manner. If the defendant wishes to challenge the decision to bring charges he/she may require the opening of this stage, trying to avoid the public trial. If the victim wishes to challenge the decision of the MP not to bring charges he/she can also ask for this stage to begin. At the end of

*Instrução* the *Juge d'Instruction* decides to press charges or not to do so, depending on his/her assessment of available evidence (Article 308 CPP). Again, the decision is legally bound. No judicial discretion is allowed at this point.

The trial stage proper follows (Articles 311 ff CPP). The judge (or 3 judges, for more serious crimes) will have had access to the evidence gathered before trial, by the prosecution, the defence or even ordered by the *juge d'instruction* if the second preparatory phase (*instrução*) has taken place. The court is supposed to know what has been gathered in the way of evidence or any other elements in the case file. This enables the first decision in the trial phase to be taken, namely to check whether the court is competent, whether the prosecution is bringing a totally unfounded case, or whether an amnesty has taken place that includes the particular case to be tried, etc (Article 311 CPP).

Trials by jury are possible in Portuguese courts but extremely rare. This is not due to plea bargaining, which does not exist as such (even if informally practised, it must be restricted to very limited occasions, for legal and traditional reasons). In formal legal terms, such an opportunity may arise in the few cases where a guilty plea is the sole basis for conviction – in exchange for sentencing as proposed by the prosecution (*processo sumaríssimo*). Confession is regarded as something slightly suspicious and usually insufficient for a conviction. It must be made in open court, during the trial session and the Code of Criminal Procedure places quite a few conditions for admission of guilt to allow the court to dispense with further evidence.

When a trial by jury does take place, the lay members (4) form a collective court with the professional judges (3) and decide on all matters, the decisions being taken by majority vote (issue of guilt, legal questions, sentencing). The jurors are selected from a list of names based on a random pre-selection of local electoral rolls. The prosecution and defence can refuse two names without any particular reason, apart from challenging candidates on grounds of partiality.

The judge is not seen as a sort of umpire who monitors respect for the rules on the part of prosecution and defence, in an adversarial type of framework. He or she will take a much more active role in the trial proceedings. The judge (or the president, the judge who presides over the three judges panel, or the jury) has the power to direct the entire *trial audience.* Moreover, judges have a certain amount of investigative power (an echo of the inquisitorial tradition?). They may order evidence to be produced or sought if they consider the case insufficiently proved, provided they do not go beyond the *facts* as reported by the prosecution (Articles 322, 323 and ff CPP).

The prosecution is seen by the Portuguese law as a somewhat *dual* entity: on the one hand, it is supposed to act under strict criteria of legal objectivity and impartiality It may, for instance, launch an appeal against conviction, if the prosecutor concludes that, in legal terms, the conviction was misguided or wrong (Article 401/1/a CPP). The prosecutors are professional magistrates, like the judges: they form two different *parallel* bodies of the (professional) magistracy, with separate governing councils. However on the other hand, the prosecutor is supposed to, in law, sustain the accusation (charges) in the sense that he/she is expected to bring solid evidence to the trial and to argue in favour of its relevance to the case. But the prosecutor is also free (in law) to, at the end of the trial, plea for the innocence of the defendant.

The defence lawyer (Articles 62 ff CPP) has a relatively less active role in the Portuguese courts, both in the sense that often he or she is designated by the judge (in the case of poor defendants, mostly) and does not have a good knowledge of the case beforehand, and also because the directive powers of the judge are more generous: questioning the defendant, the victim, and the experts is the judge's business – although prosecution and defence may suggest questions to be asked. But the questioning of witnesses, including cross-examination, is taken on by these *Parties* (a questionable concept in Portuguese criminal procedure, precisely because it is not a proper adversarial system).

The victim (or, if under age or deceased, his/her legal representative) may have an important role in the proceedings. The victim may take part in the case, in the formal role of *Assistente*. He can bring private charges, gather and offer evidence and bring appeals among other relevant powers (*e.g.* Articles 68 ff CPP).

The defendant can never testify under oath. The right to remain silent includes the possibility of lying without committing perjury. The defendant has to be warned by the court of the right to remain silent and no inference as to his/her guilt can be made from the decision not to speak (Articles 61, 140 ff and 342 to 355 CPP). The defendant may be tried in his/her absence – *in absentia* – provided he/she has been warned at some point in the procedure of such a possibility and made aware of the charges brought against him/her (Articles 332 ff). It should be stressed that these rules apply within a system in which the prosecution has virtually no discretion in deciding for or against bringing charges against someone.

There is technically no burden of proof: the judge (as noted above) can look or ask for evidence if the prosecution or the defence does not manage to present the case in a sufficiently solid and convincing manner. In case of serious doubt as to the guilt of the defendant, *in dubio pro reo*, the court must acquit. Such is the mandate of the constitutional presumption of innocence (Article 32/2 of the Constitution).

## 4. Where the essence lies: coercive measures and rules of evidence

Two topics deserve special attention: coercive measures (Articles 191 ff) and evidence rules (Articles 124 ff). Rules regarding both these categories share a higher risk of collision with the fundamental rights of citizens, suspects or defendants, and therefore demand a direct and immediate (or, at least, *a posteriori*) control. This is particularly evident in the context of coercive measures involving judicial acts limiting the defendant's personal liberty. But it also arises with certain methods of gathering evidence, such as searches, seizures and telephone tapping.

Another feature they have in common is their important role in the effectiveness of the procedure: protecting the procedure and the gathered evidence against the defendant's possibly harmful actions lies at the core of the procedure's material legitimization. Evidence is the procedure's "oxygen", vital to a range of acts such as the prosecution and indictment, as well as within the trial phase. A close analysis of both coercive measures and evidence rules allows for the understanding of any procedural system, for they illustrate the State's fundamental choices within its exercise of punitive power, as well as the limits to be observed in the pursuit of penal justice. Understanding the relationship between the State and its citizens in any legal system is made possible by the use of such a "barometer".

The CPP makes a distinction between personal coercive measures and patrimonial warrants. The formers' task is to ensure procedural integrity and effectiveness (*e.g.* investigation, evidence, witnesses, and the availability or presence of the defendant throughout the procedure); the latter contribute to the safeguarding of availability of material conditions for the payment of fines, damages or fees.

CPP includes general rules for the application of the several measures (Articles 191-195 and 204 ff), seven personal coercive measures (Articles 196-203) and two patrimonial warrants (Articles 227 and 228).

Personal coercive measures are as follows: personal identification and indication of place of residence, bail, obligation to be present at a certain time, suspension of profession or rights, prohibition of contacts or of presence in certain places, house arrest and remanding in custody.

These measures are applicable only to defendants in the course of a criminal procedure and may only be established by a court order, with the exception of personal identification and indication of place of residence (which can be applied by the Public Prosecutor or the police). The choice amongst the various measures is dependant on the seriousness of the facts imputed to the defendant, being generally framed by the principles of legality, necessity and proportionality. Moreover, all measures are compulsorily and periodically reviewed by a judge.

Despite its legally exceptional character, the use of remanding in custody is common. The law contemplates several ways of repudiating illegal measures, ranging from appeals to *Habeas Corpus* and compensation for an illegal detention or arrest (Articles 219 ff).

In principle, all kinds of evidence are permissible and the assessment of evidence is free, but in some instances the law advises the judge against an all too ready confidence in confession (Article 125 CPP). This is an historical compromise between the inquisitorial and the adversarial models, stressing the *Public Order* dimension of

Criminal Procedure. The Court must strive to reach the material, real truth of the facts (Article 340/1 CPP), and this implies a systematic doubt towards a possibly untruthful defendant. One may confess for many reasons and confessions are not necessarily genuine (Article 344 CPP).

The statements of the defendant, who never speaks under oath, are just one means of evidence amongst others (Articles 140 and 343 ff). This is partly why judges do not rely on *cross examination* of defendant and witnesses (although this is possible, Article 146/1 CPP).

Witnesses, on the other hand, always testify under oath and are liable to prosecution for perjury. In some cases, witnesses may refuse to testify on the grounds of personal *privileges* relating to family connections between themselves and the defendant. They may also be excused on grounds of *secrecy* due to professional, religious or State duties to remain silent. Professional secrecy may be lifted by the judge as opposed to State or religious duties. Witnesses are supposed to speak only about the facts they know directly. *Hearsay* evidence is expressly forbidden in the Code (Articles 128 to 139 and 348 ff CPP).

All evidence must be analysed in open Court (Article 321 CPP) but the judges (and the jury) will normally have had previous access to any documents and any other kinds of evidence. In fact, the documents are always physically present, in the shape of often voluminous files lying on the judges' desk and can and will be occasionally read and used by the judges during trial.

Freedom of evaluation (Article 127 CPP) together with presumption of innocence (Article 32/2 Constitution) lead to *in dubio pro reo*. All reasonable doubts about evidence or facts in general must be solved in favour of the defendant.

The Code allows for search and seizures under certain circumstances and within certain limits (Articles 171 ff). If they take place in a home or an office of a doctor or a lawyer, the conditions are particularly stringent, namely a court order is needed (Articles 177, 180 and 181 CPP)). Telephone tapping and other invasion of communications (letters, telegrams, faxes, electronic mail) are also possible under a court order, and their contents must be controlled by the judge (Articles 179 and 187 to 190 CPP). Admissibility in all these cases is subjected to rules relating to the seriousness of the crimes being investigated.

Exclusion of evidence is compulsory when basic rules of gathering evidence are broken or the protection of essential intimacy is violated. A mitigated version of the "fruit of the poisoned tree" is taken up by Portuguese law, as far as the long term effects of evidence exclusion are concerned (Articles 126 and 122 CPP).


## 5. What next? Looking to the future

As far as can be foreseen, the Portuguese procedural system is bound to evolve in a somewhat schizophrenic manner, oscillating between guarantees and security/neo-security mechanisms. A focus on procedural celerity can be expected, introducing some simplifications and the creation of a few limitations in the sphere of appeals. The expansion of electronic control mechanisms is expected as a replacement for penalties, envisaging lower costs for the State. The mentioned tension between political, judicial and legislative power will continue to exist regarding telephone tapping and other means of monitoring telecommunications. New issues surrounding new forms of urban vigilance (video cameras, police control at a distance) and related evidence problems are sure to arise, as well as those regarding the control of specific groups. Transnational organized crime is likely to continue its defiance of the rule of law and traditional forms of criminal justice, demanding fresh preventive measures as well as new investigation and control mechanisms. Legal systems will continue to be challenged in their effectiveness and in the ability of the police and judiciary to cooperate beyond as well as within borders.

One concluding question remains: is the so-called classical criminal justice, which we have inherited from a 19th century political, social, judicial and economic world-view and which is materialized in liberal codifications, merely a luxurious antiquity in the context of 21st century rule of law? What is startling about this problem is that it challenges the ability of European democracies to reinforce their Enlightenment inheritance while facing new social and political demands and strains.

# Bibliography

Costa Andrade, Manuel da, *Sobre as proibições de prova em Processo Penal,* Coimbra, 1992. Antunes, Maria João, and Pedro Caeiro, *Criminal Law – Suppl. 6 (May 1995), Portugal,* The Hague, 1995. Beleza, Teresa Pizarro, *Apontamentos de Processo Penal,* 3 vols., Lisbon, 1992, 1993, 1995. Figueiredo Dias, Jorge de, *Direito Processual Penal,* I vol., Coimbra, 1984 (reprinted 1st edition 1974). *Justice Across the Atlantic II. The Criminal Process in Portugal and the United States: Two Legal Systems in Pursuit of Justice* (Presentations from a Seminar at Rhode Island and Massachusetts, USA, October 1998), 1999, Lisbon. Marques da Silva, Germano, *Curso de Processo Penal,* 3 vols, Lisbon, 1999-2000.

# III
# PRIVATE LAW

# CHAPTER 12
# Contract Law

MARGARIDA LIMA REGO
CARLOS FERREIRA DE ALMEIDA

> SUMMARY: *1. Legal sources 2. Concept and general principles 3. Form and formation 4. Representation 5. Validity 6. Contents and effects 7. Performance, non-performance and remedies 8. Continuity and change*

## 1. Legal sources

The most important legislative source of Portuguese general contract law is the Civil Code of 1966. To a large extent, this Code was modelled upon the German *Bürgerliche Gesetzbuch (BGB)*. In fact, its main structure follows that of the *BGB*. Hence, we will find most of the rules concerning the formation of contracts in Book I of the Civil Code. Book II, which covers the law of obligations, is composed of a general part, setting forth the rules regulating the contents and effects of contracts, followed by a second part, dedicated to the most common types of contract.

Examining the contents of Books I and II, however, we find that, here and there, the source of inspiration can rather be traced to the Italian Civil Code of 1942 or, perhaps to a lesser extent, to the *Code Napoléon*, the influence of which is clear in the first Portuguese Civil Code of 1867.

It is important to note that, once again reflecting the influence of the German *BGB*, we find most general rules concerning the life of a contract to be drafted so as to apply to the entire law of obligations, whereas, in an even greater exercise of abstraction, the rules concerning the formation of contracts are to apply to any one or two-sided legal transaction. Indeed, with the exception of a relatively short section of the Code, which focuses on the contract as a source of obligations, only those rules regulating the most common contract types are wholly contained within the boundaries of the law of contract.

Specific types of contract are also regulated elsewhere – in other codes and statutes. Thus, for instance, some commercial contracts are regulated in the Commercial Code of 1888 and the labour contract is now regulated in the Labour Code of 2004. Significant rules of general contract law can also be found in non-codified statutes, the most important being those on standard terms and contracts of adhesion and on the sale of consumer goods and associated guarantees.

Legislation is not the only recognized source of law in Portugal. In fact usages are also relevant in a number of aspects of contract law, as are the codes of conduct in force amongst the members of certain professions.

Finally, even though formally they do not constitute binding sources of legal rules, a word should be said about the importance of case law and of legal writing – both national and foreign – in the interpretation and application of contract law.

## 2. Concept and general principles

We may define a contract as an agreement, formed by two or more parties, whose declarations to one another are able to generate for such parties legal effects of any nature – obligational or otherwise – that accord with the meaning of that agreement.

The most basic principle of Portuguese contract law is that of freedom of contract. The notion that, within the limits set forth in the law, parties may freely shape the contents of a contract is expressly contained in the Civil Code. Freedom to enter into a contract is implied throughout its provisions.

Another basic principle that permeates contract law is that of good faith. According to this principle, when making a contract, and later on, when performing that contract, the parties must comply with the requirements of good faith. As such, this principle is generally laid down in the Civil Code. However, these requirements, whilst stemming from an objective notion of good faith, are not directly set forth in any legislative source, but have rather been extensively elaborated in legal literature of Italian and mostly German influence.

The principle of good faith has also played a vital role in the shaping of the rules that regulate the consequences of a change of circumstances, and of the rules applicable to the abuse (or misuse) of rights.

## 3. Form and formation

Freedom of form is the default rule that is applicable to the making of a contract. Notwithstanding, certain types of contract such as the insurance contract are required to be drawn up in writing, whilst others must be executed by way of a public deed, as is the case with contracts for the sale or other disposition of an interest in immovable property. A contract that lacks the required form will be null and void; form is thus more than the prescribed way of evidencing the existence and contents of a contract, insofar as it is a precondition to a contract's validity.

Traditionally, a contract is said to have been concluded when a clear, sufficiently defined and firm or unequivocal offer is matched by a firm or unequivocal acceptance thereof. This model underlies the rules on formation set forth in the Civil Code. Nonetheless, there are numerous contracts in existence that contain no separate identifiable offer and acceptance, without any difficulties being raised in the application of those rules to the facts of a case.

As a general rule, contracts will become effective between the parties thereto as soon as they have been entered into.

For instance, in a contract for the sale of goods, unless the parties determine otherwise, the transfer of property will take place immediately upon conclusion. Should such transfer be subject to registration, however, it will only be enforceable vis-à-vis third parties once the transfer is registered. The parties may determine that property over the goods sold will be transferred only at a specified later date. Or they may choose to conclude a preliminary contract (*contrato-promessa*) whereby they exchange promises to enter into a contract for the sale of goods. This latter type of contract is most commonly employed when the promised contract is subject to a heavy requirement of form – such as in the case of the sale of an interest in land. The preliminary contract is a general feature of Portuguese contract law: contracting parties may exchange promises to enter into virtually any other type of contract.

Some contracts will only become effective between parties thereto once the respective object has physically or symbolically exchanged hands. Such is the case with loan contracts, regardless of whether the loan involves a sum of money or other fungible goods or the gratuitous loan of a specific thing, and such is also the case with the verbal gift contract.

It is important to note that under Portuguese contract law the negotiating parties may be subject to pre-contractual liability (*culpa in contrahendo*) prior to conclusion of the contract. This will be the case if they do not comply with the requirements of good faith in the process of their negotiations or when breaking off such negotiations.

## 4. Representation

A person may be validly and effectively bound to a contract that another person has entered into, acting in the former person's name. If that agent has been granted the authority to act in the name of the principal then no further action will be required in order for the contract to bind the principal. If that agent acts without the necessary authority to represent the principal, or acts outside the scope of that authority, the latter must then ratify the contract in order for it to have binding effect.

As a general rule, the granting of the authority to represent the principal in the making of a contract is subject to the same requirement of form as that applicable to the contract under consideration.

Where an agent acts upon instructions and on behalf of the principal, but not in the principal's name, or where an agent does not reveal that it is acting as someone else's agent, only the agent – not the principal – will be directly bound to the contract concluded with a third party. However, the principal has a duty vis-à-vis its agent to take on all the obligations undertaken by the agent when carrying out the principal's instructions or, should such an assignment be impossible, to provide the agent with the necessary means with which to fulfil its obligations.

## 5. Validity

When a contract is invalid, depending on the failing that renders it invalid, it may either become null and void, in which case it will not produce its typical effect, or may rather merely become voidable, in which case it will be treated as valid and effective until actually avoided.

Any interested party may invoke the nullity of a contract, at any time, and a court of law may declare a contract null and void *ex officio*. Conversely, a contract may only be avoided by the party in whose interest the voidability is legally prescribed, and only within a year as from the date the failing has ceased to exist, unless the contract has not yet been fulfilled, in which case it may be avoided at any time.

The party that is entitled to avoid a contract may choose to confirm its validity, expressly or implicitly, provided that the failing has ceased to exist and that it is aware both of the failing and of its right to avoid the contract.

Both the avoidance and confirmation of a contract are retroactive, as is the declaration that a contract is null and void. Consequently, once a contract is avoided or declared null and void, the parties thereto must concurrently make restitution of whatever each one has supplied to the other under the contract, or an equivalent monetary value in case restitution in kind is not possible. Such retroactive force may not, however, injure the rights of *bona fide* third parties who have onerously acquired an interest in immovable property or in registered chattels.

Partial invalidity will not entail that the whole contract is rendered invalid, unless it is reasonable to conclude that the contract would not have been entered into without the affected part. For instance, pursuant to the statute on general contract terms and contracts of adhesion, in contracts not individually negotiated by the parties, clauses contrary to good faith will be null and void, however in most cases the remainder of the contract will not be affected by such partial invalidity.

A contract that has been declared null and void, or which has been avoided, may be converted into a different kind of contract, which would be considered valid under the circumstances if the purpose of the parties when entering into the first contract would allow one to suppose that this is what they would have wanted to happen had they foreseen the invalidity.

A contract is said to be null and void if performance of the contracted obligation is impossible at the time the contract has been concluded. A contract is null and void if it lacks the required form. A simulated transaction is also null and void. However, when the parties have concluded a simulated contract, but meant to agree to a different set of terms, their true agreement will prevail, notwithstanding the nullity of the simulated contract. Such nullity is not effective in dealings with *bona fide* third parties.

A contract whose object is indeterminable, contrary to mandatory legal provisions, or physically or legally impossible to fulfil, will be null and void. A contract whose object is contrary to public policy or morality (*boni mores*) will also be null and void. If, however, only the contract's purpose is contrary to mandatory legal provisions or to public policy, or offensive of morality, it will only be null and void if such purpose was common to the parties thereto.

On the contrary, a contract will be voidable if it was entered into by a person lacking the necessary capacity to act as signatory. It will be voidable when one of the parties has been led to conclude it by another party's fraudulent misrepresentation or non-disclosure of information, by illicit threats from or usurious practice on the part of the other party, provided that such practice enables it to obtain excessive or unjustified benefits. However, in the latter case, the contract may also be modified *ex aequo et bono*.

A mistake as to the identity of the other party or as to the object of the contract makes it voidable, provided that, at the time of contracting, the other party knew or ought to have known that their identity or the object of the contract constituted essential information to the mistaken party, so that, had the truth been known, no contract would have been concluded, or it would have been entered into on substantially different terms. A mistake concerning other motives also renders the contract voidable, but only if all contracting parties had recognized such motives to be essential to the contract. A mistake as to the circumstances that make up the basis of the agreement will be given the same treatment as a fundamental change of circumstances taking place after its inception (see below).

## 6. Contents and effects

The contents of a contract should be interpreted objectively, that is to say, a statement will be interpreted to have the meaning that would be accorded to it by a reasonable person in the position of the addressee, save if the person making that statement could not reasonably have anticipated such meaning. In the latter case, one may conclude that in fact no agreement has been reached, or if it can be established that the addressee was aware that the person making that statement intended it to have a particular meaning, such meaning will prevail.

Where the meaning of a statement gives rise to doubt, the meaning that should prevail is that which is less prejudicial to the disposing party, in the case of gratuitous contracts, and that which entails the greatest balance between the parties' undertakings, in the case of onerous contracts.

Contract terms should be interpreted within the context of the whole contract. Where doubt arises as to the precise meaning of a specific contractual term not individually negotiated, the meaning that should take preference is that which is most favourable to the party who has not supplied it. In any case, terms that are the result of individual negotiation prevail over those that are not.

A contract term may be express or implied. Implied terms are said to be those that can be derived without doubt from indirect demonstrations of the intention of the parties. Silence may only be interpreted to amount to an indirect demonstration of intention, and hence as a contractual statement, in those cases where such value is attributed thereto by a statutory or contractual provision or by any applicable usages.

A contract term that has not been subject to individual negotiation is deemed to be excluded from a contract when: it is not adequately communicated to the adhering party before the contract is entered into; it is not sufficiently explained to the adhering party; due to its graphic layout, its heading, or the context in which it appears, it would not have been apparent to an average contracting party; or, when it is inserted in a form after the signature of any of the contracting parties.

A party will not cease to be bound to carry out its contractual obligations simply because performance has become more onerous than expected. If, however, the circumstances upon which the parties have founded their decision to conclude their contract have suffered a fundamental (abnormal) change, and the risk of such occurrence was not one that, according to the contract, the party affected should be required to bear, so that to require performance would gravely affect the requirements of good faith, then the affected party is entitled to have the contract modified *ex aequo et bono* or, alternatively, to rescind it, unless the other party opposes such rescission but accepts the modification, in which case the latter will take preference over rescission.

A third party may require performance of a contractual obligation when its right to do so has been agreed upon by the contracting parties. However, the existence of such a right is not implied in every case that a third party will directly or indirectly benefit from the performance of a contractual obligation; intention to confer a true right upon the third party is required. The third party may choose either to accept that right or to renounce it. Acceptance must be notified to both contracting parties, whilst renunciation need only be notified to the promisor. The promise is freely revocable by the contracting parties at any time until the third party has expressed its acceptance thereto, or at any time until the promisee has died, in the case of a promise that is to be fulfilled posthumously.

## 7. Performance, non-performance and remedies

Unless otherwise agreed by the parties, performance of a contractual obligation may be carried out by the debtor or by a third party, regardless of whether that third party has an interest in performance. As a general rule, performance must be tendered to the creditor.

Unless the parties agree otherwise, the place of performance of a contractual obligation to pay money is the place where the creditor has its domicile at the time of performance. The place of performance of a contractual obligation to deliver a given chattel is the place where it was located at the time when the contract was concluded. The place of performance of any other contractual obligation is the place where the debtor has its domicile when performance is due.

A contractual obligation must be performed at the time or within the period of time fixed in the contract. Where none has been fixed, the creditor may require performance at any time, and the debtor may perform at any time. If a period of time has been fixed, it will be deemed as fixed for the benefit of the debtor, in the sense that the debtor may waive that benefit and perform its contractual obligation at an earlier time.

Where the debtor is bound to perform several obligations of the same kind to the same creditor and the performance tendered is not sufficient to discharge all such obligations, it is for the debtor to designate to which obligations its performance is to be appropriated. If no such designation is made at the time of performance, it will be appropriated to the obligation that is due. If several are due, appropriation will be made to that obligation for which the creditor has the least security, thereafter to that which is the most burdensome for the debtor, then to that which was the first to fall due, and finally to that which arose at an earlier date. If none of these criteria applies, performance will be appropriated proportionately between all obligations.

Performance of a contractual obligation gives the debtor the right to demand that the creditor acknowledges its receipt thereof.

Non-performance of a contractual obligation will be excused if performance becomes impossible for reasons that do not result from the debtor's fault. An impediment to perform will discharge the debtor unless it is only temporary and the creditor's interest in performance is unaffected by the delay. If performance becomes partially impossible the debtor will be discharged by performing its obligation to the fullest extent possible, unless the creditor's interest in performance is justifiably lost. The creditor's contractual obligations will be proportionately reduced where only partial performance is rendered.

When non-performance of a contractual obligation is not excused, the aggrieved party may resort to one or more of the remedies set out in the law. Different remedies may be accumulated, provided that they are not incompatible. For instance, a party is not deprived of a right to damages by exercising its right to any other remedy, although in the case of accumulating damages with termination the applicable criteria and measure of damages is the subject of debate in case law and legal literature.

A person bound by a synallagmatic contract is entitled to withhold performance of its contractual obligations until the other party effects counter-performance, unless the contract requires the former party to perform first.

However, first and foremost, pursuant to the general principle laid down in the Civil Code, the aggrieved party is entitled judicially to enforce its rights under the contract and demand performance.

Where the obligation involves payment of a sum of money or delivery of goods, performance of such obligation will be enforced. Where the obligation involves an action to be taken and that action may be taken by a third party without injury to the creditor, performance of such obligation by a third party will take place at the expense of the non-performing party. Where the obligation involves an undertaking not to take some action, the result of such action will be destroyed at the expense of the non-performing party. Where the obligation involves entering into a contract, the judgment will take the place of the non-performing party's contracting statement. Lastly, where the obligation involves the taking of some action that may not be taken by a third party without injury to the creditor, the non-performing party may be sentenced to the payment of a daily sum of money until that action is effectively taken.

Specific performance is not always available to the aggrieved party. Destruction of the result of an action carried out in breach of contract will not take place if the non-performing party would suffer a considerably more significant loss from such destruction than that already suffered by the aggrieved party. An obligation to enter into a contract other than a contract for the onerous transfer or constitution of an interest in a building or in part thereof will not be enforced if the parties have provided otherwise in their agreement. An obligation to take some action that may not be taken by a third party will not be enforced where such obligation requires the non-performing party to possess special scientific or artistic qualities.

The aggrieved party may choose to terminate the contract if the non-performance is serious and definitive. A minor defect, or a simple delay in performance, is not an accepted ground for termination. In the case of delay, the aggrieved party will be entitled to terminate the contract only if it has justifiably lost interest in performance, or if it has given notice to the defaulting party of an additional period of time within which performance could still be carried out, after such period of time has elapsed. Similarly, if partial performance has been tendered, the aggrieved party may terminate the entire contract only if it has no interest in partial performance.

Notwithstanding the absence of an express legal provision to that effect, an abundance of case law has recognized that the aggrieved party may terminate the contract even before performance by the defaulting party becomes due, if the defaulting party has expressly or implicitly declared an intention not to perform.

Termination is excluded if the party purporting to terminate the contract is solely or overwhelmingly responsible for the other party's non-performance or if a circumstance for which the other party is not responsible materializes at a time when the former is in default through non-acceptance.

Termination of the contract releases both parties from their obligations to effect and to receive future performance, and it will have retroactive effect from the date of the contract's conclusion unless this contradicts the intention of the parties or the purpose of the termination.

Although consensus is far from being reached in this matter, an increasing number of authors argue that termination should not be retroactive in those cases where the purpose of the termination is not to put the aggrieved party as closely as possible into the position in which it would have been had the contract never been concluded, but rather to put the aggrieved party as closely as possible into the position in which it would have been had the contract been fully and properly performed, except that the aggrieved party has justifiably chosen to contract a third party to continue where the defaulting party has left off.

If the aggrieved party is unable to make restitution of whatever it has received under the contract, it will not be entitled to terminate the contract – but only, so one could argue, to the extent that the purpose of such termination would call for its retroactiveness.

As a general rule, a party's right to terminate the contract must be exercised by notice to the other party.

A party that accepts a tender of defective or partial performance is entitled to a reduction in price. Such reduction will be proportionate to the decrease in the value of the performance.

Finally, according to the general principle set forth in the Civil Code, the party who unjustifiably fails either to perform its contractual obligations, performs defectively, or performs at a later time than that which has been originally fixed, will be liable for all the loss caused to the other party, unless it is able to prove that it was not at fault in doing so.

The general measure of damages is an amount that will put the aggrieved party as nearly as possible into the position which it would have been in had the contract been fully and properly performed. However, if the aggrieved party chooses a remedy which is incompatible with such measure of damages, a different measure will be applied, namely reparation that will put the aggrieved party as closely as possible into the position in which it would have been had the contract never been concluded. In either case, such damages should cover both the loss that the aggrieved party has suffered and the gain of which it has been deprived.

Notwithstanding the above, the general principle laid down in the law is that the aggrieved party will only be paid a sum of money if it is impossible, inadequate or too burdensome for the non-performing party actually to put the aggrieved party as closely as possible into the position in which it would have been had the contract been fully and properly performed, or had the contract never been concluded, as natural reconstitution will take preference over pecuniary compensation. In practice, however, a sum of money will usually be awarded to the aggrieved party, such general principle being interpreted to mean that when calculating such sum of money the cost of cure will take preference over the loss of value. But this will not always be the case. Also in line with such general principle is the rule that the aggrieved party is entitled to require from the supplier of defective goods that they be repaired or replaced by goods that conform to the contract.

The non-performing party will not be liable for the loss suffered by the aggrieved party to the extent that the latter contributed to the occurrence or escalation of its own loss.

## 8. Continuity and change

For the most part, Portuguese rules on contract law have passed through different political and economic periods relatively unscathed. The current Civil Code was approved under an authoritarian regime, which supported a protected economy, but its underlying principles on contract law are not so different from the liberal principles upon which the Civil Code of 1867 had been constructed. Those rules were even adapted to serve as the legal framework of the open and competitive European market.

Change and modernization are nonetheless both necessary and inevitable, and they have indeed already begun to take place under the influence of European law, particularly in the areas of consumer protection, competition and the power of regulatory authorities. Moreover, some aspects of non-performance require simplification and modernization, following the guidelines set out by the European Principles on Contract Law.

## Bibliography

ALMEIDA COSTA, Mário Júlio, *Direito das obrigações*, 9th ed., Coimbra, 2001. ANTUNES VARELA, João de Matos, *Das obrigações em geral I*, 10th ed., Coimbra, 2000, II, 7th ed, Coimbra, 1997. FERREIRA DE ALMEIDA, Carlos, *Contratos I, Conceito, fontes, formação*, 3rd ed., Coimbra, 2005. GALVÃO TELLES, Inocêncio, *Manual dos contratos em geral*, 4th ed., Coimbra, 2002. MENEZES CORDEIRO, António, *Tratado de direito civil português*, I *Parte Geral*, Tomo I, *Introdução. Doutrina Geral, Negócio Jurídico*, 3rd ed., Coimbra, 2005. MENEZES LEITÃO, Luís, *Direito das obrigações I, Introdução. Da constituição das obrigações*, 4th ed, Coimbra, 2005. Idem, *Direito das obrigações II, Transmissão e extinção das obrigações. Não cumprimento e garantias do crédito*, 3rd ed., Coimbra, 2005. MOTA PINTO, Carlos, *Teoria geral do direito civil*, 4th ed. by A. Pinto Monteiro and P. Mota Pinto, Coimbra, 2005. *Principles of European Contract Law. Parts I and II*, ed. by Ole Lando and Hugh Beale, The Hague, Boston, London, 2000.

# CHAPTER 13

# Law of Torts

ANA PRATA

SUMMARY: *1. General framework 2. The requirements of Article 483/1 of the Portuguese Civil Code 3. Compensation*

## 1. General framework

The general rule of the Portuguese law of torts is set out in Article 483/1 of the Portuguese Civil Code (hereinafter CC). According to this legal provision, the right to reparation depends on the following requirements:

In the first place, the law requires the breach of a legal duty. Secondly, that breach must involve fault. Lastly, damage must have been caused by unlawful and intentional or negligent behaviour. Evidence of damage must be produced and a causal relation between the damage and the behaviour must be identified. In short, the legal cause of the damage must be an unlawful and faulty behaviour.

Unlike other national laws (such as the French Civil Code), the CC considers the fact that a subjective right of another person has been violated independently from the question of fault; "unlawfulness" and "fault" are two independent concepts.

Regardless of the fact that this is taken into account in some rules relative to torts included in the CC, but which are to be considered separately and autonomously from the above-mentioned article, as well as in some rules not included in the CC, the afore-mentioned framework may be considered as the general principle in the matter of torts.

In Portuguese law, therefore, there is a general principle or a general clause on torts, as for instance in the French Civil Code or in the Italian Civil Code, but unlike in the German *BGB*.

Article 483/2 sets out the exceptional existence of the obligation to compensate without fault.

The so-called strict liability (liability without fault) is foreseen in the CC mainly in relation to traffic or train accidents. There are, nevertheless, other legal provisions foreseeing situations of strict liability – where the person who causes the damage has acted without fault and his behaviour either does or does not violate the law.

## 2. The requirements of Article 483/1 of the Portuguese Civil Code

### 2.1 *Unlawfulness*

It is a requirement that a person has acted in breach of an absolute right, such as a property right or a personal right. There must be an action or omission against a right that shall prevail against everyone.

There may be an obligation to make reparation in cases where the affected right is a family law-related right. But it should be said that both authors and courts have tended to deny the existence of civil liability in cases of violation of family law-related personal rights, in situations where the law does not expressly admit such liability.

The unlawful act may also result from the breach of a legal rule protecting a private interest which does not carry any subjective right. Traffic rules may be considered an example; these include several provisions imposing conducts relative to the safety of people and assets, but do not grant a person any subjective right. If damage to a person or to an asset owned by a person results from the unlawful behaviour of a driver, the person who has suffered the damage or who owned the damaged asset has the right to be compensated by the driver.

This characteristic human scenario may be excluded by some circumstances foreseen in the law, which exceptionally remove the unlawful characteristic of the respective act.

These circumstances, such as acting in self-defence or acting in flagrant necessity, exclude the unlawful characteristic of an act that would otherwise be considered unlawful.

The plaintiff must prove the unlawfulness.

## 2.2 *Fault*

Regardless of the fact that the legal concept of fault is an objective concept that can be clearly understood in the context of civil law, authors and courts often construe this concept as close to the criminal concept of guilt, as a moral judgement of censure.

Article 487/2 of the CC determines that a person is considered to act with fault when such person does not act with the required due diligence. The due diligence required is the diligence that a *bonus pater familias* would have had if he had been in the same situation and with the same qualities and knowledge as the person who acted.

Since fault is assessed by way of a comparison with the hypothetical behaviour of *bonus pater familias*, it may happen that a behaviour which would normally be considered reckless should – in a specific situation – be considered as not faulty, due to the fact that something has occurred that would lead the *bonus pater familias* to behave the same way as the person did. Take, for instance, the case of a person who was driving a car, exceeded the speed limit and had an accident. Later, it is proved that the person was in a hurry to see his son who was in hospital having suffered a heart attack. If the court considers that the *bonus pater familias* is likely to have been very disturbed by the fact that his son was in hospital and, for such reason, would have driven the same way as that person did, then the person's conduct will not be considered as faulty.

As a general rule, it falls upon the injured party to prove the existence of a faulty act.

In some situations, however, the law presumes the existence of fault. This legal presumption reverses the burden of proof. Accordingly, in such cases, it is the defendant who must prove that he acted without fault in order to discharge his obligation to compensate the victim. In cases where someone is not in a condition to understand or freely to choose the behaviour that caused the damage, there is no possible fault and, therefore the burden of proof may also be reversed. But in this case, the person responsible is the person who – if any – ought to have taken care of the person who was not in a condition to understand or freely choose the behaviour, and the law presumes the fault of the former.

The above relies on the assumption that, in order to consider that someone has acted with fault, it is required that the person, in the specific situation, is free to decide and has the natural capacity to understand what the law requires him to do and the possible consequences of his act.

Portuguese law presumes that children up to seven years of age and persons who are legally disabled due to a mental illness or disease cannot be held liable.

Some support can be found in the law in order to construe fault as a moral judgement, as previously mentioned.

On the one hand, when the behaviour from which damage arises is considered to be only merely negligent, the law allows for a commensurate right to damages. Then, if more than one person is responsible, in order to determine the *quota* of the compensation of each offender, the law uses a criterion based on the degree of each offender's fault. Finally, when there are non-economical losses, one of the criteria used by law to evaluate damages is the degree of fault of the offender's fault.

Even in the matter of so-called strict liability (liability without fault), one can perceive this concept of fault as a moral judgement, as it is often meant that the liability of the person who caused the damage is excluded if it is found that faulty behaviour contributed, albeit slightly, to the damage. In these cases, most authors and court decisions consider that only the person who has carried out the negligent behaviour must compensate all harm, even if its act is not the cause of all, but only of one small part of it; in the same way, if a negligent behaviour of the plaintiff is found to exist, its right to damage is denied. The historical background of civil liability explains this view, since, as it is common knowlege, civil liability generated from and exists in dependence of criminal liability.

## 2.3 *Damage*

There are different kinds of damage to be considered for the purpose of determining compensation.

Portuguese law allows compensation for non-economical losses such as the pain and suffering or psychological traumas/problems resulting from the act from which the obligation to compensate arises. Court decisions even accept an indemnity for death itself, which is independent from the damages for the suffering of the victim before the death and is also independent from the damages which the deceased victim's relatives are entitled to claim in respect of their own pain and suffering.

Since death is the deprivation of a right – the right to life – which cannot be restored, damages for death can only be understood as having a punitive purpose, which has dubious basis in the Portuguese legal framework for torts.

Nevertheless, the amounts fixed by the Portuguese courts are often low, especially compared to the amounts fixed by courts in other European countries, not to mention the USA.

Damages can be claimed and awarded for actual detriment, as well as for consequential losses if these are predictable.

The legal rules governing damage and the relevant compensation are the same regardless of whether damage arises from an unlawful act or a lawful one, and also regardless of whether damage results from the violation of an absolute right or from the breach of a contract.

## 2.4 *Relation between the act and the damage*

There must be a causal relationship between the unlawful and faulty act and the damage; the act must be recognized as the legal cause of damage.

To establish this causal relation, courts and authors understand that the act must have been, specifically, a *sine qua non* condition of the damages. Furthermore it also has to be, in abstract, a potential cause for that kind of damages. Even if the text of the law is not very clear, the law in action is unequivocal in this sense.

## 3. Compensation

In principle, the right to damage is merely compensatory in purpose. Compensation is intended to place the injured party in the same situation he would have been if he had not suffered the damages.

As a general rule, the law requires a specific reparation, *i.e.* the law requires that the victim has the right to be given what he lost or what has been damaged. Only where this is not possible, or to the extent that it is not possible, will the compensation be assessed and paid in money. Notwithstanding, the law allows for a monetary compensation in cases where the restoration would be too costly to the offender.

Regardless of the fact that, as a general rule, Portuguese law provides for restoration of the situation of the victim, the majority of damages are compensated in money. This may appear to be due to the fact that specific indemnities are often too costly, but in fact, the case is that victims seldom claim a specific compensation and the courts rarely decide in this way.

### 3.1 *Persons entitled to claim damages*

The person entitled to claim damages must be the owner or holder of the right affected by the behaviour.

Therefore, if, for instance, a person is injured, such person is entitled to claim damages. His relatives, however, will have no right to claim damages even if they have suffered losses related to the fact that such person has been injured. In cases where the injured person needs assistance and one or more relatives have to provide care and, for such reason, are prevented from working, no compensation is payable to them.

The same applies to the employer of the injured person. An employer has no right to claim damages, even in situations where he has suffered any loss due to the fact that his employee has been injured (for instance, if only the injured employee is capable of performing certain tasks, his absence will cause the employer significant damages).

Exceptionally, in the case of the death or serious injury of a person, the law entitles certain third parties to claim damages. This applies to those who took care of the victim (usually, doctors or other medical assistants) or to those who were entitled to receive alimony from the victim.

This also applies to the victim's relatives, who have the right to claim damages in order to redress their pain and suffering in cases where the victim's death is caused by behaviour from which the obligation to damages arises.


### 3.2 Periods of limitation of the right to damages

The rules concerning the periods of limitation for the right to damages vary and are contingent on the liability considered (in contrast with the other rules concerning the right to damages, which, as mentioned above, are the same regardless of the kind of liability in question).

In the matter of torts – *i.e.* when the obligation to compensate results from the violation of an absolute right – there is a special rule for the relevant period of limitation.

This rule sets out a period of limitation of three years from the moment in which the victim becomes aware of his right. Since Portuguese law, as a general rule, considers that the awareness – as well as the ignorance – of the law is irrelevant, the awareness of the right previously mentioned above means awareness of the facts entitling the person to such right.

Besides the above-mentioned period of limitation, Portuguese law establishes a further period of limitation to the right to damages, which is the ordinary period of limitation. This period of limitation is twenty years from the date on which the violation occured.

The articulation of these two periods of limitation must be calculated as follows. The ordinary period of limitation begins (even if the victim is not yet aware of the fact) when the fact causing the damages occurs. The special period of limitation begins when the victim becomes aware of the damage caused by a human, unlawful and probably faulty behaviour. The right to claim damages terminates upon expiry of one of above mentioned periods of limitation.

For the purpose of determining the periods of limitation, the law does not consider that the moment when the victim knows who caused the damage is relevant. Therefore, a difficult problem may arise. A victim may know that someone caused damages, but may be unaware of who it was. For this reason, the victim may not be able to bring an action against the offender while the period of limitation is running and, consequently, his right to damages will terminate if the period of limitation elapses.

Understandably, this situation is unfair.

The reason underlying the legal solution contained in the special rule, which establishes such a short period of limitation, is that the law considers it advantageous for an action to be brought in court when it is based on recent facts and recent memories, which are more reliable and, therefore, better able to recreate the situation under discussion.

In order to prevent such unfair situations, some authors and several court decisions have applied a rule whereby the period of limitation is suspended during three years, when the person who has the right is prevented from claiming such right for *force majeure* reasons. This rule means that – without exceeding the maximum period of twenty years from the fact, as previously mentioned – the victim will have three years, from the moment in which he becomes aware of the identity of the offender, to bring an action against the offender claiming compensation.

In short, Portuguese law establishes two periods of limitation of rights. One starts when the violation occurs and is set out for a period of twenty years from such moment. The other starts at the time when the victim becomes aware of his right to be compensated (as previously mentioned, this must be construed as the moment when the victim becomes aware of the facts entitling him to be compensated) and lasts for a period of three years. The period of limitation first elapsing determines the termination of the right to damages.

# Bibliography

ALMEIDA COSTA, Mário Júlio, *Direito das Obrigações*, 9th ed., Coimbra, 2001. PRATA, Ana, *Cláusulas de Exclusão e Limitação da Responsabilidade Contratual: Regime Geral*, Coimbra, 1985. Idem, *Notas sobre Responsabilidade Pré-Contratual*, Coimbra, 2002. ANTUNES VARELA, João de Matos, *Das Obrigações em Geral II*, 7th ed., Coimbra, 1997. CALVÃO DA SILVA, João, *A Responsabilidade Civil do Produtor*, Coimbra, 1999. CARNEIRO DA FRADA, Manuel António, *Teoria da Confiança e da Responsabilidade Civil*, Coimbra, 2004. GALVÃO TELLES, Inocêncio, *Direito das Obrigações*, 7th ed., Coimbra, 1997. MAYA DE LUCENA, Delfim, *Danos não patrimoniais: o dano da morte*, Coimbra, 1985. PEREIRA COELHO, Francisco Manuel, *O Enriquecimento e o Dano*, Coimbra, 1999. PESSOA JORGE, Fernando de Sandy, *Ensaio sobre os Pressupostos da Responsabilidade Civil*, Coimbra, 1995.

# CHAPTER 14

# Property Law

Rui Pinto Duarte

SUMMARY: *1. Introduction 2. Ownership 3. Transfer of ownership and of other rights* in rem *4.* Usufruto, uso e habitação *5.* Superfície *6.* Servidões *7. Timeshare 8. Mortgage and pledge 9. Other security rights 10.Possession 11. Land registration 12. Future trends*

## 1. Introduction

As may be observed in other languages with the words of the same etymological origin, the word *propriedade* in Portuguese has several meanings and may be used to designate either a right or the object of a right. In legal language, it is used almost always to designate the right of ownership, *i.e.* the highest right *in rem*. In day-to--day language however *propriedade* is also used to designate things, in particular immovables.

The main Portuguese legal concept in this area is that of *direitos reais* or *direitos das coisas*, equivalent to *derechos reales, droits réels, diritti reali* and *Sachenrecht*. As in the legal literature of other continental European countries, the core of this concept relies on the idea of a direct and immediate authority over things effective *erga omnes* - which encompasses not only rights to use (*direitos reais de gozo*) and rights of security (*direitos reais de garantia*) but also, at least according to a major current of opinion, some rights to acquire (*direitos reais de aquisição*). It goes without saying that possession (*posse*) also belongs to this field, although its exact location is disputed.

As in the case of its continental equivalents, the branch of law named *direitos reais* does not cover some of those topics that are considered by English lawyers to fall within the scope of property law, *inter alia* succession on death and marriage settlements.

The category *direitos reais de gozo* comprises not only ownership but also the rights known by the Latin words *ususfructus, usus, habitatio, superficies* and *servitutes*, as well as one of the types of the rights to use immovable properties on a timeshare basis. The category *direitos reais de garantia* comprises mortgages, pledges and the equivalents of priorities and liens. The category *direitos reais de aquisição* comprises mainly rights to acquire when they are effective against third parties.

The vast majority of the rules on *direitos reais de gozo* are inserted in the third book of the Civil Code, entitled *Direito das Coisas,* but the rules on *direitos reais de garantia* appear in the second book of the Civil Code dealing with the law of obligations, on the grounds of their securing this type of relations.

The idea that rights *in rem* are subject to a *numerus clausus* principle has an express basis in the Civil Code. Indeed, Article 1306 states that save as otherwise stated in the law restrictions cannot be created with real nature on the right of property or on rights that correspond to parts of the same.

The first article of the Civil Code dealing with the right of ownership (Article 1302) states that it can only relate to tangible things. The following article begins by saying that copyright and industrial property are ruled by special laws but adds that the rules of the Civil Code are applicable to these rights on a subsidiary basis. Some authors construe the category of *direitos reais* as embracing only tangible things and others extend it to intangible things. It should be stressed that the Civil Code permits both the *ususfructus* and the pledge of credits and of other rights.

Portuguese law does not favour fiduciary ownership. Trusts do not exist, except in the context of the legislation of the Free Trade Zone of Madeira.

## 2. Ownership

Article 1305 of the Civil Code, entitled "contents of the right of ownership", begins by stating that the owner benefits from the rights to use, to enjoy and to dispose of his things in a full and exclusive manner, but adds "within the limits of the law and observing the restrictions imposed by it". This formulation is compatible with the evolution of law, including the development of regimes that restrict the use of land. Portuguese courts and legal authors have debated whether the right to build is co-natural to the ownership of land or if it only exists when an administrative law or act permits construction on the land in question.

Co-ownership (*compropriedade*) is of course admitted by Portuguese law but its stability is not favoured. Indeed each co-owner has the right to put an end to co-ownership and agreements waiving such right have a maximum duration of five years. The model of *compropriedade* corresponds to the English ownership in common – not to the English concept of joint ownership.

A special reference must be made to *propriedade horizontal,* the normal legal instrument for the division of buildings into flats. The law states that the parts of a building that can constitute independent units may belong to different owners under this regime and describes this by saying that each of such owners (*condóminos*) is the exclusive owner of his flat and co-owner of the common parts.

It should be stressed that in spite of the word *horizontal,* the division of the buildings can be either horizontal or vertical. Moreover the regime may be applicable to complexes of separate buildings.

Rules on *propriedade horizontal* give to each *condómino* a kind of ownership that is very close to full ownership. Legal writers discuss if *propriedade horizontal* is a *species* of ownership or if it should be characterized as a different right *in rem.*

## 3. Transfer of ownership and of other rights *in rem*

Transfer of ownership is a topic that cuts across private law and shall be addressed here only in connection with basic aspects of its relation with contracts.

The Civil Code says that, in principle, contracts effect by themselves the transfer of rights *in rem*. However the Civil Code sets out some deviations from this rule, *inter alia* for cases where, at the time of the contract, the object of the contract does not exist, is not fully determined or belongs to a third party.

Contracts are in any case the instruments of the conveyance of property. When their object is land they must take the form of a notarial deed.

The code on land registration says that facts subject to registration only produce effects vis-à-vis third parties after registration. This concept of third parties has been narrowed down by many writers and by the courts, meaning that registration is generally not the crucial factor when the rights over a certain piece of land are disputed between two or more persons.

The law accepts that parties may derogate the rule whereby contracts bring about the automatic transfer of ownership, mainly by stipulating the reservation of title until full payment of the price.

## 4. Usufruto, uso e habitação

The law defines usufruto as the right to enjoy a thing that belongs to another person, fully but temporarily and without altering its form and substance.

*Usufruto* may be constituted by contract or by will.

When it is constituted in favour of a corporation, its duration may not exceed thirty years. When it is constituted in favour of an individual it may not exceed the duration of his life. Nevertheless *usufruto* may be transferred, such transfer not altering its duration.

Almost anything may be the object of *usufruto,* but its main field of application is land.

Portuguese rules on *usus* and *habitatio* were inspired by the Italian Civil Code. The *direito de uso* consists of the faculty of using a thing belonging to another person within the limits of the needs of its holder and of his family. This right is called *direito de habitação* when its object is a home. *Direito de uso* and *direito de habitação* are not transferable.

## 5. Superfície

The law defines *direito de superfície* as the right to build or to maintain a construction on land belonging to another person or to cultivate or plant on such land.

The *direito de superfície* has two dimensions: the right to build or to plant and the right over the building or the plantation. Prior to the existence of the building or of the plantation the right consists of the faculty to build or plant. Once the building or the plantation exists, the right consists of the ownership of the same (but not of the soil).

Law says *direito de superfície* can be either perpetual or temporary, but in practice all *direitos de superfície* tend to be temporary.

## 6. Servidões

The Portuguese descendant of the Roman *servitus* is *servidão*. The law defines it as a charge imposed on a piece of land for the benefit of another piece of land belonging to a different owner. The term embraces English law's easements, *profits à prendre* and restrictive covenants effective *erga omnes*.

*Servidões* may relate to any kind of utilities and may result from the law, contract, will or possession.

## 7. Timeshare

The first Portuguese law on the use of immovable properties on a timeshare basis was published in 1981. It attempted to protect persons investing money in this type of development by ascribing to them a right with effects against third parties. The original name of this right was *direito de habitação periódica* but this was changed to *direito real de habitação periódica* in 1989, when a new law replaced the first one, thereby acknowledging both rights with and without real nature.

## 8. Mortgage and pledge

According to Portuguese law, the distinction between mortgage (*hipoteca*) and pledge (*penhor*) depends on the nature of the object of the security. When the object of the security is an immovable or a movable subject to registration, *hipoteca* is applicable; when the object of the security is a movable, a credit or another similar right, *penhor* is applicable.

The effects of mortgage depend on it being registered. The effects of the pledge of tangible things depend in principle on the delivery of its object to the creditor. In some cases, such delivery may be replaced by the delivery of a document that confers title to the object of the pledge. Pledge in favour of banks may be effective without delivery of the object.

The mortgagee does not have a right to take possession of the property in the event of default in payment of the security, but only a right to cause the judicial sale of the property and to be paid by the proceeds of such sale. In the case of a pledge, the law accepts that the parties may stipulate that the sale is made out of court.

## 9. Other security rights

Portuguese law establishes other security rights besides mortgage and pledge. The most relevant are *privilégios creditórios* and *direito de retenção*.

*Privilégios creditórios* result directly from the law. They consist of the right of a creditor to be paid from certain property with priority over the other creditors. Their object can be immovable or movable. They may or may not be effective against third parties. Portuguese legal writers consider them as *rights in rem* when they have this kind of effect.

There is no common regime for *privilégios creditórios*. Some prevail over contractual security rights and others do not grant such prevalence.

The most important *privilégios creditórios* are those that secure tax and social security credits.

*Direito de retenção* also results directly from the law. It consists of the right of a creditor that is in possession of a thing belonging to the debtor to retain it until payment is obtained, as well as the right to cause the judicial sale of the thing in question and be paid with priority out of the proceeds of the sale. It can relate to either immovable or movable things.

## 10. Possession

Portuguese legal writers are still discussing the nature of possession. It is variously contended that it is a mere fact, a right *in rem* or another kind of right. In addition, the role of *animus possidendi* is still a subject of debate, mainly because the Civil Code makes contradictory references to it.

The Civil Code regulates possession in the first title of its book dealing with *direito das coisas*. This title is divided into six chapters, of which one contains the rules on the defence of possession and another contains the rules on the acquisition of ownership as a consequence of possession (*usucapião*).

Possessory rights are very widely defined, to include *inter alia* fruits and income, as well as remedies against disturbance.

## 11. Land registration

The Portuguese land registry presents, amongst others, the following features: it is the responsibility of the administrative authorities, more precisely of departments of the Ministry of Justice (the *conservatórias de registo predial*); it is geographically decentralized; and it is organized by reference to the pieces of land, each piece of land having a number.

The list of facts subject to registration is very wide and includes all those that determine the constitution and the transfer of rights *in rem*. However there are substantial areas of territory (mainly in the countryside) not covered by the land registry.

## 12. Future trends

Over recent decades the impact of public law on property law (more precisely on land law) has grown very significantly. In all probability, this impact will continue to grow, mainly due to town and country planning.

Another foreseeable tendency is the development of the influence of European law on property law. This tendency is becoming apparent, *inter alia* in certain rules on securities consisting of movable property and will develop in keeping with the pace of consolidation of European Union.

At a different level, it is foreseeable that the rules on land registration will be amended, with registration playing a larger role in the transfer of ownership.


## Bibliography

CARVALHO FERNANDES, Luís A., *Lições de Direitos Reais*, 4th ed., Lisbon, 2003. HENRIQUE MESQUITA, Manuel, *Obrigações Reais e Ónus Reais*, Coimbra, 1990. MENEZES CORDEIRO, António, *Direitos Reais*, Lisbon, 1993 (reprint of the original dated 1979). OLIVEIRA ASCENSÃO, José, *Direito Civil. Reais.*, 5th ed., Coimbra, 1993. ORLANDO DE CARVALHO, *Direito das Coisas*, Coimbra, 1977. PINTO DUARTE, Rui, *Curso de Direitos Reais*, 2nd edition, Cascais, 2006.

# CHAPTER 15
# Intellectual Property Law

CLÁUDIA TRABUCO

SUMMARY: *I. Intellectual property law II. Copyright law 1. Origins and development of Portuguese copyright law 2. Basic rules 3. Content and nature of the rights 4. Copyright and related rights 5. Qualification for protection 6. Term of protection 7. Ownership 8. Exclusive rights 9. Transmissions and licensing 10. Evolution: perspectives III. Industrial property law 1. Origins and development of Portuguese industrial property law 2. Basic rules 3. Extent of industrial property law 4. Types of industrial property rights 5. Content and nature of the rights 6. Registration 7. Term of protection 8. Transmission and licensing 9. Evolution: perspectives*

## I. INTELLECTUAL PROPERTY LAW

In the context of "Intellectual Property", the Civil Code subjects both copyrights and industrial property rights to special legislation and states that its provisions can be applied on a subsidiary basis to those rights when compatible with their nature and without prejudice to their special regimes.

Nevertheless, in Portuguese Law, the category "Intellectual Property" is essentially derived from an organization of subjects in the Civil Code of 1966, rather than from a denomination given to an integrated study of its various components. In contrast to common law countries, there is no joint analysis, on the part of faculties of law and Portuguese legal literature, of all the forms through which the human intellect can be expressed and of their protection.

## II. COPYRIGHT LAW

### 1. Origins and development of Portuguese copyright law

Following the triumph of the ideals of the liberal revolution, and the consequent abolition of privileges concerning the development of publishing activities, the property rights of authors over their own texts were recognized in the Constitution of 1838. However authors would have to wait a further 13 years to see Article 23/4 of the Constitution regulated (Decree of 8 July 1851).

With the approval of the Civil Code of 1867, the rules concerning authors' rights were inserted in the Code, in the form of several dispositions protecting literary and artistic works. These rules were only replaced in 1927 (Decree No. 13.725, of 27 May) by a new autonomous set of provisions concerning the protection of literary and artistic works, which established a permanent property right in relation to these kinds of works.

In light of the need to match the principles and rules established both by the Berne convention of 1886 and the Universal Convention on Copyright, signed in Geneva in 1952, a new Code was approved in 1966 (Decree-Law No. 46 980, of 27 April). This Code, re-establishing the temporary protection of authors' rights (50 years after an author's death) and acknowledging the exclusive right of authors to the economic exploitation of their respective intellectual works, would be in force until its replacement by the present Code.

### 2. Basic rules

**2.1** The essential principles and rules concerning copyright law presently reside in the Copyright and Related Rights Code, approved by the Decree-Law No. 63/85, of 14 March, and most recently amended in 2004 by the Law No. 50/2004, of 24 August.

The Code is complemented by several autonomous pieces of legislation, regulating specific kinds of work (namely software and databases), special rights (namely rental rights, lending rights and the rights to broadcast via satellite and to retransmit by cable) as well as other matters, including the registration of literary works, the compensation for the use of reprography and other processes of mass reproduction, and the organization, functioning and control of the collecting societies in charge of the collective management of works and of subject-matter of related rights.

**2.2** Portugal is a signatory to most of the international conventions in the field of copyright. In addition to adhesion to the Paris Act of 1971 of the Berne Convention in 1911, Portugal is also party to the Universal Convention in 1956. Both these conventions significantly influenced Portuguese copyright law, as did the Rome Convention of 1961 on the protection of artists, phonogram producers and broadcasting organizations, notwithstanding the fact that adhesion to this last instrument was only formalized quite recently in 2002. Portugal is also a contracting party to the Agreement on Trade-Related Aspects of Intellectual Property Rights (TRIPS) and to the WIPO treaties of 1996 (WIPO Copyright Treaty and WIPO Performances and Phonograms Treaty).

Most aspects of the material protection of copyright are currently determined within the European Union sphere.

Since 1991 several directives have profoundly influenced the shaping of copyright law, in particular in the following areas: protection of software and databases; regulation of renting and lending rights; certain rules applicable to broadcasting via satellite and retransmission by cable; term of protection of copyright and related rights; standards of protection of several economic rights in the Information Society; and resale rights for the benefit of the author of an original work of art. Only the latter still awaits complete transposition into national law.

## 3. Content and nature of the rights

Copyright is a subjective right, which gives its owner both the possibility to exercise the faculties or powers that are legally endorsed, and the possibility to demand respect of that right from all other individuals. It is also a fundamental right, recognized as such by the Constitution.

In the context of copyright law, this right encompasses both personal and economic elements, which explains the severe difficulties that have arisen in defining its legal nature. Legal doctrine oscillates between its characterization as a special property right over an immaterial good (the work), or even a special kind of right *in rem*, and an exclusive or monopoly right, reserving to its owner certain activities correspondent to the economic exploitation of an intellectual work.

## 4. Copyright and related rights

Since 1985, copyright legislation has also covered the rules on neighbouring rights of artists, phonogram and videogram producers and broadcasting organizations. Some doctrine adds to these the rights of the producer of a show, in connection with its economic exploitation via public communication.

The object of these rights is variable according to the purpose of their protection: the protection of artists' performances aims at safeguarding a creative activity; the protection of both phonogram and videogram producers and broadcasting organizations focuses on the sounds and images fixed in a material support, in the first case, and on the broadcast itself, in the second case, and aims at compensating their respective financial investments. The related rights are independent from copyrights but the application of the copyright legal regime is subsidiary to those rights.

## 5. Qualification for protection

Copyright protects intellectual creations from the moment of their expression in a perceptible form. The object of protection is not the creation in itself but the form of expression of the work. Ideas, data, facts and mere information do not qualify for protection, since it is the personal treatment that the author gives to those materials that is eligible for copyright protection. However the work may be expressed in any form because fixation in a material support is not a condition for protection.

The fundamental requirement for the defence of a work within the framework of copyright is its original nature. This means that the work must present a minimum level of creativity and individuality, which varies considerably from work to work but is still connected, to a certain degree, to "the personal brand of the author".

The law specifically discards other characteristics as conditions for the protection of work, such as merit, gender, or public registration. Apart from the special case of newspapers and other periodical publications, works are not subject to an obligatory act of registration in order to qualify for protection.

## 6. Term of protection

Copyright is an exclusive temporary right. The general term established by the law for its protection is 70 years after the death of the author. From that date onwards the work is considered to be in the public domain and its use becomes free, except for the safeguarding of personal rights.

The term of protection for related rights expires 50 years after either: the representation or performance by the artist; the first fixation of the phonogram or videogram by its producer; or the first broadcast by the broadcasting organization.

## 7. Ownership

The original ownership of an intellectual work belongs, in principle, to the author as its creator. However the law establishes and regulates some special cases of ownership, such as works made for hire (either ordered and financed by an external entity or resulting from a task performed within the context of a labour contract). In these cases some doctrine admits the occurrence of an original attribution of the right to a person, in most cases a legal person, other than its creator. The same is said to occur in the so-called "collective works", promoted and organized upon the initiative of a natural or legal person but involving the intervention of several individuals within the creative process.

The Code also regulates other cases of multiple authorship, arising from collaboration among the participants or incorporation of a pre-existing work in a new intellectual creation, with the authorization but without the collaboration of the author of the former work.

## 8. Exclusive rights

Copyright comprises both personal (or moral) rights, connected with the author's personality, and economical rights, related to the exploitation of the work's economic potential. The moral rights of the author are independent from the economic rights, and subsist in the author's legal sphere even after the transmission or extinction of the latter rights.

**8.1** Personal rights are inalienable and may not be prescribed or renunciated. The Copyright Code acknowledges the following personal rights of the author: the right to disclose, or conversely not to disclose, the work; the right to withdraw the copies of the work from the market when justified by acceptable moral reasons; the right to the paternity of the work, which encompasses the right to be mentioned in all the versions of the work as its author; the right to the work's integrity, including the right to oppose to its destruction, mutilation, deformation or other modification of the work and, in general, to oppose any act which depreciates or affects the honour and reputation of the author; and also the right to modify and to oppose any non-authorized modification of the work.

**8.2** The author has an exclusive right to enjoy and use the intellectual work, which covers the right to exploit the work economically, either directly or through a third party.

The law confers upon the author the exclusive right to choose the processes and conditions of use of the work and establishes a non-exhaustive list of possible forms of economic exploitation. Among these forms, which are not subject to any categorization, are uses that can be traced back to the main internationally recognized economic rights of the author, namely: the right to reproduce the work; the right to distribute, rent and publicly lend material copies; the right to communicate the work to the public; and also the recently established right of making the work available to the public in such a way that members of the public may access it from a place and at a time individually chosen by them, which covers most of the uses allowed by the information technology networks.

The exclusive economic right of the author is circumscribed by several limitations destined to promote other social interests, such as the promotion of public information public, investigations, education and culture, or to safeguard rights and liberties of other individuals, such as the freedom of expression and the right to the intimacy of the private life. Consequently, the Code enumerates several "free uses", which are not subject to the author's consent, even though some of them entail payment of a fair compensation to the holder of the right.

## 9. Transmissions and licensing

The author may use and economically exploit his work, but he will most often find it more convenient to charge a third party to undertake that task. The law establishes two fundamental ways in which the author can dispose of his work and subjects them to different formal and substantial requirements.

The first is the authorization for the use of the work. This permits the third party to use and exploit the work within the conditions and for the objectives determined in the contract, but does not imply a transmission of the author's right. These licences can either be exclusive or non-exclusive, but the Code presumes their non-exclusivity. The second is the transmission of the economic aspects of the author's right, which can be total or partial (that is, limited to certain forms of use) and either temporary or permanent.

The economic rights of the author can also be the object of usufruct, pledge and seizure.

## 10. Evolution: perspectives

An expected development in the field of Portuguese copyright law is the adoption of new legislation with the objective of creating the conditions for the enforcement of intellectual property rights in general, which naturally also concerns the field of industrial property.

In the European sphere, new projects are also foreseen in the domain of the harmonization of legislation concerning the collective management of copyright and related rights, in view of the changes brought about by the Information Society and also in the context of the theme of the review of the *acquis communautaire* of Copyright Law. The latter refers to the need to improve the operation of the legal framework and its coherence, in particular by comparing the earlier directives to the higher standards of protection for the owners of right established more recently by the Information Society Directive.

## III. INDUSTRIAL PROPERTY LAW

### 1. Origins and development of Portuguese industrial property law

Following the abolition of royal privileges conceded to some inventors, which represented neither a systematic nor a normal process of protection, the first piece of legislation concerning Industrial Property Law in Portugal was the Decree of 16 January 1837, which regulated the property of new inventions. This law was substituted by the Decree of 31 December 1852, which was partially revoked by the Civil Code of 1867. The subject of trademarks in the fields of industry and commerce was first addressed by the *Carta de Lei* of 4 June 1883, regulated by a Decree of that same year.

The regulation of industrial property in general was only assembled in a legal statute in 1894 (Decree of 15 December, regulated in the following year and replaced, with very small changes, in 1896 by the *Carta de Lei* of 21 March). The first Industrial Property Code came to light in 1940 (Decree No. 30 679, of 4 August 1940). In 1995 a new Industrial Property Code (approved by the Decree-Law No. 16/95, of 24 January) replaced the Code of 1940.

## 2. Basic Rules

**2.1** The essential principles and rules concerning industrial property law presently reside in the Industrial Property Code, approved by the Decree-Law No. 36/2003, of 5 March.

The above-mentioned Code states that industrial property fulfils the function of assuring the loyalty of competition through the attribution of private rights to the different technical processes of production and development of wealth.

**2.2** Even though the protection of industrial property rights is subject to the principle of territoriality, which means that each State is competent to determine which rights can be recognized as industrial property rights and to establish the criteria for their protection, it is now possible to detect a well-established process of internationalization of the rules applicable to these rights.

The first and most important international regulation of industrial property was the Paris Convention for the Protection of Industrial Property of 1883, of which Portugal was one of the founders. Several other international law instruments, to which Portugal is a contracting party, established international exclusive rights concerning systems of international registration of trademarks, geographic indications, as well as inventions. In 1994, the Portuguese authorities also ratified the specific annex of the Agreement that created the

World Trade Organisation, which established relevant mechanisms aiming at the effective enforcement of intellectual property rights.

In the context of EU law, several efforts to harmonize national regulations are worthy of mention, particularly regarding trademarks, designs and models, and biological inventions. In two cases the EC legislator went further and created supranational exclusive rights by Regulation: the communitary trademark and the communitary designs and models.

## 3. Extent of industrial property law

The protection conferred by industrial property law is directly related to two basic aims: the attribution of the power to explore economically certain immaterial realities, either in a exclusive or in a non-exclusive fashion, and the imposition of a duty upon all agents operating in the market to behave honestly in the development of their respective activities.

These ideas gave rise to the fundamentals of industrial property, which are, respectively, the protection of industrial property rights and the repression of unfair competition. Despite some hesitations in the context of previous legislation, current doctrine expresses a consensus favourable to the autonomous treatment of these two realities. Even if the law does not accurately define margins between these fundamentals, the repression of an act of unfair competition is not subordinated to the recognition of a violation of industrial property law. In parallel, the violation of one of the private rights conferred by the Code may occur in the absence of competition.

Notwithstanding their autonomy, the two fundamentals are reunited under the heading of industrial law due to their common function, which is to guarantee the necessary conditions for fair competition in the market.

## 4. Types of industrial property rights

Private rights protected by the Industrial Property Code can be divided into two major categories: the protection of innovations, and the protection of signs of business goodwill. The first category includes the protection of patents, utility models, semi-conductor products' topographies, and designs or models. The second covers the protection of trademarks, rewards, names and insignias of establishments, logotypes and geographic indications.

## 5. Content and nature of the rights

These rights can be characterized as exclusive rights according to which the law reserves to their owners the exclusive economic exploration of their object, that is, immaterial goods. In other words, these rights set the boundaries of the economic activities reserved to their owners.

The core of these rights lies in their potential for economic benefit, from which not only the circumscription of their sphere of protection may be derived but also some duties incumbent to owners concerning the need for their economic use.

## 6. Registration

In the Portuguese Industrial Property Code, the effects of registration are determined for each exclusive right. The Code sets out a system whereby the object of the rights is only directly and exclusively attributed to the owner after registration. The proof of those rights is made by titles corresponding to the different modalities of industrial property rights. However, the registration of the rights merely implies a presumption of the completion of the basic elements for attribution.

This system of constitutive registration does not include rewards and geographic indications. These rights may be registered but this public act of registration pursues a different intent: it guarantees the authenticity of their corresponding titles and in both cases has a mere declarative effect.

The Industrial Property National Institute is the competent authority for the registering of industrial property rights, either with constitutive or merely declarative effects.

## 7. Term of protection

The duration of protection is established by law for each right: 20 years for patents, 6 years for utility models (with possible prorogation), 10 years for semi-conductor products' topographies, 5 years for models and designs (with possible prorogation), 10 years for trademarks (with possible prorogation), and 10 years (with possible prorogation) for names and insignias of establishments and for logotypes. The law recognizes the right to unlimited protection for geographic indications.

## 8. Transmissions and licensing

The industrial rights consisting in patents, utility models, registration of semiconductor products' topographies, models and designs and trademarks, as well as the rights resulting from their request, may be transmitted either globally or partially. These rights may also be the object of exclusive or non-exclusive licences concerning their exploitation.

Rights over the names and insignias of establishments can only be transmitted with the whole or the part of the establishment to which these rights are attached.

## 9. Evolution: perspectives

New instruments of European harmonization are expected in the field of industrial law. These instruments will require an accurate transposition into Portuguese law. One of the most important instruments concerns the approval of a proposal for a new directive on the protection by patents of computer-implemented inventions, which will harmonize the way in which national legislators deal with inventions using software.

Another issue worthy of mention is the proposal on the Community Patent, which aims to grant inventors the option of obtaining a single patent legally valid throughout the European Union. This development is long overdue and has recently received a new impulse.

# Bibliography

ASSOCIAÇÃO PORTUGUESA DE DIREITO INTELECTUAL, FACULDADE DE DIREITO DE LISBOA (org.), *Direito da Sociedade da Informação,* Vols. I to IV, Coimbra, 1999, 2001, 2002, 2003. ASSOCIAÇÃO PORTUGUESA DE DIREITO INTELECTUAL, FACULDADE DE DIREITO DE LISBOA (org.), *Direito Industrial,* Vols. I to IV, Coimbra, 2001, 2002, 2003, 2005. CORNISH, William R.; *Intellectual Property: Patents, Copyright, Trade Marks and Allied Rights,* 4th edition, London, 1999. DIETZ, Adolf; *El Derecho de Autor en España y Portugal* (translated from "Das Urheberrecht in Spanien und Portugal", Baden-Baden, 1989), Madrid, 1992. OLAVO, Carlos, *Propriedade Industrial,* Coimbra, 1997. OLIVEIRA ASCENSÃO, José, *Direito Comercial – Direito Industrial,* Vol. II, Lisbon, 1988. Idem, *Direito de Autor e Direitos Conexos,* Coimbra, 1992. Idem, *Concorrência Desleal,* Coimbra, 2002. STERLING, J.A.L., *World Copyright Law,* London, 1998. STROWEL, Alain, *Droit d'Auteur et Copyright – divergences et convergences,* Brussels, 1993.

# CHAPTER 16
# Family Law

LUÍS LINGNAU DA SILVEIRA

SUMMARY: *1. Brief historical background 2. The current Constitution 3. Marriage 4. Unmarried cohabitants 5. Parents and children 6. Adoption 7. Future areas of reform*

## 1. Brief historical background

The first Civil Code, approved in 1867 by liberal legislators, introduced the civil marriage in Portugal for those that did not wanted to marry in a Catholic ceremony. The family structure of the Code nevertheless reflected the traditional supremacy of the husband and father. Divorce was not admitted.

The Republican revolution of 1910 heralded some clear innovations in the field of Family Law, in coherence with its ideological roots. Civil marriage became the only legally relevant form of marriage. Catholic marriage was permitted, but had only a religious value. Divorce was moreover introduced and regulated in a specific law: the Law of Divorce.

Portugal underwent a deep political change in 1926, albeit maintaining a formal Republican structure, inspired by the authoritative theory of the "Estado Novo"("New State"). This change was consecrated in the Constitution of 1933, which declared that the religion of the Portuguese nation was Catholicism.

In accordance with this declaration, in 1940 Portugal celebrated a *Concordata* with the Catholic Church, an international agreement conceding a very special position to this religious institution in the Portuguese State. Regarding family matters, Portugal accepted the Catholic marriage as legally relevant in Portuguese internal law, with its special conditions and legal characteristics. This meant, above all, that those who decided to marry in the Catholic Church could not divorce. Divorce became possible only for those deciding to marry in civil form.

The Civil Code of 1966, although it represented an important legal "monument", maintained the legal system of the *Concordata*. This Code enshrined very conservative principles and defined the structure of the family according to a hierarchical model, endorsing the supremacy of the husband and father, as the "head of the family". Divorce – only admitted for those bound by civil marriage – was limited, with divorce by mutual agreement being abolished.

Once the system of the *Estado Novo* had been abolished in 1974, one of the first objectives of the governments of the new democratic regime was the appropriate regulation of the many social difficulties created by the prohibition of divorce in Catholic marriages. Acting upon these concerns, Portugal in 1975 contracted with the Catholic Church an Amendment to the *Concordata*, establishing that Catholic marriages could be dissolved by divorce in the same way as civil ones.

## 2. The current Constitution

The Constitution (published in 1976 and amended on several occasions) considers the family to be such an important institution that it defines the principles constituting the basis of its legal regulation.

The most relevant of these principles are, according to Article 36 of the Constitution: the right of every person to constitute a family and to marry, under circumstances of full equality; the equality, in rights and duties between husband and wife, and in that which concerns the assistance and education of their children; the prohibition upon discrimination, both in the law and in administrative practice, against children born outside of marriage (and even to refer to them as "illegitimate children", as they had been referred to in the past); the right and obligation of parents to assist and educate their children; the prohibition upon separating children from their parents, except through a judicial decision that recognizes that the latter are not accomplishing their parental duties; the attribution to civil legislation of the right to rule on the conditions and effects of all marriages, including their dissolution through death or divorce.

It therefore became a constitutional rule that all marriages could be dissolved by divorce, even Catholic ones.

## 3. Marriage

**3.1** There are currently two modalities of marriage: the civil marriage and the Catholic marriage. Persons baptized in the Catholic religion may choose between civil or Catholic marriage ceremonies. Non-baptized persons can naturally only marry under civil law (excepting "mixed marriages" allowed by Canonic Law).

Two persons married under civil law can afterwards marry in Catholic form if Canonic law so allows. But two persons married under Canonic law cannot marry afterwards under civil law.

The civil marriage may be contracted by observing the formalities of civil law or of any of the (non-Catholic) religions considered as "radicated" (being officially recognized) in Portugal. The conditions and effects of these modalities of marriage are the same, all of them being established in the Civil Code.

The possibility of contracting religious, non-Catholic marriages was introduced by the Freedom of Religion Law, approved in 2001.

According to the current text of the Civil Code and the recent Concordata (contracted between the Portuguese Republic and the Catholic Church in November 2004), the Catholic marriage exists as an autonomous modality. This means that not only the formalities, but also the validity, of this type of act are subject to Canonic law, as applied by the courts of the Catholic Church.

Nevertheless, the Catholic marriage must also respect the conditions established in the Civil Law: this means that it must abide by both civil and Canonic law requirements. All the effects of Catholic marriages are regulated by civil law – including the possibility of dissolution by divorce.

**3.2** The agreement to marry is a legally accepted contract, which is not subject to any kind of proof, but this does not give rise to any right to demand the contracting of marriage.

If one of the contracting parties does not want to marry, or loses the capacity to do so, each must return gifts received from the other party. And if one of the parties refuses to marry without a "just motive" he has to compensate the other partner (or his/her parents) for the expenses or obligations contracted in connection with the marriage.

**3.3** As the Catholic marriage is subject to Canonic law, its validity is a matter for the consideration of the Catholic courts. Hereinafter our comments will only refer to the civil marriage.

Marriage is a contract celebrated by two persons of different sexes, with the intention to create a family, through a full communion of life. A marriage is a strictly personal contract; both parties must be present – or at least one of them together with the representative of the other one.

The capacity to marry depends upon the fulfilment of two types of conditions.

In the event that the first type of conditions is not fulfilled, a marriage is not only impeded, but, if contracted, becomes voidable. According to these conditions: no party to the marriage can be under 16 years of age; no party can be known to be insane or declared so by a court decision; no party can be married to another person; no party can have been convicted of murder against the husband or wife of the other; parties cannot have a relationship of consanguinity (full adoption being equivalent) or affinity in direct line, nor be brothers/sisters.

The second type of conditions only impedes the marriage (which does not become voidable if contracted in the absence of their fulfilment). According to these conditions: minors (under 18 years of age) must obtain authorization for the marriage from their parents or guardians; if an earlier marriage is dissolved, annulated or declared void – in the case of Catholic marriages – parties are allowed

*Family Law* 233

to marry again only after a period of 180/300 days (men/women) has elapsed; uncles or aunts cannot marry their nephews; guardians or administrators cannot marry the persons whose interests they take care of; persons accused of the murder of the husband or wife of the other party cannot marry the surviving spouse. The first, third and fourth of these impediments can be excused by the civil registrar if there is sufficient justification to do so.

Civil marriages normally take place in a civil registrar's office (or in another place authorized by the registrar, who as a rule must be present to solemnize the marriage).

Both parties must be present, or at least one of them together with a representative of the other party. The ceremony must be public. During the ceremony the registrar must ask if anyone present knows of any impediment against the marriage.

There is also a special form of marriage called an urgent marriage, which may be invoked in cases of reasonable fear of death of one of the parties or imminent delivery. In the above case a marriage may take place without fulfilment of the previous procedure intended to ascertain the capacity of the parties and the presence of the registrar is also not necessary.

The celebration, which has to be public, takes place in the presence of four witnesses. The act must afterwards be ratified by the registrar for the legal existence of the urgent marriage to be recognized.

Marriage has two important types of effects: personal and patrimonial. Concerning personal effects, the basic rule governing all the personal relations between spouses is the principle of equality. This principle encompasses the specific duties of fidelity, cooperation, respect, cohabitation and maintenance.

Spouses have the duty to agree in choosing the matrimonial home; if they do not reach agreement the courts must decide. The duty of maintenance covers the agency of necessity and the duty to contribute to supporting the costs of the family. The courts consider that the duty of maintenance is not limited to the basic necessities of life, but shall correspond to the standards of each family.

Each spouse keeps his or her surname, and may also, in terms of absolute equality, choose to add the surname of the other, if the latter so agrees, or if the court so decides, after considering the reasons presented.

Concerning patrimonial effects, the rules related to property rights, the administration of goods, sale of goods and real estate must be outlined.

Excepting some special situations where separation of property is imposed by law (e.g. if at least one of the spouses is 60 years old or more) the main rule is that spouses may, before a wedding, choose – through a pre-nuptial settlement – a system of property division. If they do not make such a contract, the so-called "community of acquired goods" applies. Under this system, the spouses maintain the ownership of goods they had before marriage, and of those obtained whilst married by inheritance or gift. Goods acquired during marriage are part of the "community" – including the respective salaries.

Concerning the administration of goods, it may be said, in general, that each spouse has the sole administration of his or her own goods or real estate, whilst they have joint administration of the common goods and real estate.

There are, nevertheless, some special rules. For instance, each spouse has the administration of the salaries he or she earns and of the goods he or she uses in the course of work, even if they are legally common goods or belong to the other spouse.

The right to sell goods is related to the capacity of administration over them; each spouse can, as a rule, sell his or her goods, whilst common goods may only be sold by both spouses, jointly.

The sale of real estate is subject to strict legal protection. This means that real estate can only be sold by both spouses, irrespective of the correspondent ownership, excepting the system of property separation under which each spouse can sell their own real estate.

Divorce is now applicable, as stated above, to all modalities of marriage – civil and religious. There are two types of divorce: divorce by agreement of the spouses and divorce by a court decision. The former type covers more than 90% of all divorces.

The procedure of divorce by agreement takes place before the office of the civil registrar. No grounds to the agreement need to be presented, although certain conditions must be fulfilled, without which the civil registrar will not be able to approve the agreement to divorce. There must be agreement as to: the destination of the marital home; the agency of necessity(the provision of financial support/ alimony) to the spouse that needs it; and parental responsibility over minor children (if there is no agreement on this subject a court decision ruling this subject shall be necessary).

There are two types of grounds for the divorce by court decision.

One is the faulty violation of any of the marital duties, to such a serious or consistent extent that it puts the possibility of life in common at risk. The second ground is the occurrence of one of certain defined situations that according to the law correspond to marital breakdown. These situations are: "de facto" separation for at least three years, or one year if the defendant does not contest the petition of divorce; the absence, without information as to the whereabouts, of one of the spouses for at least two years; the insanity of one of the spouses for a period of at least three years and to so serious a degree that it puts the possibility of life in common at risk.

The law rules that the civil registrar and the judge may always attempt to bring about the reconciliation of the spouses. However there are no legal norms regarding mediation. Nevertheless parties to a divorce already have the "de facto" possibility of requesting the intervention of a mediation office of the Ministry of Justice.

Divorce terminates the personal and patrimonial effects of marriage (similarly to death). A spouse declared by the court as being the responsible (or the mainly responsible) party in the divorce, and similarly a spouse that demanded divorce on the grounds of insanity of the other, can be ordered to pay compensation for damages caused by the divorce itself. This compensation should not be confused with the compensation payable due to damages caused by the facts that constitute the grounds of divorce. The court may, considering the interests of the children or the needs of the spouse, grant to him/her the matrimonial home, even if it belongs to the other one or to both of them.

## 4. Unmarried cohabitants

A special law, approved in 2001, regulates the position of unmarried cohabitants, either of the same or different sexes, if the period of cohabitation lasts for at least two years. The situation of unmarried couples is not registered and can be proved by any legal means.

There is no patrimonial relationship between unmarried cohabitants, and neither one can be a successor to the other. The main legal effects of unmarried cohabitation concern: the right to a survival pension; the right to absences or to take leave, as an employee or civil servant, for reasons related to the other cohabitant; the right to stay in the home used by the couple, in case of death of the other cohabitant; and the right to be taxed as a couple.

Unmarried cohabitants of different sexes can adopt, but those of the same sex cannot adopt as a couple (although each of them can do so as an individual person).

## 5. Parents and children

As previously stated, the main reform concerning the relationship between parents and children occurred as a consequence of a principle consecrated in the Constitution (1976), and subsequently introduced as an amendment in the Civil Code (reform of 1977).

This is the principle of absolute equality between children born inside or outside the marriage of their parents. The traditional difference of status between "legitimate" and "illegitimate" children was, in this way, abolished.

The reform of the Civil Code published in 1977 introduced a radical change in the identification of legal parentage. It declared that for this purpose not only blood tests would be admitted, but also any other scientifically accepted means of proof.

This substituted the original prohibition of the Code (1966), denying any relevance to artificial insemination in the establishment of parentage. Moreover, on the other hand, the reformed version logically recognized the value of DNA tests in this area.

In establishing parentage, there is a presumption that the children of a married woman (taking into account the normal pregnancy period) are the children of her husband. This presumption can only be rebutted through a court decision.

Children of unmarried parents can obtain this status through a declaration made by one or both parents. If this declaration is not made parentage can only be established by a court decision. Normally, it is the interested person that introduces the court procedure in order to obtain such a decision. However, if there are sufficient indications that someone is the father or mother of a certain person, the office of the state prosecutor can also take the initiative, investigating and instigating the court procedure to establish parentage (in the case of a possible father, the state prosecutor must take this initiative during the two first years after the birth of the child).

Parental responsibilities over their children belong to both parents, if they are married. If they do not agree in exercising their responsibility, the court must intervene and take a decision. If the parents are not married, the responsibility rests with the parent who is in charge of the child.

Parental responsibilities include not only the representation of the children (if minors) but also the duty to care for their health and security, maintain and educate them and administrate their goods.

Parents cannot, without due reason, deprive their children of normal conviviality with ascendants, brothers or sisters.

The rule that majority is attained at the age of 18 is subject to some exceptions. Children have freedom of religion when aged 16. But, on the other hand, if they obtain majority in the course of their studies, parents are responsible for their education during the normal period needed to complete their studies or training.


## 6. Adoption

Adoption must always be decided by the courts (preceded by a preparatory procedure coordinated by the social security services). Adoption depends on the consent of the person to be adopted if he/she is more than 12 years old. There are two forms of adoption: full adoption and restricted adoption.

Full adoption places the adopted person in the position of a son or daughter of the adoptant(s). Full adoption can only be requested: by two persons, of more than 25 years of age, married for more than 4 years without separation; or by a person of more than 30 years of age, or 25 years of age if the child is the son or daughter of his or her spouse. In any case, adoptants cannot be more than 60 years old. The biological parents can declare that they do not wish for their identity to be revealed to the adoptant(s). The identity of the adoptant is not revealed to the biological parents of the person to be adopted.

Restricted adoption involves only certain legal effects of the parental relationship. Restricted adoption can only be requested by persons over 25 years of age and under 60 years of age.

## 7. Future areas of reform

Among the principal areas in which reform is needed, the following should be highlighted: the introduction of mediation, especially in the context of divorce and separation cases; the enlargement of the personal, patrimonial and succession effects of cohabitation; and the revision of the rules relating to the establishment of paternity and maternity, in accordance with the recent advances in scientific knowledge.

## Bibliography

ANTUNES VARELA, João de Matos, *Direito de Família*, Coimbra, 1999. PEREIRA COELHO, Francisco and Guilherme de Oliveira, *Curso de Direito de Família*, vol. I, 3rd ed., Coimbra, 2003. PIRES DE LIMA, Fernando Andrade, and João de Matos Antunes Varela, *Código Civil Anotado*, vol. IV, 2nd ed., Coimbra, 1992. SANTOS, Eduardo dos, *Direito de Família*, Coimbra, 1999.

# CHAPTER 17

# Law of Sucessions

JOSÉ JOÃO ABRANTES

SUMMARY: *1. Concept, sources and brief historical notes 2. Types of succession 3. The process of succession 4. Inheritance petition 5. Alienation of the inheritance 6. Administration, liquidation, and partition of the inheritance 7. Future trends*

## 1. Concept, sources and brief historical notes

**1.1** Within the legal framework, successions law regulates the occurrence of succession; the process of entitling one or more persons to assume the legal relationships of a deceased person and the subsequent devolution of the assets that pertained to that person.

**1.2** The most important source of Portuguese successions law is Book V (articles 2024-2334) of the Civil Code. Notwithstanding, succession-related legal norms can be found in other books of this code as well as in other documents, for instance in provisions of the New Urban Lease Regulations [*Novo Regime de Arrendamento Urbano* (NRAU)] concerning the conveyance of the right to a housing lease through succession and in some provisions of the Public Notary Code (in particular concerning the process of entitlement of heirs and legatees and the instruments of approval, deposit and disclosure of closed wills), while the existence of normative provisions concerning fiscal matters within the succession legal framework should also be mentioned.

**1.3** Portuguese successions law follows the individualist model of its Roman law origins, emanating the principles of free will and the right of ownership – albeit with strong concessions to the family model of germanic origin, particularly in terms of the so-called *sucessão legitimária* that has unquestionable autonomy as opposed to the 1867 Civil Code (Seabra Code), in which it was considered as a mere limitation to the freedom of bequest and therefore regulated in the chapter concerning testamentary succession. It should also be noted that the last great reform of the Civil Code of 1966 (the reform embodied in Decree-Law No. 486/77 of November 25 enacted on July 1 1977) was essentially centred on family law and successions law. Although this reform did not question the essence of the model it did represent a rather significant alteration to the legal framework in force, namely in certain aspects that resulted from the new legal and constitutional system brought into being by the 1974 Revolution (such as non-discrimination among legitimate and illegitimate relatives, the legal position of the surviving spouse or the higher relevance conferred upon the nuclear family).

## 2. Types of succession

**2.1** Means of entitlement to succession recognized by Portuguese law are the law, testament and contract.

Legal succession is legitimate or imperative (*sucessão legitimária*) depending on whether or not it can be overturned by the will of the author.

The rules governing inheritance establish five classes of legitimate successors in the following order: spouse and descendants; spouse and ascendants; brothers, sisters and their descendants; other collateral relatives up to the fourth degree; and the State.

There are certain rules governing the order of devolution upon death that are applied both to legitimate and to imperative succession:

a) Preference of classes: the successors within each class take preference over those of the following class;

b) Preference of degree of relationship: within each class the closer relatives take preference over the more distant relatives;

c) Succession per capita: the relatives within each class succeed per capita or in equal parts (exceptions stem from succession *per stirpes* and the division among full and half brothers and sisters, where the share of the former is double that of the latter).

The surviving spouse is a legal heir and is thus included in the first class of successors, except in cases where the author dies without descendants and leaves ascendants, in which case the surviving spouse is integrated within the second class. In such case the surviving spouse is called together with the descendants, or in cases where there are no descendants the spouse is called together with the ascendants (with the exception of any applicable right of representation).

The surviving spouse has the right to be ranked first, at the time of succession, in claiming the right to live in the family home and make use of its respective contents. However, should the value of these preferential attributions exceed the corresponding value attributable through succession then the surviving spouse owes reimbursements and possible joint use to the co-heirs.

The descendants, together with the spouse, constitute the first class of successors.

The partition of the inheritance between the spouse and the children is performed per capita, although the spouse's share cannot be less than one-quarter of the estate.

The descendants of children who could not or did not wish to accept the inheritance are entitled to the succession in their representation and each receives that which their respective ascendant would have inherited.

In cases where deceased children or children who waived their rights have no descendants their part of the estate is added to that of the remaining children.

The ascendants of the decedent only succeed when there are no descendants and they constitute, together with the spouse, the second class of successors.

The ascendants are entitled to the entire estate if there is no spouse. If there is a spouse they are only entitled to one-third of the estate (while the spouse is entitled to two-thirds).

Should any of the ascendants be unable or unwilling to assume the succession, the respective part will be added to that of the other ascendants and only in cases where there are no other ascendants will this part be added to that of the spouse.

In cases where there is no spouse and no descendants or ascendants, the brothers and sisters of the decedent are called or, in representation thereof, the descendants of these siblings (nephews and nieces). The entitlement of these successors varies in accordance with whether they are full or half brothers or sisters; the share of each of the full brothers and sisters is equal to double the share of each of the half brothers and sisters.

In cases where there are no heirs in the preceding classes, the remaining collateral relatives, up to the fourth degree, are called. The closest relatives are accorded preference.

The State holds the title of legitimate successor (and may also be a testamentary successor) and it constitutes the final class of successors. The entitlement of the State depends on the non-existence of any of the foregoing classes of successors and this fact must be verified judicially through a special process, known as a "settlement of estate in escheat in favour of the State" (*"liquidação da herança vaga em benefício do Estado"*). Only after liquidation of the estate, i.e. settlement of liabilities, will any remainder be allocated to the State.

The acquisition of the inheritance by the State as a legal successor is performed *ipso jure*, without either the need to accept or the possibility to decline the inheritance.

**2.2.** Imperative legal succession is based on an unassignable reserve (*legítima* or *quota indisponível*), which constitutes the part of the estate of the decedent that cannot be freely disposed of by the decedent. This part is mandatorily reserved for the so-called *herdeiros legitimários* e.g. the spouse, descendents and ascendants according to the afore-mentioned order under legitimate succession.

The portion of each *herdeiro legitimário* varies in accordance with his status within the defined order of succession. Thus, the portion of the spouse, when not dividing the estate with descendants or ascendants, is half the estate. However, in cases where there are descendant children, the portion is two-thirds of the estate (the partition is performed per capita, while safeguarding the spouse's right to at least one-quarter of the unassignable share). The portion of the children, when there is no surviving spouse, is half or two-thirds of the estate depending on whether there was only one child or two or more children. The portion of the spouse and the ascendants, in cases of competition, is two-thirds of the estate. The portion of the ascendants, when there is no spouse, is half or two-thirds of the estate, depending on whether the parents, or ascendants in second and further degrees, are called or not.

Calculation of the unassignable reserve (*legítima*) should take into account not only the value of the existing assets of the estate of the decedent on the date of demise (*relictum*) but also the value of conferred assets (*donatum*), as well as any expenses subject to restitution and debts of the estate.

Restitution (*colação*) is, for the purpose of equality, reallocation of assets to the estate that were conferred upon descendants who wish to succeed the decedent and who on the date of the conferral were presumable *herdeiros legitimários* of the conferrer.

All gifts made by the decedent during life and *post mortem* can be contested by the legal heirs, as far as they offend their reserve. The process is defined by law, and the respective proceedings are subject to a limitation period of two years after the acceptance of the inheritance by the *herdeiro legitimário*.

**2.3** Voluntary succession can be testamentary or contractual. Contractual succession is only allowed under exceptional circumstances foreseen in the law. Such is the case for gifts (upon death) granted within marriages that have been included in a prenuptial agreement. This agreement may involve the appointment of an heir or nomination of a devisee or legatee in favour of either of the engaged persons, performed by the other engaged person or by a third person, or in favour of a third person performed by either of the engaged persons. Due to both the irrevocability and bilateral nature of succession agreements, these are ranked in second place in the succession hierarchy, immediately after the so-called *sucessão legitimária* and prior to the expressed will of the decedent in testament, which is a unilateral act and freely revocable.

However, the general rule is a ban on succession agreements with the effect that in principle nobody can renounce the succession of a live person through a contract or dispose of his/her own succession or the succession of a third person.

**2.4** Testamentary succession is based on the existence of a will. Anyone who has not been declared incapable to do so by law can draw up a will. Non-emancipated minors (as well as persons disqualified for reasons of mental illness) cannot draw up a will. This means that the minimum age for drawing up a will is, in general, 18 years of age – however, minors who have been emancipated (through marriage) may also draw up a will.

There are common forms and special forms of last will and testament. Among the common forms are the 'public' will (that is drawn up by and lodged with the Public Notary) and the 'closed' will (drawn up and signed by the testator or someone with power of attorney, or drawn up by a third party with power of attorney and signed by the testator and approved by the Public Notary within the terms of the law). Special forms include the military will, the seafarer's will, the will drawn up on board an aeroplane and the will drawn up during a public emergency.

An index of all wills made in Portugal can be found at the General Register Office (*Conservatória dos Registos Centrais*) where notaries must register all last wills and testaments in which they have intervened, identifying (through a standard form) the author and signature date.

All special forms of last will and testament have time limits. Two months after the special circumstances – i.e. the circumstances that impeded the testator from drawing up a will in accordance with the common form – cease, the special form of last will and testament loses its effectiveness.

**2.5** Portuguese law distinguishes between the appointment of heirs and the nomination of legatees. An heir succeeds in all, or in a share of all, the assets of the decedent. A successor to the remainder of unspecified assets is also considered an heir. A legatee inherits specified goods or assets.

The legal qualification is imperative, i.e. it depends on the tangible configuration of the inheritance and not on the qualification made by the testator.

Heirs and legatees are subject to different rules. In addition to the rules concerning the responsibilities for the debts of the estate (in contrast to heirs, legatees have only a limited responsibility regarding the charges from the legacy itself or in cases where the entire estate is distributed in legacies), we have for example the right of accretion, a right that is only fully recognized with respect to heirs (the only case where this right is conceded upon legatees is when they have been nominated regarding the same object).

## 3. The process of succession

**3.1** Succession is opened at the time of death of the author and at the last place of domicile. Note that in cases of more than one person dying during the same event, Portuguese law (Article 68 of the Civil Code) establishes the presumption of simultaneous death (in case of doubt, it is presumed that both died at the same moment), from which can be concluded that any legal effect depending on one person surviving the other is non-existent.

**3.2** Acquisition of the inheritance is performed by means of acceptance, regardless of how material possession is carried out, with retroactive effect to the moment the succession is opened.

Acceptance can be express or tacit. Express acceptance occurs when in a written document the successor, called to the inheritance, declares their acceptance or assumes the title of heir. Acts of administration carried out by a successor do not imply tacit acceptance of the inheritance.

Acceptance can be either unconditional or in favour of the inventory.

Should the designated successor die without accepting the inheritance, the right of acceptance is transmitted to his/her heirs provided they accept the inheritance of the deceased.

The right to accept the inheritance expires 10 years after the successor was notified, or, in cases of appointment subject to condition, upon verification that condition.

The inheritance cannot be accepted under conditions or terms or in part. This means that should a person be called to an inheritance simultaneously, or successively, under two entitlements (e.g. a will and under law), he/she may not accept under one entitlement and refuse under another, but rather he/she must accept or refuse it under both entitlements. The only exceptions are when a person is called to the inheritance simultaneously or successively by will and under the law. The inheritance may be accepted or refused under the first entitlement despite having been accepted or refused under the second entitlement, if at that time, the person called ignored the existence of the will. When the legal successor is also called to the inheritance by will the available share may be refused and it may be accepted as an unassignable reserve.

Acceptance can be annulled for reasons of fraud or coercion but not due to an error. Acceptance is irrevocable.

The effects of refusal are retroactive to the moment of the opening of the succession, whereby the successor is considered as not having been called (except for the purpose of representation). Refusal must be an express statement and is subject to the same form required for alienation of the inheritance. The inheritance cannot be refused under conditions, terms or in part, except in the two cases mentioned above. Refusal can be annulled for reasons of fraud or coercion but not due to an error and it is irrevocable.

Creditors of a person that refuses to accept an inheritance can subrogate and accept the inheritance in his/her name. In this case the surplus is attributed to the immediate heirs (and not to the person that refuses).

## 4. Inheritance petition

Inheritance petition proceedings are a type of claim allowing an entitlement to heirship to be judicially recognized. The restitution of all the assets of the estate or part of them is simultaneously claimed against whoever possesses them as heir, or under any other entitlement, or even without entitlement.

## 5. Alienation of the inheritance

The heirs can jointly dispose of the inheritance as a whole, certain assets of the inheritance or a share of the inheritance.

Alienation can only take place after acceptance and before the partition of assets.

The alienation of the inheritance, or of a share of the inheritance, is subject to the normal rules for the legal transactions involved (e.g. free of charge or against payment, *inter vivos* or *mortis causa*). The form required for the alienation is, in principle, the same as the form required for any such business dealing. However, alienation will always be subject to minimum formalities and must be carried out by deed if the inheritance or share of the inheritance contains assets that must be conveyed in this manner or be registered by private document if this is not the case.

The alienation of a share of an inheritance is subject to the preferential rights of the other co-heirs.

## 6. Administration, liquidation, and partition of the inheritance

**6.1** An inheritance is an autonomous estate until it has been dissolved into the estate of the heirs and is liable for the debts of the testator and only for these debts (for which purpose only these assets are liable).

An inheritance can remain undivided for a considerable period of time. Problems of administration can arise and the undivided estate should be jointly administered by the heirs or by the so-called *cabeça-de-casal* on behalf of all.

Nomination of a *cabeça-de-casal* is obligatory, but the legal rules concerning the designation are subsidiary.

Exercising the role of *cabeça-de-casal* is personal and non-transferable and the *cabeça-de-casal* has the right to be reimbursed for administration expenses.

In general, the powers of the *cabeça-de-casal* are limited to ordinary administration, including the right to demand surrender of the assets for administration and the possibility of resorting to judicial means for the maintenance or restitution of ownership. Beyond these powers, rights concerning the inheritance belong to the heirs as a whole.

The role of *cabeça-de-casal* ceases with the liquidation and partition of the inheritance.

**6.2** Heirs are liable for the expenses of an inheritance (while legatees are in principle only liable for the expenses of the legacy itself or for the whole inheritance when it is distributed in legacies).

The law expressly identifies inheritance expenses as: the expenses regarding the funeral and requiem of the decedent, the expenses concerning the will, expenses connected with the administration and liquidation of the inheritance, and the debts of the author of the succession and legacies.

Two situations should be identified. In cases where the inheritance is undivided, i.e. when the inheritance has not yet been shared out, the assets are collectively liable for meeting the expenses of the inheritance, which means that creditors should address the heirs as a whole. After the inheritance has been shared out, joint liability ceases and each heir is liable only in proportion to his/her share.

The heirs are only liable within the scope of the inheritance (*intra vires hereditatis*): they are only liable with assets from the inheritance and not with personal assets. However, in cases where their acceptance is unconditional the heirs have the burden of proving the estate does not have enough assets to meet all the expenses. In cases where the acceptance is in favour of the inventory, the creditors have the burden of proving that there are other assets besides the assets in the inventory.

The autonomy of the assets is maintained during five years, after which time the inheritance is dissolved into the estate of the heirs.

**6.3** Partition consists of apportioning certain assets to the share of each heir.

Partition can be performed in two ways. An out of court agreement among all interested parties must, as with all matters concerning real estate, be registered by deed. In court, a special proceeding (inventory) is drawn up in order to establish a list of the assets that should be apportioned for the purpose of liquidation and distribution. This proceeding can be requested by any interested party (any co-heir or the surviving spouse) or by the Public Prosecutor in cases of incapacity or absence of an heir.

## 7. Future trends

No major reforms are foreseeable in the near future. However, a reassessment might be timely, to consider the improvement and development of the succession process, together with some pertinent social aspects.

For instance, from the point of view of the present socio-economic reality is *sucessão legitimária* justified? Consideration should be given to the succession situation of the surviving spouse (should it be maintained, e.g. as regards the other legal heirs? should the terms of marriage, namely separation of assets, be reflected in terms of succession by positively or negatively conditioning the succession position of the spouse?). A review might also extend to the succession effects of cohabitation and the legal succession situation of those spouses, descendants and ascendants that, because of their natural or judicial incapacity (minors, incompetents) or due to their advanced age, deserve special judicial protection. Certain schemes, such as partition inter vivos (aimed at increasing recourse to this friendly composition of succession interests without neglecting its perils and inconveniencies) should be reviewed, as should the matter of restoration and of the gifts that offend the unassignable reserve.

## Bibliography

CAPELO DE SOUSA, Rabindranath, *Lições de Direito das Sucessões* I, 4th ed., 2000, and II, 2nd ed., Coimbra, 1997. CARVALHO FERNANDES, Luís, *Lições de Direito das Sucessões*, Lisbon, 1999. GALVÃO TELLES, Inocêncio, *Direito das Sucessões – Noções Fundamentais*, 6th ed.,

Coimbra, 1991. GOMES DA SILVA, Nuno Espinosa, *Direito das Sucessões* (cyclo-styled), Lisbon, 1978. LEITE DE CAMPOS Diogo, *Lições de Direito da Família e das Sucessões*, Coimbra, 1997. OLIVEIRA ASCENSÃO José, *Direito Civil. Sucessões,* 5th ed., Coimbra, 2000. PAMPLONA CORTE-REAL Carlos, *Direito da Família e das Sucessões*, vol. II ("Sucessões"), Lisbon, 1993. PEREIRA COELHO Francisco M., *Direito das Sucessões*, 4th ed., Coimbra, 1992.

# CHAPTER 18
# Commercial Law

RUI PINTO DUARTE
ASSUNÇÃO CRISTAS

SUMMARY: *1. Introduction 2. Major differences between commercial law and civil law 3. Negotiable instruments 4. Commercial register 5. Insolvency 6.* Estabelecimento comercial *7. Commercial jurisdiction 8. Future trends*

## 1. Introduction

Portuguese lawyers agree on the existence of a branch of private law called commercial law. As in other countries, there is no agreement on a material definition of this branch of law, but authors' opinions generally converge on the idea that the focus of contemporary commercial law is on economic undertakings. Given that the practical consequences of this disagreement are of very little significance, we can proceed without discussing the definition.

The first Portuguese Commercial Code was published in 1833. It is known as "Ferreira Borges Code" in homage to its author. This Code was influenced by the French Commercial Code of 1807, but it did more than merely adapt the French model. The reasons for some of the specific characteristics of the first Portuguese Commercial Code included the fact that Portugal had no Civil Code at that time (and had none until 1867). The Ferreira Borges Code therefore had no elder brother to relate to, and being alone in the world of Portuguese modern Codes was forced to regulate more questions than some similar Codes in other countries.

The second Portuguese Commercial Code (generally known as the "Veiga Beirão Code", after the minister responsible for it) was published in 1888. Less than half of it is still in force.

The Portuguese Commercial Code of 1888 delineates its scope through a mixed system. Article 1 states that commercial law governs commercial transactions, irrespective of whether the persons involved are merchants or not. Nevertheless, Article 2 considers as commercial transactions not only the transactions described in the Code but also the transactions performed by merchants in general, even if they are not described in the Code. Consequently, although the Portuguese system for determining commercial law is *prima facie* "objective", it is in fact half "objective" and half "subjective".

The category of merchant comprises both individuals engaged in commercial activities and commercial companies.

Since 1986, individual merchants may limit their liability by creating a so-called *"estabelecimento individual de responsabilidade limitada"* – which is not a legal entity but a mere separate business property (however this possibility is rarely used, people preferring to incorporate one-person limited liability companies).

Originally, the Veiga Beirão Code was divided into four books: general provisions, specific commercial contracts, maritime commerce and bankruptcy. In 1899, the book on bankruptcy was replaced by a separate Bankruptcy Code. From then on, the Veiga Beirão Code has undergone many amendments. Currently, not only have all its provisions on stock and commodities exchanges, bills of exchange, promissory notes, cheques, registers and companies been replaced, but also very important parts of its provisions on maritime commerce, insurance contract and other subjects have been substituted by different pieces of legislation. This means that the Code is now a small part of commercial law and that its relevance is not very great.

The Veiga Beirão Code was enacted when Portugal already had a Civil Code, forging links between both. As a result, many of the provisions of the Commercial Code, mainly those dealing with contracts, are drafted as deviations from the provisions of the Civil Code which are seen as the standard rules. The replacement in 1966 of the first Portuguese Civil Code by a new Code has had little impact on this system of linkage.

It may almost go without saying that the concept of commerce underlying Portuguese law is far wider than that used by economists or in everyday language. Indeed, as is also the case in other countries, the Portuguese Commercial Code governs not only commerce in the narrow sense, but also (some aspects of) other economic activities such as manufacturing, banking, insurance and transportation.

## 2. Major differences between commercial law and civil law

The reasons for the emergence of commercial law were essentially the same in all countries. In those legal systems that have developed a distinction between civil law and commercial law the major differences between these two branches of private law tend to be similar, allowing for a general understanding that commercial law favours expediency in business and the strength of the creditors' position. Let us see how this works in the context of Portuguese law.

In Portuguese civil law, when not otherwise stipulated, co-debtors are severally obliged. In contrast, under commercial law, co-debtors are jointly and severally liable.

The stronger protection of creditors is also apparent in the rules on guarantee (*fiança*). In civil law, unless otherwise established, the guarantor may refuse payment until the creditor exhausts the assets of the debtor unsuccessfully, but in commercial law the guarantor has no such right.

The rules on interest due in the event of late payment also show the same tendency, the interest rate for commercial credits being higher than that for civil credits.

One aspect of the favouring of business expediency is that commercial law has less exigent rules on the formal requirements of contracts. This may be exemplified by the rules on loans: those subject to civil law must consist of a document signed by the borrower if the amount involved is in excess of € 2,000 and must consist of a notarial deed if the amount involved is in excess of € 20,000, whereas those entered into between merchants may be proved by any means.

The degree of protection afforded to the *bona fide* acquirer provides another example of the expediency favoured by commercial law. In contrast to the general tendency in continental Europe, in Portuguese law the principle *en fait de meubles la possession vaut titre* does not prevail. Nonetheless, those who acquire *a non domino* enjoy stronger protection when the seller is a merchant.

Different but convergent examples of the differences between commercial law and civil law can be found in the rules on sale and purchase, *inter alia* in the greater flexibility accorded by commercial law to the sale of goods of which the seller is not the owner.

## 3. Negotiable instruments

In Portuguese legal literature the main concept in this area is that of *títulos de crédito*, derived from the Italian concept of *titoli di credito,* mainly through the writings of Vivante and Ascarelli. This concept is wider than similar concepts used in other legal literatures, including the English concept of negotiable instruments. Indeed it encompasses a heterogeneous variety of instruments, such as bills of exchange, promissory notes, cheques, shares, debentures, bills of lading and warehouse warrants. The utility of such a concept is more than ever open to discussion. On the one hand, some of these instruments do not need nowadays to take the form of documents. On the other hand, some of these instruments are also securities and this characteristic implies a regime different from that applicable to those instruments that are not securities.

As regards bills of exchange, promissory notes and cheques, it should be noted that Portugal is a party to the Geneva conventions and that the uniform laws approved by these conventions are in force in Portugal.

## 4. Commercial registration

From an organizational point of view, we may point to the following two characteristics, amongst others, of the Portuguese system for commercial registration: it is the responsibility of the administrative authorities, more precisely of departments of the Ministry of Justice (the "Conservatórias do Registo Comercial"); and it is geographically decentralized.

The law states that individual merchants and companies (as well as other business entities) are subject to registration. Nevertheless, individuals (with the exception of those who have created a "estabelecimento individual de responsabilidade limitada") are not directly penalized for not registering themselves and indeed the large majority of individual merchants are not registered.

Overlapping partly with the commercial register is a national register for legal entities (*"Registo Nacional de Pessoas Colectivas"*), which is responsible *inter alia* for the task of authorizing company names.

## 5. Insolvency

As we have already seen, in 1899 the provisions on bankruptcy (*"falência"*) were detached from the Commercial Code by means of the creation of a specific Code on this matter. In 1905, this Bankruptcy Code was incorporated in a pre-existing Code of commercial procedure. In 1932, an act was passed establishing for the first time in Portugal insolvency for non-merchants (calling it *"insolvência"*, so as to underline its difference from bankruptcy of merchants).

In 1935, a new and separate Bankruptcy Code was enacted. In 1939, a Code of Civil Procedure was published incorporating both rules on bankruptcy and on the insolvency of non-merchants. Insolvency law (in a broad sense) then experienced a period of stability until 1986, when an act was passed changing the "philosophy" in this legal field, by creating a "special procedure for the recovery of undertakings and for protection from creditors", with the aim of enhancing the chances of survival of undertakings in a poor financial state, by way either of agreement with their creditors or of reconstruction as determined by these creditors. In 1993, a Code entitled *"Código dos Processos Especiais de Recuperação de Empresa e da Falência"* (Code on the Special Proceedings for Recovering of Undertakings and on Bankruptcy) was published, going further along the same path.

The present regime derives from the *"Código da Insolvência e da Recuperação de Empresas"* (Code of Insolvency and of the Recovery of Undertakings), enacted in 2004, under the influence of the German *Insolvenzordnung* of 1994, of the Spanish *Ley Concursal* of 2003 and naturally of the relevant European Regulations and Directives.

The 2004 Code marks a break with previous concepts and trends, mainly with the idea that this kind of proceeding may serve as "protection against creditors". Indeed, it is no longer feasible to adopt reconstruction measures before a declaration of insolvency. These measures may only take place under an "insolvency plan" agreed by the creditors after such a declaration.

Some of the other most important features of the 2004 Code are the specific provisions on the insolvency of individuals, including non-merchants. These seek to make it possible for the insolvent person to make "fresh re-start" after a five-year period, during which time his income (except the minimum necessary for subsistence) is assigned to a trustee responsible for its distribution among the creditors.

## 6. Estabelecimento comercial

A very important concept in the context of Portuguese commercial law is that of *estabelecimento comercial* – which corresponds broadly to Spanish, French, Italian and German concepts of *establecimiento mercantil, fonds de commerce, azienda commerciale* and (in one of meanings of the word) *Handelsgeschäft.*

The reason for this importance is that *estabelecimentos comerciais* as such (*i.e.* as a whole) are often taken as the object of contracts, mainly of sales and of leases. We should pay special attention to two of the factors that determine this way of drawing up transactions. The first results from the conjunction of the fact that many businesses are carried on in leased premises with the rule that the assignment of the contractual position of tenant does not depend upon the consent of the landlord when such position is assigned in the context of the assignment of a business. The second reason derives from a rule on value added tax, whereby the transfers of goods within the framework of the transmission of a *estabelecimento comercial* are exempted from such tax.

The regime of the *estabelecimento comercial* is not to be found in the Commercial Code, but in other laws, *inter alia* those on leases. Besides the expression *estabelecimento comercial*, the key words in the area are *trespasse* and *cessão de exploração* (or *locação de estabelecimento*). The former designates any kind of *inter vivos* transfer of ownership of a *estabelecimento comercial* and the latter the lease of a *estabelecimento comercial.*

## 7. Commercial jurisdiction

The traditional commercial courts were abolished in 1932. Insolvency courts were created in 1996 and in 1999 the commercial courts were restored, although only in the judicial districts of Lisbon and Oporto. Their competence includes bankruptcy, internal disputes of companies, competition and industrial property.

## 8. Future trends

When it entered into force in 1888, the Portuguese Commercial Code comprised rules on companies, negotiable instruments, stock and commodities exchanges and bankruptcy. These subjects are now addressed and dealt with by other pieces of legislation, some of which have been codified.

Whereas almost all the provisions of the Commercial Code that are still in force deal with contracts, the future of the Portuguese Commercial Code is dependant on the decisions to be taken on the legislation on contracts (currently dispersed through the Civil Code, the Commercial Code and many specific acts, as explained in the chapter on contract law).

The increasing fragmentation of commercial legislation has brought about the emergence of new branches of legal studies. It is not clear whether commercial law will survive the development of these new branches. What happens abroad will determine the path taken in Portugal. At the present time, there still seem be a number of reasons for maintaining commercial law as a living discipline: not only does it enable the joint study of those divisions of the Commercial Code that are still in force, but it is also the appropriate "place" for an introductory and panoramic approach to a very large area of private law.


## Bibliography

COUTINHO DE ABREU, Jorge Manuel, *Curso de Direito Comercial*, vol. I, 5th ed., Coimbra, 2004. FERRER CORREIA, António, *Lições de Direito Comercial*, vol. I, Coimbra, 1973 (cyclo-styled); vol. III, "Letra de Câmbio", Coimbra, 1975 (cyclo-styled). MENEZES CORDEIRO, António, *Manual de Direito Comercial,* 2 vols., Coimbra, 2001. OLAVO, Fernando, *Direito Comercial*, vol. I, 2nd ed., Lisbon, 1974, vol. II, 2nd part, "Títulos de Crédito em Geral", Coimbra, 1977. OLIVEIRA ASCENSÃO, José, *Direito Comercial*, vol. I, "Parte Geral", Lisbon, 1986/87 (cyclo-styled); vol. II, "Direito Industrial", Lisbon, 1988 (cyclo-styled); vol. III, "Títulos de Crédito", Lisbon, 1992 (cyclo-styled). PUPO CORREIA, Miguel J. A., *Direito Comercial*, 8th ed., Lisbon, 2003.

# CHAPTER 19
# Company Law

RUI PINTO DUARTE

SUMMARY: 1. *Introduction* 2. *Civil companies versus commercial companies* 3. *Types of commercial companies* 4. *Companies and other legal forms of carrying on economic activities* 5. *The* Código das Sociedades Comerciais 6. *Some aspects of the regime applicable to all commercial companies* 7. Sociedades anónimas 8. Sociedades por quotas 9. *Future trends*

## 1. Introduction

The Portuguese legal concept of *sociedade* is similar to the Spanish, Italian, French and German concepts of *sociedad, società, société* and *Gesellschaft* (less clearly in the last case). It encompasses equivalents of both the partnerships and companies of English law.

On the one hand the idea of *sociedade* refers to a type of contract and on the other hand it refers to a type of legal entity. The purpose of such a contract and of such an entity may be either commercial or civil but, in any case, there must be (unlike, for example, in German law) an economic purpose.

Evolution over the last two decades has caused the concept of the *contrato de sociedade* to be widened, to include also the cases where law admits the creation of a company by a unilateral act.

In this text the word "company" shall be used to translate *sociedade,* although as noted above the English concept of company is different from the Portuguese concept of *sociedade.*

## 2. Civil companies *versus* commercial companies

As in other countries, Portugal traditionally draws a major distinction between civil companies *(sociedades civis)* and commercial companies *(sociedades comerciais)*. The former are governed by the Civil Code and the latter by the *Código das Sociedades Comerciais* (the Companies Code that in 1986 replaced the part of 1888 Commercial Code dealing with companies, as well as other subsequent legislation).

Outwardly, the crucial difference between civil companies and commercial companies lies in their purpose. Commercial companies must have a commercial purpose and civil companies may not have such a purpose. Nevertheless, it should be stressed that companies with a civil purpose may adopt a commercial form and that in doing so they become subject to the rules on commercial companies.

As the regimes for the various types of commercial companies are quite different from one another, it is difficult and almost irrelevant to make a general comparison between civil companies and commercial companies. The most relevant difference is that all types of commercial companies are legal persons, while ordinary civil companies do not have (according to the majority opinion) legal personality, although they enjoy a certain degree of "patrimonial autonomy". However, besides ordinary civil companies (*i.e.* those governed only by the Civil Code), there are special types of civil companies ruled by other laws (such as, for instance, *sociedades de advogados* – "law firms"), which are legal persons.

## 3. Types of commercial companies

Commercial companies must adopt one of the types specified by law (they are subject to what in German is called *Typengesetzlichkeit*), these types being:

- *sociedades em nome colectivo,* which correspond to the French, Spanish and Italian types with similar names;
- *sociedades por quotas*, which correspond to the German *GmbH*, to the French *société à responsabilité limitée* and to the Spanish and Italian types with names similar to the latter;

- *sociedades em comandita simples,* which correspond to the French, Spanish and Italian types with similar names;
- *sociedades em comandita por acções,* which correspond to the French, Spanish and Italian types with similar names;
- *sociedades anónimas* – which correspond to the French and Spanish types with similar names, to the Italian *società per azioni,* and to the German *Aktiengesellshaft,* and, less closely, to the UK public company limited by shares.

The name of each company must permit identification of the type to which it belongs. The names of *sociedades anónimas* must end with the expression *"sociedades anónimas"* or with the letters "S.A." and those of *sociedades por quotas* with the word *"Limitada"* or with the abbreviation *"Lda".* The names of *sociedades em nome colectivo* must either include the names of all their members or include the name of one or some of them and a reference that indicates the existence of other members, such as *"e Companhia".* The names of *sociedades em comandita* must include the name of at least one of the members with unlimited liability and the word *"comandita".*

As in other continental European countries, *sociedades em nome colectivo* and *sociedades em comandita simples* have existed at least since the Middle Ages. *Sociedades anónimas* descend from the companies that were created by royal charter, the first law allowing their incorporation without previous authorization having been published in 1867. *Sociedades por quotas* were created in 1901 under the strong influence of the German *Gesetz bettrefend die Gesellschaften mit beschränkter Haftung.*

*Sociedades em nome colectivo* and *sociedades em comandita* (either *simples* or *por acções*) are currently of little economic significance. That is why this text deals mainly with *sociedades anónimas* and *sociedades por quotas* (hereinafter also *"SA"* and *"SpQ"*).

The differences between the types of commercial companies relate mainly to the rules governing the liability of their members for the debts of the company, to the rules on the transfer of holdings in their capital and to the structure of the company bodies.

## 4. Companies and other legal forms of carrying out economic activities

According to concepts adopted by Portuguese legal rules, not all legal entities with an economic purpose are companies. Entities with charitable objectives, *i.e.* foundations, clearly lie outside this category. But even among self-interested entities with an economic purpose there are some that Portuguese law does not characterize as companies. This is the case of *cooperativas, agrupamentos complementares de empresas, entidades públicas empresariais* (all of which are types of legal entities) as well as of *estabelecimentos individuais de responsabilidade limitada* (which do not constitute a legal entity).

Until 1980, the *cooperativas* were ruled by the Commercial Code and were characterized as a special type of company, as in other legal systems. In that year a *Código Cooperativo* was adopted that has removed the *cooperativas* from the primary scope of company law – albeit establishing that commercial law, including the law on *sociedades anónimas,* was applicable to them on a subsidiary basis. The second *Código Cooperativo,* which came into force in 1996, has retained these principles, merely replacing the reference to commercial law with a reference to the *Código das Sociedades Comerciais.*

The *agrupamento complementar de empresas* (hereinafter *ACE*) is a type of legal entity created in 1973 under the strong influence of the French *groupement d'intérêt économique.* It is intended as a means for enhancing collaboration among pre-existing undertakings and may not have as a primary goal the generation of a profit in its accounts. Underlying the creation of the *ACE* was the (disputable) assumption that Portuguese law did not allow for non-profit-making companies, namely because the definition of company in the Civil Code (Article 980) sets out – following the definition of the original text of the corresponding article in the French Civil Code (Article 1832) – that the purpose of members of companies is to divide among them profits arising from the activity of companies. The *ACE* is therefore a kind of Portuguese ancestor of the European Economic Interest Grouping.

Undertakings that are entirely owned by the State may adopt the form of a company or the form of *entidades públicas empresariais (EPE)*. The law characterizes this type of entity as "legal persons of public law" with an "entrepreneurial nature". Although their bodies are similar to those of *sociedades anónimas,* we might say that in practical terms they are less autonomous from the State than State undertakings that take the form of a company.

The *estabelecimento individual de responsabilidade limitada* (hereinafter also *EIRL*) was created in 1986, a few days before the publication of the *Código das Sociedades Comerciais*. It is not a company or any other kind of legal entity, but a mere separate undertaking belonging to an individual. The influence of the French *entreprise unipersonnelle à responsabilité limitée (EURL)* may be observed in its name and purpose.

Indeed, although in 1986 some European legal systems, including those of Germany and France, already provided for single-member private limited liability companies as a means to the limitation of the liability of individuals merchants, Portuguese legislation opted to follow a different path, echoing the suggestions made by a number of writers in the early decades of the twentieth century. Most probably it was due to this Portuguese legal device that Article 7 of the 12th European Directive of 1989 allowed Member States the possibility of not providing for single-member companies if their legislation offers individual merchants other means for limiting their liability. Nevertheless in 1996 the *CSC* was amended in order to admit the single-member *SpQ*. The *EIRL* was never embraced by the Portuguese business community, and since the creation of the single-member *SpQ,* it has become almost a dead letter.

## 5. The *Código das Sociedades Comerciais*

The *Código das Sociedades Comerciais* (hereinafter also "*CSC*") of 1986 was intended to replace old and fragmentary laws, transposing the European Directives on companies in force at the time (*i.e.* the 1st, 2nd, 3rd, 4th, 6th, 7th and 8th Directives). Additionally, it took into account the drafts of European Directives then under discussion, which have not been finally approved (*i.e.* the drafts of the 5th and 9th Directives).

It is divided into eight parts, entitled:
- general part;
- *sociedades em nome colectivo;*
- *sociedades por quotas;*
- *sociedades anónimas;*
- *sociedades em comandita;*
- *sociedades coligadas (i.e.* groups of companies*);*
- provisions on crimes and offences; and
- final and transitional provisions.

The *CSC* contains the most important rules on commercial companies and is the centrepiece of Portuguese company law. However, there are many other pieces of legislation relevant to companies. These include the *Código dos Valores Mobiliários* (Securities Code), worthy of mention because it contains rules on public companies (*i.e.* companies open to public investment).

Since 1986, the *CSC* has undergone several amendments. Taken together, they have materially transformed the contents of the Code, although each one of them has had a limited reach. The most relevant of these amendments was perhaps that brought in by the very recent Decree-Law 76-A/2006, of 29 March 2006, which entered into force on 30 June 2006. This statute introduces changes in different fields, and particularly in the following: formal requirements concerning the *contrato de sociedade* and alterations to it, removing the requirement of notarial deeds; winding-up of companies; merger and division; and, last but not least, management and supervision of SA.

## 6. Some aspects of the regime applicable to all commercial companies

The general part of the *CSC* consists of 174 Articles. This shows clearly that Portuguese law has many provisions applicable to all companies irrespective of their type. The authors of the Code attempted to draft the largest number of general provisions, including by submitting all types of companies to many of the rules that European Directives only impose upon *SA* and in some cases upon *SpQ*.

In this section we shall outline various aspects of the main rules potentially applicable to all types of commercial companies. In the following sections we shall address some specific aspects of *SA* and *SpQ*.

### 6.1 *Formation of companies*

All companies result from a legal act known in Portuguese law as *contrato de sociedade* – even when this act is unilateral.

The *contrato de sociedade* comprises that which in English law is divided between the *memorandum of association* and the *articles of association*. For the sake of simplicity however, we shall often translate *contrato de sociedade* as "articles of association".

The minimum number of parties to a *contrato de sociedade* is two in the case of *sociedades em nome colectivo* and of *sociedades em comandita simples*. Single-member *SpQ*s are admitted with the requirement that the company name contains the word *unipessoal*. The main rule on *SA*s (and on *sociedades em comandita por acções*) states that five members are required for incorporation, but an *SA* or *SpQ* wholly owned by another *SA* may be incorporated by a unilateral act.

The principal rules applicable to the formation of all types of companies are:
- the company name must first be authorized by the *Registo Nacional de Pessoas Colectivas;*
- the *contrato de sociedade* must be drawn up in writing and the signatures of the parties notarized (until Decree-Law 76-A/2006 the *contrato de sociedade* generally had to consist of a notarial deed)
- the company must be registered with the relevant Commercial Registry;
- the *contrato de sociedade* must be published on an official internet site as well as in an ordinary newspaper;
- legal personality results from final registration.

The content of the *contrato de sociedade* required by the CSC is very similar to the minimum requirement of the 2nd European Directive.

The cash contributions of the founders of the *SA* and of the *SpQ* must be deposited with a bank prior to the "*contrato de sociedade*". In these types of companies, contributions in kind must be valued by a chartered accountant, according to rules transposing the 2nd European Directive.

The formation of a company is traditionally quite time-consuming and all measures taken so far to speed up the process have enjoyed only limited success. In July 2005, a law was published enabling the formation of the *SA* and the *SpQ* in a single day, provided a number of conditions are met. Under these rules, as long as the parties are willing to adopt a text of a *contrato de sociedade* corresponding to an officially approved model, the powers to carry out all the formalities required lie with the Commercial Registry. Establishing a name for the company under these rules is easy, as pre-approved names are available to those who choose this alternative route. However, these rules do not apply if there are contributions in kind or if the formation of the company (because of its purpose) is subject to any form of authorization.

### 6.2 *Capital*

All companies must have a fixed capital determined by the articles of association (the sole theoretical possible exception being *sociedades em nome colectivo* without capital contributions).

The CSC extends to all types of commercial companies many of the rules that the 2nd European Directive establishes for the *SA*. It would therefore be pointless to elaborate on this subject and we shall only address some of the particulars of Portuguese law.

First, the minimum capital required. For the *SA* and *sociedades em comandita por acções,* the minimum is € 50,000 and for the *SpQ* it is € 5,000. No similar requirement exists for *sociedades em nome colectivo* or for *sociedades em comandita simples.*

The percentage of the capital that must be paid up on execution of the *contrato de sociedade* is 30% for the *SA* and 50% for the *SpQ*.

Increases and decreases in capital are considered special cases of amendment of the articles of association, subject to the provisions generally applicable to such amendments and to other specific rules.

The capital may be increased by means of new contributions or through capitalization of reserves. The capital may be reduced to adjust it to the actual equity of the company or to pay back to the members a part of their contributions. In the latter case, the operation is subject to a judicial authorization.

In capital increases by means of new cash contributions, the members of the *SA* and the *SpQ* have subscription rights. The exclusion of such rights is feasible through a resolution of the general meeting on the grounds of the "interest of the company".

A curiosity suggestive of Portuguese economic problems is the fact that until January 2005 provisions concerning the transposition of Article 17 of the 2$^{nd}$ Directive (on "serious loss of the subscribed capital") were not in force. After completion of a tortuous path, a rule was adopted on this date corresponding to the softest solution admitted by the European rule.

### 6.3 *Resolutions of the members*

In its general part, the CSC allows resolutions of the members of the companies to be adopted either at the general meeting *(assembleia geral)* or without such a meeting, if all members agree in writing with the contents of the resolution. This means that not all resolutions of the members of companies are adopted at general meetings. For the sake of simplicity of language, over the following pages we shall speak only about resolutions adopted at general meetings, but these references are to be interpreted as encompassing all kinds of resolutions of company members (except where otherwise indicated or implied).

The formalities for convening the general meeting *(stricto sensu)* vary depending on the type of company. In the case of the *SpQ*, the means of convening is by registered letter (with advance notice of at least 15 days) and in case of the *SA* the means are publication on an official internet site (from 1 January 2006 onwards) as well as in a ordinary newspaper (with advance notice of at least one month). However, if all shares are registered shares, the articles of association may stipulate that general meetings are convened by registered letter or (pursuant to Decree-Law 76-A/2006) even by e-mail (with advance notice of at least 21 days).

The convening formalities may be avoided if all members take part in the general meeting and agree to hold the meeting without observing such formalities.

For the *SpQ*, the *CSC* also allows resolutions to be adopted by circular, but this proceeding is not used in practice.

Other particulars concerning resolutions of the members shall be given in the specific sections on the *SA* and the *SpQ*.

### 6.4 *Liability of the members of the company for its debts*

Members of the *SA* and of the *SpQ* are not liable for the debts of the company, once the company is registered. However members of the *SpQ* are liable for the payment of the contributions of the other members. Portuguese law also enables that the articles of association of a *SpQ* state that one or more of its members are liable for the debts of the company but this possibility is not used in practice. Members of *sociedades em nome colectivo* and the *comanditados* of *sociedades em comandita* are jointly and severally liable for the debts of the companies – but such liability can only be enforced following enforcement of the liability of the company.

### 6.5 *Liability of the directors and of other persons entrusted with control of management and with auditing*

The *CSC* rules both the liability of the directors towards the company and liability of the directors towards the creditors of the company.

The main rules of the *CSC* on the liability of directors to the company are (more onerous since Decree-Law 76-A/2006) as follows:
- liability depends on the violation of duties deriving from law or the articles of association;
- liability depends on intention or negligence, the burden of proof (of the non-existence of intention or negligence) falling on the directors concerned;

- there is no liability if the relevant act was performed in accordance with a resolution of the general meeting;
- the directors involved are jointly and severally liable;
- proceedings to enforce such liability may be started by the company, upon a resolution of the general meeting or (for the benefit of the company) by any shareholder owning 5% or more of the capital.

Portuguese authors continue to discuss the extent to which the law imposes a general duty of good management on *administradores* and *directores*.

The main rules of the *CSC* on the liability of directors to the creditors of the company are as follows:
- liability depends of the violation of legal rules or contractual provisions designed to protect the creditors;
- liability exists only when the assets of the company become insufficient to satisfy its creditors;
- liability exists even if the relevant acts of the directors have been performed in accordance with a resolution of the general meeting and may not be excluded by any act of the company.

Members of the boards charged with the auditing are jointly and severally liable with the directors involved, both to the company and to the creditors whenever the damage would not have occurred if they had fulfilled their duties. They can also be independently liable under terms similar to those applicable to the directors.

Chartered accountants are also liable to the company and to the creditors of the company according to rules similar to those applicable to the directors.

### 6.6 *Right to information*

The right to information is hardly dealt with in the general part of *CSC,* but the Code has provisions on this subject for each type of company. In the *SpQ*, each member has a strong right to demand information. In the *SA*, the contents of this right depend on the percentage of the shareholding. Only shareholders (or groups of shareholders) with 10% or more of the capital may demand information not disclosed in the financial statements and other documents made public by the company.

### 6.7 *Amendment of the articles of association*

The *CSC* governs the amendment of the articles of association both in the general part and in each of the parts dedicated to the specific types of companies. Rules included in the general part address mainly the formal requirements for all amendments and general aspects of increases and decreases of capital.

### 6.8 *Merger and division*

The CSC governs the merger and division of companies, applying to all types of companies the solutions set out by the 3rd and the 6th European Directives for public limited liability companies. Decree-Law 76-A/2006 has simplified the relevant proceedings, which were previously very bureaucratic and time-consuming.

### 6.9 *Dissolution and liquidation*

Under Portuguese law, the voluntary winding-up of companies consists in principle of three steps: dissolution, liquidation and the division of assets. When the company has no liabilities the liquidation can be avoided and the division of assets may take place simultaneously with dissolution.

The main causes of dissolution are:
– a resolution of the members;
– if the articles of association limit the duration of the company, expiry of the stipulated period;
– a judicial declaration of insolvency

Liquidation is carried out by liquidators, whose main duties are to collect debts, to turn assets into cash, to honour the obligations of the company and to prepare the division of the surplus. The general meeting may authorize the liquidators to continue the business of the company temporarily.

### 6.10 *Groups of companies*

Portugal belongs to the short list of the countries where groups of companies are governed by private law. As we have already seen, Part VI of the CSC is devoted to *sociedades coligadas,* a (not successful and not commonly used) translation of the German expression *verbundene Unternehmen.*

This concept encompasses different scenarios for affiliated companies, ascribing duties and liabilities, which increase in line with the power of the relevant company over the other. A company that owns 100% of another company is liable for its debts.

## 7. Sociedades anónimas

As mentioned above, we shall now address some particulars of the *SA*, beginning with their management and supervision, not only because the rules on these subjects are the most relevant from a practical point of view, but also because these rules reveal some degree of originality.

### 7.1 *Management and supervision*

Prior to the enactment of Decree-Law 76-A/2006, the CSC already permitted more than one management and supervision model for *SA*. One of these models, corresponding to the Portuguese tradition, consisted of a board of directors (or in some cases of a single director) and a board of auditors (or a single auditor). The other model, inspired by the German system of *Aufsichtsrat* and *Vorstand*, consisted of a supervisory board (*conselho geral*) and a board of directors (or in some cases of a single director).

Sometimes the first model was described as a one-tier system of management, contrasting with the second, characterized as a two-tier system of management. Indeed, the first model envisaged the possibility of dividing the directors into "executive" and "non-executive" and could therefore accommodate a two-tier system of management.

Following the enactment of Decree-Law 76-A/2006, the CSC is even more generous in the range of models it offers for structuring the management and supervision of SA. The Code itself says that it offers three models, but in reality the following eight possibilities exist:

- single director (*administrador*) and single auditor (*fiscal único*) – necessarily a chartered accountant;
- single director and board of auditors (*conselho fiscal*) – comprising at least one chartered accountant;
- board of directors (*conselho de administração*) and single auditor – necessarily a chartered accountant;
- board of directors and board of auditors – comprising at least one chartered accountant);
- board of directors, board of auditors and chartered accountant (*revisor oficial de contas*);
- board of directors, auditing committee (*comissão de auditoria*) and chartered accountant;
- executive board of directors, supervisory board (*conselho geral e de supervisão*) and chartered accountant;
- single director, supervisory board and chartered accountant.

Models including a single director are permitted only in companies where the capital does not exceed € 200,000.

Listed companies and companies with "big figures" must adopt one of the models in which there is a chartered accountant acting out of any board of the company. In these companies, some (and in some cases the majority) of the members of the board of auditors, of the auditing committee and of the committee of the supervisory board charged with "financial matters" must be independent from the shareholders.

The main differences between models including *conselho geral e de supervisão* and the others are:

- when there is no *conselho geral e de supervisão*, the *administradores* must be elected by the general meeting, whilst when there is *conselho geral e de supervisão* this power belongs in principle to this board, although the articles of association may ascribe it to the general meeting;
- when there is a *conselho geral e de supervisão*, all directors must be executive, whilst when there is no *conselho geral e de supervisão* the board of directors may be divided into executive and non-executive members;
- the articles of association may give the *conselho geral e de supervisão* powers to intervene in management matters, prohibiting the *administradores* from acting in some matters without the consent of the *conselho geral e de supervisão*, whilst similar powers may not be given to the *conselho fiscal*.

Legal entities may be elected to the *conselho de administração* and to the *conselho geral e de supervisão*, but such entities must designate individuals to hold the office in question, and the persons so designated "hold office in their own name". The members of the *conselho fiscal* must be individuals, with two exceptions: law firms and firms of chartered accountants.

The *conselho de administração* must have a chairman, who is however is a mere *primus inter pares*.

The term of office of all members of the boards of management and supervision is limited to a maximum period of four years, although this term is renewable without limitation.

Pursuant to the amendments carried out by Decree-Law 76-A/2006, meetings of the boards of management and supervision of *SA* may take place with recourse to telematic means.


### 7.2 General Meeting

The main responsibilities of the general meeting of shareholders of *sociedades anónimas* are:
- to amend the articles of association;
- to decide on the allocation of results;
- to approve the annual accounts;

- to make an annual assessment of the management of the company; and
- to elect and dismiss the *administradores* except if there is a *conselho geral e de supervisão,* in which case, as mentioned above, this responsibility may be ascribed either to the general meeting or to such *conselho geral e de supervisão.*

The general meeting may not take decisions on management issues unless the management body requests it to do so.

The general meeting of an *SA* has a kind of permanent subbody, called the *mesa da assembleia geral,* composed of at least a chairperson and a secretary. Convening and conducting meetings falls within the powers of the chairperson. It is also the chairperson who, together with the secretary, drafts and signs the minutes of the meetings.

Pursuant to amendments of Decree-Law 76-A/2006, the general meetings of *SA* may also be held using telematics.

### 7.3 *Shares and their transfer inter vivos*

The capital of an *SA* is divided into shares *(acções)* with a minimum par value of € 0.01 each.

Shares can be either registered shares or bearer shares and both can be represented by certificates or electronically.

The articles of association may provide for different classes of shares, including non-voting preference shares.

In the absence of any clause on this matter in the articles of association, shares are freely transferable. However, the articles of association may restrict the transfer of shares, *inter alia* subordinating it to the consent of the company or ascribing a right of first refusal to the other shareholders.

The formalities for the transfer of shares vary depending on whether they are represented by certificates or electronically and whether they are registered shares or bearer shares. In any case, these formalities are intended to facilitate the speed of the transactions.

## 7.4 *Amendment of the articles of association*

The main specific rules on the amendment of the articles of association of the *SA* are as follows:

– powers for amendment lie with the general meeting, but the articles of association may ascribe to the management body authority concurrent with that of the general meeting to increase the capital by contributions in cash, provided that such authority is limited in terms of value and time;

– resolutions on the amendment of the articles of association require two thirds of the votes cast; and

– in principle, the general meeting may only decide on the amendment of the articles of association if the votes of the shareholders participating in the meeting correspond to at least one third of the total votes; such requirement, however is not applicable if the general meeting is convened for a second time for the same purpose.

## 8. Sociedades por quotas

Moving on to the particulars of the *SpQ*, we shall address the same issues considered above in connection with the *SA*, in order to provide a comparative framework.

## 8.1 *Management and its supervision*

*SpQ* have one or more directors *(gerentes),* entrusted with the management and representation of the company. Only individuals (either shareholders or third parties) may be appointed directors.

The term of the office of the *gerentes* is open-ended, unless otherwise stipulated in the articles of association or in the resolution of election. The articles of association may attribute to the *gerentes* a special right to their office.

The articles of association may provide for the existence of a *conselho fiscal*, to which the rules on the same body in the *SA* are applicable.

Using the possibility presented by Article 51/2, of the 4th Directive, the *CSC* excuses those *SpQ* that do not exceed certain figures for balance sheet total, net turnover and number of employees from the requirement of auditing accounts.

## 8.2 *General meeting*

The main responsibilities of the general meeting of *sociedades por quotas* are:
- to amend the articles of association;
- to approve the annual accounts;
- to decide on the allocation of results;
- to make an annual assessment of the management of the company; and
- to elect and to dismiss the directors.

Unless the articles of association attribute the relevant powers to the *gerentes*, the general meeting has the power to take decisions on important transactions, *e.g.* transfer of immovable property and acquisition of holdings in other companies.

Powers to convene meetings lie with the directors. The chair of the meetings belongs to the holder of highest stake of capital. The minutes of the meetings must be signed by all the participants.

## 8.3 *Quotas and their transfer* inter vivos

The capital of an *SpQ* is divided into *quotas* (a concept that corresponds to the German concept of *Anteile*). The minimum par value of each *quota* is € 100,000.

*Quotas* may not be represented by certificates.

All members of the *SpQ* must have voting rights, which in principle are proportional to the par values of their *quotas*. *CSC* allows the articles of association to ascribe double voting rights to certain *quotas* on the condition that these do not correspond to more than 20% of the capital (but this possibility is seldom used).

The articles of association may regulate the transfer of *quotas,* making it free or restricting it. In the absence of any clause on this matter in the articles of association, the transfer of *quotas* depends on the consent of the company, to be given by the members in a general meeting, unless it is a transfer between members, a transfer between a member and his spouse or a transfer between a member and a person who belongs to his or her direct family line.

The transfer of *quotas* must be in writing and must be subsequently registered with the Commercial Registry (traditionally the transfer of *quotas* required a notarial deed, but Decree-Law 76-A/2006 abolished this requirement).

### 8.4 *Amendments of the articles of association*

The main rules on the amendment of the articles of association of an *SpQ* are as follows:
- powers for amendment lie at all times with the general meeting; and
- resolutions on the amendment of the articles of association require the votes of three quarters of the votes corresponding to the total capital (or more if the articles of association so require).

## 9. Future trends

The future of Portuguese company law will of course reflect the evolution of EU law on the subject. In any case, we can attempt to predict a number of tendencies.

Concern about corporate governance will continue to be reflected in greater regulation of public companies. Globalization will require corporate mobility and the appearance of transnational types of companies (of which the European Company is a mere forerunner). The digital world will require the replacement of formalities. The attempt to render Portuguese rules more "competition friendly" will lead to alterations to the current rules on *SA* and *SpQ*, perhaps through the creation of a simplified sub-type of *SA*, as implemented in other countries and as is currently being discussed at the level of European law.

## Bibliography

Coutinho de Abreu, Jorge Manuel, *Curso de Direito Comercial*, vol. II, "Das Sociedades", Coimbra, 2002. Ferrer Correia, António, *Lições de Direito Comercial*, vol. II, "Sociedades Comerciais, Doutrina Geral", Coimbra, 1968 (cyclo-styled). Menezes Cordeiro, António, *Manual de Direito das Sociedades I*, "Das Sociedades em Geral", Coimbra, 2004. Oliveira Ascensão José, *Direito Comercial*, vol. IV, "Sociedades Comerciais", (cyclo-styled), Lisbon, 1993. Pereira de Almeida, António, *Sociedades Comerciais*, 3rd ed., Coimbra, 2003. Pinto Furtado, Jorge, *Curso de Direito das Sociedades*, 5th ed., Coimbra, 2004. Ventura, Raul, (Several books under the generic name) *Comentário ao Código das Sociedades Comerciais*, Coimbra, 1987-1994.

# CHAPTER 20
# Labour Law

José João Abrantes

SUMMARY: *1. Introduction 2. Brief historical background 3. The current crossroads and the outlook for labour law*

## 1. Introduction

**1.1** The scope of labour law focuses on subordinated and remunerated labour.

The basis is the labour contract, "through which a person obliges himself/herself to provide his/her activity against remuneration to another/other person(s) under his/her/their authority and guidance" [Article 10 of the *Código do Trabalho* (Labour Code), hereinafter referred to as LC].

Under this contract the employee concedes the availability of his/her labour against a salary and places himself/herself under the authority and guidance of the employer who may give him/her orders and set out guidelines and instructions concerning the "where, how and when" of the provision of labour. On the other hand, within certain legal constraints (and in particular the contractual objective of the contracted activity) the employee owes obedience to the employer "as regards everything that concerns the execution and discipline of the job", except where these orders and instructions are revealed to be contrary to his/her rights and guarantees (Article 121/1/d of the LC).

This entrusting of a person "to the authority and guidance" of (an)other person(s) confers singularity upon the labour contract and distinguishes it from the rendering of a service, the legal form of autonomous remunerated labour.

As in any contractual relationship, besides the main obligations of providing and remunerating the respective activity, the contract also imposes other obligations on the employee and the employer, both through requirements stated in the law as well as through undetermined concepts, with prominence being given to the general principle of good faith when honouring the contract (Articles 334 and 762/2 of the Civil Code and 119 of the LC), which requires that all parties in a contractual relationship heed the purposes of the counterpart to which the contract is instrumental and show them due consideration (in other words, as far as their satisfaction depends on compliance with the stated obligation) when carrying out the contractual programme.

**1.2** Not all subordinated labour falls within the scope of labour law, only that which is provided in fulfilment of a labour contract. Labour provided by civil servants, although subordinated, is excluded from the sphere of labour law and is subject to administrative law. However, the division between public law and private law when regulating labour is gradually disappearing as the regime of public legal relationships is becoming more and more permeable to the penetration of principles and procedures from labour legislation.

**1.3** On the other hand, it should be mentioned that due to legitimate social considerations, attempts are being made to extend the protection provided by labour legislation to certain employees who are legally not subordinated but are economically dependent and to whom the concept of weak contractual party as described in the legislation can be ascribed. Several pieces of legislation have, up to a certain point, assimilated or compared these situations with those of subordinated labour. This applies to working at home or handicrafts, to which the Portuguese legislator, in line with other legislators, has granted a regime in accordance with Article 13 of the LC.

## 2. Brief historical background

**2.1** Labour law made a late appearance in Portugal, which is understandable considering the slow pace of industrial development. The regulation of "remunerated service" (predecessor of the labour contract) in the 1867 Portuguese Civil Code (Articles 1391–1395) is based on the fiction of full equality between the parties, with no clear differentiation from the "provision of service contract". Strikes and lock-outs were forbidden by the Penal Codes of both 1852 and 1886.

Between the 1850s and 1870s, the country experienced trade and industrial development hand in hand with the creation of various class associations, the initiation of strikes as a form of industrial action, and the circulation of socialist ideals, etc. However, the State began to intervene in labour relationships in the last decade of the 19th century, primarily due to the development of labour organizations and class struggle that had already manifested itself. The Decree of 10 February 1890, concerning female and child labour, and the Bill of 9 May 1891, concerning trade unions, date from this period. Before this, on 14 August 1889, a Decree created a specialized labour authority (regulated by 3 decrees of 19 March 1891) – the so-called *tribunais de árbitros-avindores* (Courts of Labour Arbitration).

It was already in the 20th century that a Decree of 3 August 1907 instituted the concept of 24-hours rest in the consecutive working week (only for commerce and industry).

**2.2** The 1st Republic was characterized by great legislative progress; in particular a Decree of 6 December 1910 regarding strikes and the Law No. 83 of 24 July 1913 (work-related accidents) and Law No. 494 of 16 March 1916 (creating the Ministry of Labour and Social Security). The enormous expansion of the labour movement at the time provided an impetus to this legislation.

The creation of the International Labour Organization in 1919 triggered an impressive flow of legislative instruments, in particular Decree No. 5.616 of 7 May 1919 concerning the duration of work in the civil service, commerce and industry.

On 27 December 1924, Decree No. 10.415 recognized the right to collective bargaining.

**2.3** The *Estado Novo* (New State), based on the idea of a corporative state, undertook production of legislation on a vast scale, anchored and informed by the principles laid down in the Constitution of 1933 and by the *Estatuto do Trabalho Nacional* [National Labour Statute (Decree-Law No. 23.048 of 23 September 1933): proscription of class struggle (Articles 35 and 39 of the Constitution) and solidarity between capital and labour beseeching social peace and mutual cooperation (Articles 11, 5 and 22 of the *NLS*)].

This led to a clear distortion of collective rights that culminated in: the imposition of exclusive trade unions (Decree-Law No. 23.050 of 23 September 1933), the prohibition of strikes and lock-outs (Decree-Law No: 23.870 of 18 March 1934) and the initial prohibition and later limitation (subject to administrative control) of collective bargaining (Decree-Laws No. 36.173 of 6 March 1947 and No. 43.182 of 23 September 1960).

On the other hand, legislation concerning individual rights revealed susceptibility to other European countries' doctrine and jurisprudence. On 10 March 1937, the first legal regime governing the labour contract was published, the famous Law No. 1.952, which remained in force until 1966.

The final years of the regime saw a certain liberalization at the trade union level, allowing for considerable development of trade union action within the corporative unions themselves along with a growing strike movement. The regime tried to modernize itself in response to the pressures from Portuguese capitalism, which generated the following legislation: the LCT [Labour Contract Law (Decree-Law No. 47.032 of 27 May 1966, afterwards substituted by Decree-Law No. 49.408 of 24 November 1969)]; the Law on the Duration of Work (Decree-Law No. 409/71 of 27 September 1971); Decree-Law No. 49.212 of 28 August 1969 concerning collective bargaining; and Law No. 2.127 of 3 August 1965 regulated by Decree-Law No. 360/71 of 21 August 1971, concerning work-related accidents and professional illnesses.

**2.4** The "25 April 1974" [the day on which a military coup replaced the almost 50 year-old autocratic regime (*Estado Novo*) in Portugal with a parliamentary democracy] rang in a new era for Portuguese labour law. In the immediate aftermath of the revolution job security and limitations on employers' discretional power were assumed as objectives of legislative policy, above all reflected in the laws concerning the cessation of the labour contract. Except for some features, most objectives can be aligned with a generalized legislative movement that dominated Western legislation at the time, mainly distinguished by restrictions on the liberty of employers regarding unilateral dismissal.

Over recent years we have seen great changes in the legislative policies regarding labour, in a movement towards deregulation, favouring technical and organizational priorities, in particular those related to the efficiency of the production process, not only in Portugal but in many other countries. Whilst initially presented as temporary measures to deal with an emergency situation, these changes were then later assumed as independent from the setting in which they had been framed and inserted into the objectives of neo-liberal-type legislative policies. We think we can safely affirm that these objectives formed the basis for the present Labour Code (approved by Law No. 99/2003 of 27 August 2003) and the respective Regulation (Law No. 35/2004 of 29 July 2004).

## 3. The current crossroads and the outlook for labour law

**3.1** The neo-liberal movement, invoking the inappropriateness of workers' protection and the rigidity of labour legislation, argued for the weakening of the individual and collective rights of employees.

This is essentially the orientation of the Labour Code in which, notwithstanding some occasional benefits for employees, structural changes in the law favour employers.

However, it is not only unfair to blame labour legislation for the deficient functioning of the productive system but also inaccurate to claim that the essence and social role of this field of law has lost its purpose. If one agrees with the mere adjustment of certain legal norms to new conditions that are perfectly compatible with the traditional philosophy of this field of law, one has to disagree, in our opinion, with everything leading to a subversion of the fundamental principles and values of traditional legal regulation, in particular when bearing in mind the social role ascribed by the Constitution.

The protectionist and special character of this field of law is still justified; even today labour relations consist of relationships between parties with asymmetric powers, a relationship of power-subjection, in which the liberty of one of the parts may appear vulnerable to the stronger economic and social power of the other.

The clear differences between the powers of employers and of employees form the basis of not only the current legislation but also of the relevance the Constitution grants to employees' rights.

The Constitution contains the fundamental principles of labour law and is (also) the supreme source of this branch of law, where the labour relationship is conditioned by values that grant constitutional dignity to matters concerning the grand issues of labour law, *i.e.* respect for labour-related fundamental rights, in particular for collective rights.

**3.2** The Labour Code strayed from these concerns and in many cases took an opposing stance to that which followed from constitutional requirements. Although one can find some sporadic benefits for employees – e.g. the recognition of the plurality of employers (Article 92) or the express pronouncement of the applicability of the general regime for contracts to labour contracts (Article 96) – in our opinion the philosophy underlying this legislation deserves severe criticism in itself, as it seems to rely on a concept of the individual, society and the State that ignores the fact that legislation protecting the employee is an integral part of modern democracy.

Employers' powers were reinforced in the domain of individual rights, in favour of a flexibility concept that considers these individual rights as a mere discretionary power of corporate management, leading to precarious job security, variable working hours, and geographical and functional mobility of employees, etc.

In some of these important matters (e.g. mobility), where the role of the law in establishing minimum requirements for protection is imperative, it is even accepted that this protection may be removed by individual agreement (Articles 314/2, 315/3 and 316/2).

Significant changes were also introduced with regard to dismissal. The possibility of re-opening disciplinary proceedings in cases of unlawful dismissal, due to nullification of the proceedings (Article 436/2) and (partial) non-compliance with the principle of reintegration of the employee (Articles 438/2 and 3, and 439/4 and 5) is controversial even from a constitutional point of view. Furthermore these changes could be in conflict with the constitutional guarantee of job security that, in our opinion, implies the nullification of dismissals without just cause and the subsequent right of the employee to reintegration.

Regarding collective rights, the LC weakened the collective dimension of the labour relationship, in particular when it depreciates the role of collective conventions as an instrument of social progress and imposes expiration of rights (Article 557), increases administrative intervention in collective conflicts, as seen in the case of obligatory arbitrage (Article 567 et seq.) or in the provision of minimum levels of service during strikes (Article 559), etc.

Article 4 of the LC is a crucial element that reformulates the principle of a more favourable treatment of employees. According to this article – and unlike the legal regime established in Article 13/1 of the old LCT – legal norms can be disregarded, provided this does not result in the converse of the norm. The non-application of the law is only permitted when more favourable conditions for the employee are established. This raises doubts concerning its constitutionality in light of the right of collective bargaining as a fundamental workers' right ingrained in a State of democratic law (the so-called *Estado de direito democrático*).

**3.3** These are three inter-related matters (amongst others) that we consider important enough not to be overlooked in the revision of the Code that was announced by the new Government voted into office in February 2005.

Neo-liberal logic does not stem from Portuguese fundamental law. The Portuguese Constitution clearly places respect for workers' rights as the cornerstone of labour law, without overlooking or underestimating the importance of a minimum of flexibility that all productive systems need. This respect should be upheld above other aims and values such as profitability, economic rationality, etc.

The road to the modernization of labour legislation should match the civil rights of workers with the capacity of companies to adjust to the demands of ever-increasing competitiveness, while recognizing that these rights should have a primordial role in linking social progress with economic growth.

The great challenge for today's labour law is the rediscovery of its fundamental purpose; the achievement of social justice for all, in a movement towards full citizenship, in other words a citizenship that is not only civil and political but also economic, social and cultural. Indeed, as Pierre Mauroy said some years ago, "reconciling the economic with the social is a demand that no modern nation can avoid, because ... there is no productive efficiency without the promotion of the world of labour, without the recognition of its aspirations and its rights. There is no freedom of enterprise without freedom in the enterprise".

## Bibliography

ABRANTES, José João, *Direito do Trabalho. Relatório*, Coimbra, 2003. Idem, *Estudos sobre o Código do Trabalho*, Coimbra, 2004. Idem, *Contrato de trabalho e direitos fundamentais*, Coimbra, 2005. LEITE, Jorge, *Direito do Trabalho*, vol. I, Coimbra, 1998 (reprinted 2001), vol. II, Coimbra, 1999. LOBO XAVIER, Bernardo, *Curso de Direito do Trabalho*, 3rd ed., Lisbon, 2004. MONTEIRO FERNANDES, António, *Direito do Trabalho*, 12th ed., Coimbra, 2004. ROMANO MARTINEZ, Pedro, *Direito do Trabalho*, Coimbra, 2002.

# CHAPTER 21
# Private International Law

EUGÉNIA GALVÃO TELES
MARIA HELENA BRITO

SUMMARY: *1. Sources 2. The choice of law process in general 3. Specific choice of law rules 4. Conclusions and future developments*

## 1. Sources

National statutes remain the main source of private international law in Portugal. The core rules are codified in the 1966 Portuguese Civil Code (*Código Civil*). Chapter III – *Rights of Foreigners and Conflict of Laws* – of the first title of the Code's first Book begins by setting out a number of rules that generally govern the choice of law process. Subsequently, under the heading *Choice of Law Rules*, one finds several specific choice of law rules on various topics: personal law, obligations, property, family law and succession.

The Civil Code (hereinafter, CC) is not exhaustive, and additional rules are to be found in other codes such as the Companies Code (*Código das Sociedades Comerciais*), the Securities Code (*Código dos Valores Mobiliários*), the Copyright and Related Rights Code (*Código do Direito de Autor e dos Direitos Conexos*), the Industrial Property Code (*Código da Propriedade Industrial*), the Employment Law Code (*Código do Trabalho*) and the Insolvency Code (*Código da Insolvência e da Recuperação de Empresas*). Besides these, rules relevant to the choice of law process may be founded in various scattered statutes.

International conventions are also a significant source of private international law rules. In view of the fact that Article 8/2 of the Portuguese Constitution provides for the automatic recognition of international conventions, the rules contained therein are applicable as such and take precedence over the relevant national provisions. The most important convention on conflicts is the 1980 Rome Convention on the Law Applicable to Contractual Obligations. Additionally, some Hague Conventions on choices of law are applicable in Portugal.

More recently, there has been an increase in European Union legislation concerned with private international law issues in general and the choice of law process in particular. This phenomenon has generated quite a number of conflict rules, which have originated more or less directly from Community acts – Directives and, increasingly, Regulations. When applying the above-mentioned rules, a number of decisions taken by Portuguese courts should be considered. Regarding Community rules, the case law of the European Court of Justice may be relevant. In order to gain a proper perspective on the legal development one also has to consider the work of commentators.

The present text is restricted to the description of the choice of law process, and does not examine the rules on jurisdiction. These rules are, however, critical, as they decide whether a Portuguese court has international jurisdiction. Portuguese courts have jurisdiction if so provided by national rules, Community regulations or international conventions. All rules on jurisdiction are fixed and definite; there is no room to decline jurisdiction because of *forum non conveniens*. The main rules on international jurisdiction are to be found in Regulation 44/2001 on Jurisdiction and Enforcement of Judgments in Civil and Commercial Matters, and, where this regulation does not apply, in the Portuguese Civil Procedure Code (*Código de Processo Civil*) – Articles 65 and 65-A.

As for foreign judgments, there are provisions for their automatic recognition in a Community context, namely under Regulation 44/2001 referred to above. Where this Regulation does not apply, foreign judgments are subject to recognition and enforcement proceedings, as described in Articles 1094 to 1102 of the Civil Procedure Code.

The Portuguese Voluntary Arbitration Act (*Lei da Arbitragem Voluntária*) contains a section on international arbitration (Articles 32 to 35). Article 33 refers specifically to the law to be applied by the arbitrators to the substance of the dispute. As Portugal is a party to the 1958 New York Convention on the Recognition and Enforcement of Foreign Arbitral Awards, the rules contained therein regulate the recognition and enforcement of *foreign* – in the sense of the Convention – arbitral awards.

## 2. The Choice of Law Process in General

### 2.1 *General Features*

The Portuguese system of choice of law is largely composed of traditional rules based on a bilateral model. They are also classical rules, in the sense that they typically use a localization process to establish the proper law. They are not, in general, *policy* or *materially-oriented rules*, even if it is possible to identify some alternative rules that are more or less inspired by the *better law* approach.

Whilst the *closest connection* appears as a vital guiding principle, the majority of the choice of law rules employ fixed connecting factors, more or less detailed, and not open-ended references. Nevertheless there is a trend towards more flexible solutions, in particular in rules that originated in the Community.

The Portuguese conflicts system tends also to be rather analytical. Due to this characteristic, a case involving foreign elements frequently gives rise to a plurality of issues requiring the application of different choice of law rules.

### 2.2 *Characterization*

The introduction of an express rule on characterization is one of the most notable solutions of the 1966 CC. Article 15 establishes that the reference to a law comprises only those substantive rules that, according to their content and function in that law, correspond to the legal category referred to in the choice of law rule.

This rule introduces the so-called *selective reference* solution, by establishing that a choice of law rule does not refer to all material rules of the designated law, but only to those which correspond in content and function to the category used by the choice of law rule. Moreover, under this rule the process of characterization is to be performed in accordance with the *lex causae*, as it states that the applicable substantive rules take sense from the system to which they belong, even if the *lex fori* is essential when interpreting the legal category referred in the choice of law rule. It seems clear that Article 15 maintains a fairly flexible approach towards characterization.

### 2.3 *Renvoi*

The Portuguese rules on *renvoi* (Articles 17 to 19 of the CC) result in quite a complex scheme. Notwithstanding the affirmation of the exclusion of *renvoi* as the primary rule (Article 16), Portuguese courts are however required to recognize a reference of the foreign conflicts law back to Portuguese law (Article 18/1) or a reference to the law of a third State if, under the conflicts law of this third State, its substantive law is also applicable to the dispute (Article 17/1). This solution is generally justified with reference to the uniformity of decisions principle. The system is furthermore complicated by special restrictive provisions for *renvoi* in matters governed by personal law (Articles 18/2 and 17/2/3).

*Renvoi* ceases when it affects the validity of a transaction or the legitimacy of a status (Article 19/1). There is no *renvoi* in case of choice of law by the parties (Article 19/2). Choice of law conventions generally exclude *renvoi*, as it is the case in the Rome Convention on Contractual Obligations (Article 15).

### 2.4 *Reference to a State with more than one Legal System*

When a rule refers to the law of a person's nationality, and it corresponds to a State comprising several territorially based legal systems, it is necessary to determine the applicable law. In doing so a Portuguese court has to refer to the solutions of the foreign complex legal order itself, or, in their absence, to the legal unit of the law of the person's habitual residence, when situated in the State of its nationality (Article 20/1/2 of the CC). If the habitual residence is not situated in the State of nationality the majority of commentators contend that the court should refer to the legal unit with which the person has the closest connection.

Under Article 19 of the Rome Convention, each territorial unit shall be considered as a country for the purposes of identifying the applicable law.

### 2.5 *Fraudulent Avoidance of the Applicable Law*

The Portuguese CC provides for the intentional manipulation of connecting factors leading to the avoidance of the law that would otherwise apply (Article 21). The sanction is the irrelevance of such manipulation, with the application of the law that would be applicable. This solution is disputable when the fraud refers to a foreign law that does not react to the fraud.

### 2.6 *Incidental or Preliminary Question*

The CC does not deal expressly with the incidental or preliminary question. The majority of commentators support the application of the relevant choice of law rules of the forum to establish the law governing the subsidiary question. Yet, reference may be made to the substantive rules or the choice of law rules of the law applicable to the main issue, in the cases where there is an express provision in this sense.

### 2.7 *Application of a Foreign Law: Ascertainment, Interpretation and Proof of the Foreign Law*

When the choice of law rules refer to a foreign law, the foreign law is a matter of law, not of fact. Hence, it shall be ascertained and applied *ex officio* by the court, even if the assistance of the parties is required (Article 348 of the CC).

The foreign law is to be construed as such, i.e. according to its own canons of interpretation (Article 23/1 of the CC). If the court is unable to establish the contents of the foreign law, it must have recourse to the subsidiary connecting factors, if any, before reverting to its own domestic rules (Article 23/2).

## 2.8 *Exclusion of Foreign Law. Public Policy Exception and Internationally Mandatory Rules*

Once ascertained, the foreign law may be excluded if it is deemed to violate fundamental principles of Portuguese public policy (Article 22/1 of the CC). Before reverting to the application of its own law, the court must however try to bring the foreign law into conformity with Portuguese public policy, whether by disregarding the offensive rules or by applying more appropriate foreign rules (Article 22/2).

The rules of the foreign governing law may also be excluded in consequence of the necessary application of certain Portuguese mandatory rules, whenever these apply unilaterally to an international case. The ability to apply the so-called *internationally mandatory rules* of the forum is expressly covered by Article 7/2 of the Rome Convention and other conventions and Community instruments, but it is also generally recognized as a general principle.

More problematic is the issue of the so-called recognition and application of foreign mandatory rules. Although Portugal has made use of the reservation to Article 7/1 of the Rome Convention, which establishes a system of recognition of third country mandatory rules, the Portuguese position is not straightforward. There are a number of scattered rules that provide for the recognition of foreign mandatory rules in specific matters – such as Article 6/5 of the Portuguese Employment Code and Article 16 of the 1978 Hague Convention on Agency. The issue has not been considered in general terms within case law. Recent commentators have tended to accept the interference of foreign mandatory rules in the choice of law process.

## 3. Specific choice of law rules

### 3.1 *The Law of Natural Persons. The Law of Nationality*

The choice of law process relating to natural persons has its starting point in the concept of *personal law* of Article 25 of the CC. This provision does not contain a connecting factor – for the relevant connecting factors, one has to refer to Articles 31/1 and 32 – but describes a set of legal categories composing the scope of the personal law: status and capacity, family relations and succession.

Article 25 is complemented by rules addressing some specific issues relating to natural persons: defining the limits of personality (Article 26), personality rights (Article 27) and the effects of a change in the connecting factor on majority (Article 29). As for family relations and succession, the general provision of Article 25 is to be complemented with Articles 49 to 61 and 62 to 65, respectively.

Portugal still adopts the principle of nationality in personal law matters (Article 31/1). When a person has more than one nationality, Portuguese nationality shall prevail. When both nationalities are foreign, the nationality of the State where the person has his habitual residence, or, when he resides habitually in another State, that of the State with which the person maintains a closer connection – Articles 27 and 28 of the Nationality Act (*Lei da Nacionalidade*) – shall prevail. Some commentators propose that the automatic preference for Portuguese nationality should be limited, so as to allow for the application of a foreign law when there is a manifestly closer connection with the foreign country and a minor connection with Portugal. It is also suggested that Community case law, i.e. the *Micheletti* case (C-369/90), should be considered, resulting in the priority of Member State nationality over non-Community nationality.

There are, however, departures from the principle of nationality, mostly for the benefit of the law of the habitual residence. Habitual residence is the relevant criterion for persons that do not have any nationality (Article 32 of the CC). Similarly, specific choice of law rules refer to the law of the common habitual residence, mostly in the field of family law, where spouses and parents do not have the same nationality. Moreover, under Article 31/2, the Portuguese courts recognize transactions on personal law issues that would be valid in the courts of the habitual residence.

There are also rules that substitute altogether the personal law for other criteria. Article 47 of the CC provides for the *lex situs* to decide on the capacity to constitute or dispose of rights *in rem* over immovable property, if the courts of the *situs* apply their own law to the issue. As for contractual capacity, Article 11 of the Rome Convention implies the substitution of the personal law, normally applicable, by the law of the place of conclusion of the contract when contracts are concluded between persons in the same country, as a party may only invoke his incapacity resulting from another law under an "awareness by the other party" test. There is a parallel provision in Article 28 of the CC for transactions not covered by the Rome Convention.

### 3.2 *Family Law*

The material validity of a marriage is governed by the personal law of each spouse, as it defines the capacity to contract marriage, as well as the effects of lack of consent and/or defective consent (Article 49). Articles 50 and 51 regulate the issue of formal validity, which is normally governed by the law of the place where the marriage is celebrated (Article 50). There are, however, special rules for the marriage of foreigners in Portugal (Article 51/1) and of Portuguese citizens abroad (Article 51/2) before their respective consular agents. Another rule favours recognition of Catholic marriages (Article 51/3).

Marital relationships are generally governed by: the law of the spouses' common nationality; the law of their common habitual residence; or the law of the country with which the family life is most closely connected (Article 52). This choice of law rule is also applicable to separation and divorce, with a restrictive reference to the prior governing law where there is a change of the connecting factor (Article 55/1/2).

As for prenuptial agreements and matrimonial property regimes, Article 53 refers to the law of the common nationality or habitual residence of both spouses. Yet here the relevant moment is the date of the celebration of the marriage and the subsidiary rule refers to the first marital residence (Article 53/1/2). Portuguese rules generally do not recognize party autonomy, but there is a limited admission of choice for the benefit of Portuguese substantive regimes, upon certain conditions (Article 53/3). The ability to modify the matrimonial property regime depends on the law applicable under Article 52, with a special provision to protect third parties (Article 54).

It is for the personal law of the parent to decide upon the establishment of a parent-child relationship (Article 56/1). Special rules apply with reference to the child of a married woman. The connecting factors are, in sequence: the law of the common nationality of the mother and her husband; the law of their common habitual residence; the personal law of the child (Article 56/2). The relevant moment is the time of birth, or that of the termination of marriage, if the latter event occurs first (Article 56/3). Furthermore, it may be necessary to take into account the need for consent, either from the child, a relative or a guardian, under the connecting factors established in Article 61/1/2.

The parent-child relationship is governed by the law of the common nationality of the parents, or by the law of their common habitual residence, or by the personal law of the child, as the case may be (Article 57/1). When there is only one parent, reference is to be made to his personal law (Article 57/2).

The 1961 Hague Convention concerning the Powers of Authorities and the Law Applicable in respect of the Protection of Minors is in force in Portugal. The 1996 Hague Convention on Jurisdiction, Applicable Law, Recognition, Enforcement and Co-operation in respect of Parental Responsibility and Measures for the Protection of Children has been signed but not yet ratified.

Although Article 60/1 states that an adoptive parent's personal law governs adoption, in the case of adoption by married couples, or where a spouse wants to adopt the other spouse's child, the issue is governed by the law of their common nationality or habitual residence, or, in the absence of such, by the law of the country with which the couple has a closest connection (Article 60/2). The personal law of the adoptive parent also governs the adopter-adoptee relationship, as well as the relationship with the original family of the adoptee (Article 60/3).

The application of the governing law is, however, restricted by the law governing the relationship between the adoptee and his parents – Article 60/4. Additionally, consent from the adoptee, or a relative or a guardian, is necessary, if so stipulated by, respectively, the personal law of the adoptee or the law governing the family relationship or the guardianship (Article 61/1/2).

Portugal has signed and already ratified the 1993 Hague Convention on Protection of Children and Co-operation in respect of Intercountry Adoption. It has also approved a specific regulation, along similar lines, on international adoption.

The Hague Conventions on maintenance obligations are in force in Portugal. Special attention may be drawn to Articles 4 to 6 of the 1973 Hague Convention, which establish an alternative choice of law rule favouring the creditor.

### 3.3 *The Law of Succession*

The personal law of the deceased at the time of death generally governs intestate, as well as testate, succession (Article 62).

However, it is for the personal law of the testator at the time of the declaration to decide on his capacity to dispose of property upon death. The same law governs the need for any particular formalities upon acts of disposition made by persons with a certain age (Article 63/1). A subsequent variation of personal law will not affect the testator's capacity to revoke the will (Article 63/2).

The testator's personal law at the time of the declaration also governs the interpretation of the will, in the absence of an express indication request for the application of another law, the existence and validity of consent, as well as the admissibility of joint wills or agreements on succession (Article 64).

Formal validity of wills is particularly favoured by way of an extensive alternative rule established in Article 65/1. Attention shall, however, be given to any formal requirements of the testator's personal law that apply irrespective of the place of conclusion of the will (Article 65/2).

Portugal has signed, but not ratified, the 1961 Hague Convention on the Conflicts of Laws relating to the Form of Testamentary Dispositions. It has signed and ratified the 1973 Convention concerning the International Administration of the Estates of Deceased Persons.

### 3.4 *The Law of Contracts*

Choice of law rules for contracts are mainly to be found in the 1980 Convention on the Law Applicable to Contractual Obligations; the national rules – in particular, Articles 41 and 42 of the Civil Code – apply only when the transaction is not covered by the scope of the Convention, as defined in Article 1.

The law chosen by the parties governs the contract. This primary choice of law rule is established both in Article 3/1 of the Rome Convention and Article 41of the CC – even if the latter specifies limits that are absent from the Rome Convention. The choice of law may be expressed or implied, in which case it must be demonstrated with reasonable certainty. There is even an express recognition of the parties' ability to choose different laws for different parts of their contract, although this possibility is generally strictly construed. The parties are also free to change the chosen law or to make a later choice of law (Article 3/2), although this cannot prejudice the contract's formal validity or affect third parties rights.

The Convention does, nonetheless, establish some limits to a party's autonomy. First, choice of law in a purely national contract does not prejudice the application of all mandatory rules of the law to which the contract is exclusively connected (Article 3/3). Choice of law in consumer and employment contracts cannot deprive the consumer and the employee of the protection afforded by the mandatory rules of the law that would apply in the absence of choice (Articles 5/2 and 6/1). Finally, party autonomy may be limited by the application of *internationally mandatory rules*, under Article 7, as outlined above.

In the absence of choice, the contract's proper law is the law of closest connection (Article 4/1 of the Rome Convention). This flexible rule is supplemented by some fixed connecting factors, which are, however, always subject to rebuttal if it appears from the circumstances as a whole that the contract is more closely connected with another country (Article 4/5).

Article 4 contains two special rules: one for contracts relating to rights in immovable property, where the *lex rei sitae* is, in principle, applicable (Article 4/3), and one for certain contracts of carriage, where the Convention refers several connecting factors, each being applicable to different types of contracts of carriage (Article 4/4). In all other cases, under Article 4/2, the contract's closest connection is established with reference to the concept of *characteristic performance*. The characteristic performance is generally understood as the performance of services or provision of goods for which payment is due. It will, therefore, normally correspond to a non-monetary obligation. If the characteristic performance cannot be established, the applicable law is determined by direct application of the closest connection test (Article 4/5). Under Article 4/1, the court may establish that severable and autonomous parts of the contracts have their closest connection with different countries. Such severance is, however, expressly described as exceptional.

When the Rome Convention is not applicable, contracts are governed by the law of the parties' common habitual residence, if any, or in the case of gifts, by the law of the habitual residence of the donor. In all other cases, the law of the place where the contract is concluded prevails (Article 42 of the CC).

The Rome Convention contains a specific alternative rule promoting the formal validity of contracts (Article 9/1/2), and a quite similar rule may be found in Article 36 of the CC. Where the contract concerns rights in immovable property, Article 9/6 of the Rome Convention provides for the application of the *lex situs'* internationally mandatory rules on formal validity.

The scope of the proper law is defined in Article 10 of the Rome Convention. The proper law of the contract governs the existence and validity of the contract or of any contractual term, including a choice of law clause (Article 8/1 of the Rome Convention and Article 35/1 of the CC). Under Article 8/2 of the Rome Convention, a party may, upon certain conditions, rely upon the law of his habitual residence to establish that he did not consent to a contract or contractual term – an analogous rule may be found in Article 35/2 of the CC.

The Rome Convention also contains specific provisions on assignment (Article 12) and subrogation (Article 13).

In addition to these general rules, there are a number of specific rules for particular contracts. The Rome Convention itself provides special rules for consumer contracts (Articles 5 and 9/3) and employment contracts (Article 6, from which Article 6 of the Portuguese Employment Code draws its main inspiration). The main point of those rules is to provide protection for the consumer and employee. It should be noted that, under Community law influence, there are several choice of law rules in scattered statutes relating to consumer and employment contracts.

Agency contracts, as well as non-contractual relationships emerging from agency, are subject to specific choice of law rules, namely under the 1978 Hague Convention on the Law Applicable to Agency, in force in Portugal.

### 3.5 *The Law of Torts*

Non-contractual liability is governed by national choice of law rules, namely Article 45 of the CC, applying to torts, but also to strict liability. The main connecting factor is the place where the harmful event occurred, or where the person liable under the claim should have acted, for torts caused by an omission (Article 45/1). The law of the place of the injury takes the place of the *lex loci delicti commissi*, if the latter does not recognize liability, and liability may be established under the law of the place of the injury (Article 45/2). The application of the law of the place of the injury is subject to a foreseeability test.

Article 45/3 deviates from the *lex loci delicti commissi* for the benefit of the law of the common nationality – or habitual residence – of the person held liable and the victim, when they were only fortuitously abroad. This rule, based on the closest connection principle, is subject to the application of the *lex loci delicti commissi* mandatory rules that are applicable to all persons without distinction.

## 3.6 *The Law of Quasi-Contracts*

*Negotiorum gestio*, or agency without authority, is one possible source of non-contractual obligations arising out of an act other than a tort. When the 1978 Hague Convention on Agency is not applicable, the governing law shall be the law of the country where the principal activities of the "agent" took place (Article 43 of the CC).

As for unjust enrichment, the Civil Code makes use of a somewhat imprecise connecting factor, referring to the "law on which basis the transfer of value to the beneficiary of the enrichment took place" (Article 44). Some commentators advocate the application of the law of a pre-existing relationship between the parties, whenever it exists. This is the solution actually proposed in the Rome II Regulation referred to below.

## 3.7 *Property Law. Copyright and Industrial Property Rights*

Property rights are generally subject to the classical connecting factor of the *lex situs* (Article 46/1 of the CC). There is a special rule for items in transit, which are deemed to be situated at the place of their destination (Article 46/2), and for means of transport subject to registration, governed by the law of the place of registration (Article 46/3).

Copyright is governed by the law of the country where the work was first published, or, in the case of unpublished works, by the personal law of the author (Article 48/1 of the CC). However, in some cases this solution may be affected by the special rules contained in the Copyright and Related Rights Code. Industrial property is, in principle, governed by the law of the place of its creation (Article 48/2 of the CC).

## 3.8 *Company Law*

The personal law of a company or other legal person is the law of the country where the principal and effective seat of its central administration is situated, i.e. the place where its central management and control is exercised (Article 33/1 of the CC). The same connecting factor is adopted by Article 3/1 of the Companies Code.

It is therefore this law that regulates the issues described in Article 33/2: the capacity of the legal person; the formation, operation and authority of its organs; the means by which one acquires or relinquishes the quality of partner or shareholder; the rights and duties corresponding to that quality; the liability of the legal person towards third parties, as well as the liability of its organs and their members; the legal person's transformation, dissolution and extinction; and other questions pertaining to the law of companies. Some commentators argue that the constitution of a company or other legal person is to be ascertained according to the law of its place of incorporation, as this represents the natural solution and the issue is not referred to in Article 33/2.

Under Article 3/1 of the Companies Code, where the company's registered office is in Portugal, the company is barred from relying on a foreign law against third parties, despite the location of its effective central management abroad. This unilateral rule is construed by many commentators as being open to bilateralization, and would apply whenever a company's registered office and its central management are located in different countries.

Under Article 4 of the Companies Code, there are some requirements for companies with a foreign personal law – i.e. whose seat is situated abroad – to do business in Portugal.

Article 33/3 of the CC and Article 3/2/3/4/5 of the Companies Code regulate the issue of the transfer of seat from one country to another and Article 33/4 of the CC refers to the merger of legal persons with different personal laws.

## 4. Conclusions and future developments

A revision of the Portuguese CC is possible, even if it is not likely to take place in the near future.

A revision would probably not involve any major changes to the basic features of the Portuguese choice of law process in general. It is, however, conceivable that the solutions on *renvoi*, currently rather complicated, would be simplified. There is also a chance that the legislator would take the opportunity to clarify the Portuguese position on the recognition and application of foreign mandatory rules, as the present situation leaves room for some uncertainty. For an illustration of the form these new solutions could take, one should refer to the more recent codification of Private International Law rules in the 1999 Macau Civil Code.

It is likely that the modifications will affect the special choice of law rules more significantly, in particular under the influence of Community and international trends.

As for the matters pertaining to so-called *personal law*, it is likely that the principle of nationality will lose some of its current predominance, to the benefit of the law of the habitual residence, as may be gleaned from the proposals in the Commission Green Papers on Succession and Wills [COM(2005) 65 final] and on the Applicable Law and Jurisdiction in Divorce Matters [COM(2005) 82 final]. These Green Papers also reflect a position more favourable to party autonomy, generally ignored by the Portuguese legislator for personal law issues. It also seems probable that the trend towards more materially-oriented solutions in family law will be reflected in new solutions, in particular as regards the establishment of the parent--child relationship, adoption, and maintenance obligations – as suggested in the Commission Green Paper on Maintenance Obligations [COM(2004) 254 final].

It should also be noted that the Rome Convention's solutions may undergo some alterations if the Convention is transformed into a Community Regulation, as proposed in the Commission Green Paper on the Conversion of the Rome Convention of 1980 on the Law Applicable to Contractual Obligations into a Community Instrument and its Modernization (Rome I) [COM(2002) 654 final] and more recently in the Proposal for a Regulation of the European Parliament and the Council on the Law Applicable to Contractual Obligations (Rome I) [COM(2005) 650 final 2005/0261 (COD)].

The national choice of law rules for torts are very likely to be replaced, in the near future, by Community uniform rules, with the advent of the Regulation on the Law Applicable to Non-Contractual Obligations (Rome II) [COM(2003) 427 final 2003/0168 (COD)]. The Regulation will not have a dramatic effect on the general solution, as it refers to the law of the place where the direct damage arises or is likely to arise. There is, however, a general exception clause that introduces some flexibility, on the basis of the *closest connection test*, and a specific reference to a pre-existing relationship under the so-called "secondary connection". Neither of these features are known in the present Portuguese solution. The general rule is also complemented by special rules for particular torts, which will be a clear innovation in Portugal.

## Bibliography

BAPTISTA MACHADO, João, *Lições de direito internacional privado*, 3ª ed., Coimbra, 1985 (reimp.). FERRER CORREIA, António, *Lições de direito internacional privado*, I, Coimbra, 2000. LIMA PINHEIRO, Luís, *Direito internacional privado*, vol. I – *Introdução e direito de conflitos. Parte geral*, Coimbra, 2001; Idem, vol. II – *Direito de conflitos. Parte especial*, 2ª ed., Coimbra, 2002; Idem, vol. III – *Competência internacional e reconhecimento de decisões estrangeiras*, Coimbra, 2002. MARQUES DOS SANTOS, António, *Estudos de direito internacional privado e de direito processual civil internacional*, Coimbra, 1998. MOURA RAMOS, Rui Manuel, *Estudos de direito internacional privado e de direito processual civil internacional*, Coimbra, 2002. MOURA VICENTE, Dário, *Direito internacional privado. Ensaios*, vol. I, Coimbra, 2002, and vol. II, Coimbra, 2005.

CHAPTER 22

# Civil Procedure

José Lebre de Freitas
Mariana França Gouveia

Summary: *1. Brief historical review 2. Sources 3. Fundamental principles 4. Ordinary proceedings in first instance 5. Trends in Portuguese civil procedure*

## 1. Brief historical review

The impetus towards the codification of law, which began in France with Napoleon, reached Portugal some decades later. The first Portuguese Civil Code dates from 1867 and the first Portuguese Civil Procedure Code (CPC) dates from 1876. Both were strongly inspired by French counterparts, although Portuguese tradition exercised a strong influence as well, particularly as regards procedure law. As a result of its multitude and complexity of forms, whereby written acts predominated and a long and solemn judicial journey was the precursor to any trial, the Code was already out of date by the beginning of the 20th century.

New and faster procedural schemes indicated the need for a new Code, although this did not come into existence until 1939. Portugal was then dominated by a dictatorship, and this regime was reflected in many choices made in the new Code. The Code's rigidity soon led to a strong predominance of civil procedural law over civil law in court decisions. The same orientation was revisited in 1961, when a so-called new CPC replaced the CPC of 1939.

Even after Portugal overturned the ruling dictatorship in 1974, we would still have to wait more than 20 years (until 1995-1996) for procedural law that would reflect the modern concepts of efficiency and fair trial which had arisen in Europe after World War II. More recently, in 2003, a reform of enforcement law was undertaken, which introduced into Portugal the French experience of the *huissier*; aiming to make the enforcement easier and liberating the judges from procedural interventions that by their nature require a magistrate. As a matter of fact, litigation has grown exponentially over the last years and the courts are less and less capable of providing a quick answer to the plaintiff. The efficacy of every reform of the CPC tends to be blunted and outweighed by the dimension of this growth.

## 2. Sources

The most relevant sources of civil procedure are the *Código de Processo Civil* (Civil Procedure Code) – the last version of which was published in the Decree-Law No. 180/96, of 25 September, and the Decreto-Lei No. 38/2003, of 8 March and the *Lei de Organização e Funcionamento dos Tribunais Judiciais* (Structure and Organization of the Judicial Courts Law) – Lei No. 3/99, of 13 January.

## 3. Fundamental principles

There are some fundamental principles of Portuguese civil procedure law that are worth mentioning, such as the principle of party control or adversary procedure, the preference for oral expression, the principle of procedural economy, the principle of cooperation, and also some essential rights, such as the right of access to justice, the right to reasonable duration of proceedings and the right to a fair trial (principle of equity).

All of these ideas are in reality mixed with other policies, which transform some of them into non-absolute principles. For instance, the antonym of the principle of party control or adversary system, the inquisitorial system, has been introduced into numerous procedure rules, inclusively those relating to proof-taking. Nevertheless, the subject matter of the proceeding is determined by the parties and the court must decide within the limits of their requests (Article 264), even though the judge can request clarification of some allegations or facts in order to reach the real truth.

The Code expressly establishes that the judge controls the direction of the proceeding (Article 265) and since 1995/6, to complement this idea, a cooperation principle was established within the law (Article 266), with the following text: "During the proceeding, the court, the attorneys and the parties should cooperate to obtain, quickly and efficiently, a fair decision on the case."

This principle of cooperation was introduced into Portuguese civil procedure as a "revolutionary" idea that would bring modernity and justice to our courts. An example of the concretization of this principle is the "pre-trial" hearing, which is an oral hearing following the introductory stage, or the presentation of allegations.. The parties and the magistrate discuss the case, trying to achieve a settlement and, if no agreement can be reached, the action proceeds to final hearing and judgment. Together, in positions of equality, they organize the proof-taking, according to which facts are proved and those that remain unsubstantiated are identified.

## 4. Ordinary proceedings in first instance

The ordinary proceedings in first instance can be divided into declarative proceedings and execution proceedings. In a declarative proceeding the court decides on the merit of the litigation between the parties and in an execution proceeding this judgement, or other documents with special characteristics established by law, are enforced.

The declarative procedure can be divided into four distinct phases: allegation or introductory stage, interim phase, proof-taking and judgment.

The declarative action starts with articulation of a complaint (*petição inicial*), containing the type of relief requested and the basis of the claim, the court, and the name and domicile of the parties, among other accessory information. This complaint must be signed by the party's attorney if the value involved is greater than € 3,740. 98.

Since 1995/6, the judge does not intervene in this earlier phase of the proceeding. Thus, immediately upon its receipt, the complaint is served to the defendant. The service is generally carried out by registered mail. When it is shown to be impossible to serve the complaint via registered mail, the service is instead made through direct contact by a private individual (*solicitador de execução*).

The defendant then has 30 days to present his reply (*contestação*), where he can defend himself by alleging procedural objections, arguing that the facts are false or stating that other facts constitute an impediment to the claim or should extinguish it (peremptory exceptions). In his reply, the defendant can also present a counter-claim, setting forth new bases of action and requests that are somehow related with the subject matter of the initial claim.

If the defendant registers objections, procedural or substantive, the plaintiff can respond within 15 days (*replica*). In this response, the plaintiff can alter the basis of action and the request, even without the agreement of the defendant. If the plaintiff does so, the defendant then has 15 days to defend himself.

All these acts must be in written form. Only after they all brought before the court is the process analysed by the judge. Thus, after this allegation stage has been concluded, the judge calls for an oral hearing, a pre-trial hearing. Here, a series of different matters relating to the action are discussed by the parties and the judge, for example the procedural objections and the exact cause or causes of action. If none of the procedural objections prevails, the judge, with the collaboration of the parties, continues with the preparation of the proof-taking, which begins with the partition of proved facts and contested facts. At the pre-trial the parties must also offer the means of proof, for example the persons that will testify. Thereafter the judge indicates the day of the final hearing, which should be scheduled within the next 3 months.

At the final hearing the witnesses testify and other proofs are taken, for instance the testimonies of experts. This final hearing takes place with a single judge or with three judges, depending on the request of the parties. The parties must choose, at the pre-trial, if they want to record the hearing or if they want it to be assisted by three magistrates. In Portuguese civil procedure the decision is never taken by juries. The final hearing ends with the court's decision about contested facts and those that remain unproven.

After this judgment of fact, the parties can offer written legal allegations. The judge subsequently hands down the final judgment within a brief timeframe. The judge must describe the action, justify his decisions and condemn or absolve the defendant.

If the defendant thereafter does not pay the amount he is required to pay within the terms of the judgment, it is up to the creditor to commence execution proceedings. It is also important to note that if the creditor has a document fulfilling the characteristics described by article 46º CPC (executive title), he can directly advance to an execution proceeding, which means that this latter proceeding is not dependent on a previous judgement on the merits of the case.

Execution proceedings in Portugal begin with a requirement presented to the court, whereby the plaintiff must identify his credit, the debtor, and, if he so wishes, goods to be apprehended. Depending on the nature of the executive title, a judicial analysis of the requirement may be carried out, to verify the substantive and the procedural requisites of the claim. In other cases there may be a service of execution or an immediate seizure of the debtor's property. With the seizure of the debtor's property, possession is transmitted to the execution agent, although in certain cases, such as real estate, the possession can be transmitted to a third person.

The creditors, having a real guarantee, are then served so that they can reclaim their credits. The next phase is the sale of the property, which can be effected in various ways, but with attention to the essential objective of selling the property for the best price. The proceeds of the sale, after deduction of the execution agent's fees and other costs of the execution, are delivered to the creditor or creditors. If, after satisfying the amount reclaimed, some profits remain, they will be turned over to the debtor.

All the execution acts, such as service, levy, sale and payment, are generally completed by a private individual, the *solicitador de execução*, a new judicial role created in 2003 and inspired by the French *huissier de justice*. The judge has control over the execution, which means that he can always verify the legality of the execution agent's acts. The parties and the execution agent can also ask for his intervention when they find that it is necessary.

## 5. Trends in Portuguese Civil Procedure

The recent reforms of the Portuguese Civil Procedure Code have not been able to solve the crisis that afflicts justice in our country. The problem, however, has at least been diagnosed and it is not in law that the central problem lies. Much must be done to improve the management of the Portuguese courts, not only to undermine many ingrained habits, notably the excessive application of process rules, but also to change the courts into modern, decentralized and efficient organizations.

Nevertheless some changes in law are due to be enacted on an experimental basis. Nowadays the majority part of litigation is mass litigation, which includes the small debts of communications companies, consumer credit, car leasing and, in general, all the natural litigation of a consumer society. Recently, the government has proposed the adoption of some measures to combat this problem. From these we can envisage the creation of a special and experimental civil procedure regime, to be applied in the courts that have higher levels of litigation. This new system will strengthen the powers granted to judges concerning the management of processes, obviously drawing inspiration from the recent American Law Institute/Unidroit *Principles of Transnational Civil Procedure*, (published in 2004, number 4, the Uniform Law Review).

## Bibliography

ANTUNES VARELA, João, *Manual de processo civil,* Coimbra, 1985. LEBRE DE FREITAS, José, *Introdução ao Processo Civil*, Coimbra, 1996. Idem, *A Acção Declarativa Comum*, Coimbra, 2000. Idem; *A Acção Executiva*, 4th ed., Coimbra, 2003. RIBEIRO MENDES, Armindo; *Recursos em Processo Civil*, Lisbon, 1994. Idem, *Os recursos no Código de Processo Civil revisto*, Lisbon, 1998. TEIXEIRA DE SOUSA, Miguel; *Estudos sobre o Novo Processo Civil*, Lisbon, 1996.